MW00809518

UNDERCOVER AGENTS IN THE RUSSIAN REVOLUTIONARY MOVEMENT

Undercover Agents in the Russian Revolutionary Movement

The SR Party, 1902–14

Nurit Schleifman
Lecturer in History
Tel-Aviv University

St. Martin's Press New York

Scholarly & Reference Division,
St. Martin's Press, Inc., 175 Fifth Avenue, New York, NY 10010

First published in the United States of America in 1988

Printed in Hong Kong

ISBN 0-312-00077-4

Library of Congress Cataloging-in-Publication Data
Schleifman, Nurit, 1941–
Undercover agents in the Russian revolutionary movement.
Bibliography: p.
Includes index.
1. Revolutionists – Soviet Union – History. 2. Subversive activities – Soviet Union – History. 3. Spies – Soviet Union – History. 4. Internal security – Soviet Union – History. I. Title.
HX313.S35 1987 322.4'2'0947 86-21888
ISBN 0-312-00077-4

To my mother

Contents

List of Tables

Preface

The secret agent has been a constant figure in struggles between régimes and their opponents. In the nineteenth century police penetration of subversive organizations was widespread, especially in the Austro-Hungarian Empire, during the Metternich period, in the France of Louis-Philippe and Napoleon III, and in Prussia under Friedrich Wilhelm IV. However, while in those countries their use was limited and temporary, in Russia it became the cornerstone of the political police work. The contemporary revolutionaries were aware of its unusual scope. Indeed, the secret agent of the Russian political police was a permanent factor from the very outset of the revolutionary movement, and one whose presence cannot be disregarded in any study of its history.

The secret agent took part in the entire range of revolutionary activity: in propagandizing and in agitation, in the publication of underground periodicals, leaflets and pamphlets, and in terrorist actions. He was a member of commissions and committees of all types and at all levels, from the local organization to the central party committees, and was even to be found on commissions of inquiry that investigated suspected traitors to the party. His imprint is striking in the letters and memoirs of revolutionaries, and in the revolutionary press which constantly reported the exposure of secret agents. Every movement or party was infiltrated by secret agents; all of them had to cope with the phenomenon sooner or later.

At the same time, contradiction exists between the secret agent's prominence in revolutionary life, and the place of betrayal in the collective consciousness of the generation; the revolutionaries were not preoccupied with betrayal but with the betrayer. Their memoirs depict the exposure of agents as a rationale for a defeat or the failure of a revolutionary initiative; their letters bear witness to their immense personal grief when a comrade was exposed as a traitor.

In only one case did the issue surface as a major phenomenon with an impact on the life of the revolutionaries, with the exposure of Evno Azef, a widely acclaimed member of the SR leadership. Azef was a secret agent for about 15 years. He began his activity before the foundation of the SR party and by 1901 had already acquired a position of prominence that made him instrumental in the formation of the united party. Following the arrest of Grigorii Gershuni in 1903 he succeeded him as the head of the Battle Organization and in this capacity was also appointed member of the Central Committee. For as long as five years he turned in scores of revolutionaries and at the same time organized assassinations which caused a sensation throughout the world. Prominent examples are the murder of the Minister of the Interior V. von Plehve and that of the Grand Duke Sergei Alexandrovich. In 1908 he instigated an attempt on the life of the Tsar, but was not responsible for its failure.

Throughout the years the SRs received several warnings about Azef's true role but these were stubbornly rejected as being police intrigues. Vladimir Burtsev, an independent revolutionary firmly convinced of Azef's guilt and aided by Mikhail Bakai, a police defector, led the struggle for Azef's exposure. This brought him into severe conflict with the party leadership which firmly supported Azef and sued Burtsev before a revolutionary court of honour. During the trial Burtsev managed to meet with Alexander Lopukhin, a former Director of the Police Department, who confirmed the allegations. Lopukhin later repeated these accusations to a dumbfounded delegation of the party leadership. Azef succeeded in escaping. In 1912 he contacted his former colleagues from his hiding place, offering to stand trial before the Party on condition that his safety was guaranteed pending the outcome.[1] The affair rocked the SR party and the entire revolutionary movement. Yet in the discussion that followed the point of departure was generally apologetic or rhetorical and focused primarily on the problem as it existed in the rival political camp. Despite their sense of the pervasiveness of the secret agent, the revolutionaries did not seriously ask themselves what part the police were actually playing in revolutionary developments. Did they deliberately use agents in order to influence the revolutionary process on the basis of a defined policy, or was the effect achieved unintentionally simply through the agents' very presence in the revolutionary movement? Beyond referring to the subject for purposes of political backbiting, the revolutionaries also failed to consider seriously what conditions the secret agents needed and whether these differed from one movement to another; nor did they draw the operational conclusions which might have resulted from replies to these questions.

The revolutionaries' tendency to avoid the full import of this topic is perhaps understandable, since it undermined their revolutionary credibility in their own eyes and *vis-à-vis* their adversaries, while they themselves came across as tools in the hands of the police. This being so, they preferred to regard the plethora of secret agents in their ranks as a natural phenomenon, the inevitable byproduct of all revolutionary activity, one whose impact was restricted to the struggle between the forces of the revolution and the authorities. It is less comprehensible why the historians of the Russian revolutionary movement also adopted this approach uncritically. Not a single study exists that examines the role played by the secret agents in shaping the movement and its various components. In practice, the extensive studies of the history of the revolutionary parties in Russia continue to follow the approach of the contemporary protagonists by shunting aside the issue of the secret agent – even when they refer to the political police in order to account for a certain aspect of the developments. A striking instance is the book by Manfred Hildermeier, in which the Okhrana is cited as one of the causes of the SR party's organizational weakness.[2] This appraisal lends additional force to questions relating to the overall phenomenon of the police agents' mode of operation: did they operate similarly and equally throughout the entire revolutionary movement? What were the direct and indirect results of their activity? Were these results similar in all instances and throughout the entire period?

However there are two cases which scholars have been unable to ignore. The Azef and Malinovskii affairs are discussed in greater or lesser detail in the general historiography of Russia during the Revolutionary period, and in monographs on the SR party or the Russian Social Democrats. Roman Malinovskii was a confidant of Lenin's, a member of the Bolsheviks' Central Committee and head of the SD faction in the Fourth Duma. The Azef affair in particular had a profound impact not only on the SRs but on the entire revolutionary movement. It was the subject of a book by Boris Nikolaevsky. More recently a monograph also appeared on the Malinovskii affair,[3] after it had been discussed in several articles and in Bertram Wolfe's well-known volume.[4] But in many ways both cases were exceptional. The two protagonists attracted scholarly attention because they were central figures in the two largest revolutionary parties in Tsarist Russia. However although they constituted an integral part of the secret agent phenomenon as a whole, they have not been studied within that framework. For this reason they can hardly serve as a case study for the phenomenon in general.

The present book makes no pretence of answering the complex web of questions, nor of drawing comparisons concerning the impact of the secret agents on the various components of the revolutionary movement. Although such comparisons might well contribute to an understanding of the socio-political character of the movement, from an unusual angle, they are not feasible without a thoroughgoing and fundamental examination of the phenomenon as it existed in each and every party. This study concentrates on the agents in the SR party, and not on those indirectly connected to it like Gapon or Bogrov. Its intention is not primarily to draw attention to any specific secret agent, but to the question as a whole by describing and analysing it in a single party.

The SR party was chosen for this analysis for several reasons. Firstly, because the historiography has not been overly concerned with that party, and even when it has been studied, the question of the police impact on its history, as we saw, has received scant attention. Yet this question assumes particular importance in view of the fact that even among the revolutionaries themselves it was generally assumed that the SR party was more riddled with secret agents than any other revolutionary organization. For the SRs, this was proof of the immense threat they posed to the Tsarist régime; for their rivals, it was proof of their revolutionary weakness. Both the assumption and the interpretation call for an examination. The conclusions may throw light on previously unexplored aspects of the party's development. At the same time, an inquiry focusing on the SR party could also elucidate the aims of the Police Department's anti-revolutionary struggle. For the SR party was characterized both by the use of terrorism and by a centralist organization, whereas the anarchists and the Social Democrats were each distinguished by one of these aspects only. Terrorism and centralism, the characteristics of the SR party, combine with its internal problems to serve as the background to an examination of the effect of police infiltration on the direction of party development. The question, then, is important both in itself and as a point of departure for future comparisons with other parties.

Key roles are played in this study by the political police and the SR party. Their point of encounter is the secret agent, whose influence depended on his case officers on the one hand, and on the revolutionary party on the other. Accordingly our discussion is divided into two main sections. The first section deals with the policy and mode of deployment of the secret agents within the SR party, the RSDRP (the Russian Social Democratic Labour Party), and the anarchists, to which end comprehensive data pertaining to police infiltration of these groups have been collected and compared. The latter part discusses the party and its response to the police infiltration of its ranks via the secret agent.

In the main, the research is based on two archives and one large collection: the archives of the Okhrana's Foreign Agency, located at the Hoover Institution at Stanford, California; the archives of the Socialist Revolutionary Party, located in the International Institute of Social History, Amsterdam, and the Nicolaevsky Collection, also at the Hoover Institution. The Okhrana Archives contain the full correspondence between the Foreign Agency and the Police Department for the period from 1885 to 1917, agents' reports which served as the basis for the Foreign Agency's official reports to St Petersburg, together with correspondence with the Foreign Agency's case officers outside Paris, including the small representation in Berlin. The archives contain also a large collection of circulars which the Police Department distributed among all the investigative institutions under it, press clippings, surveys of the various revolutionary parties, letters of revolutionaries that were intercepted and copied, and more. All told, the archives include 97,143 documents, 163,802 biographies, 287 books and 456 newspapers, circulars and periodicals. Its scope alone indicates the importance of the archives, both within the framework of police activity and as a source for the historian. It contains information on the political appraisals of the Police Department and of its representatives in Paris, on the nature of the connection between the secret agents and the Foreign Agency, and between the latter and the centre. In addition, inferences may be drawn from its documentation concerning the accepted reporting procedures between the Foreign Agency and the Police Department in St Petersburg, and the extent to which these reflect the relations between the department and the investigative bodies in Russia. All this is in addition to the vast amount of detail concerning events in the parties' centres abroad, and about gatherings of the *émigré* groups and their conferences.

Reliance on the archives of the Okhrana's Foreign Agency raises problems typical of the use of police material; scrutiny and sorting are essential. A good deal of the information that reached the police was based on unconfirmed rumours or on erroneous assessments by secret agents. The present study therefore makes a constant effort to verify the information from these archives against material from additional sources – first and foremost the archives of the SR party. It should be noted that due to the nature of the material it was not possible to ascertain the full names of a number of the persons involved.

In contrast to the situation at the Foreign Agency archives at the Hoover Institution, classification and cataloguing has only recently begun of the material in the SR archives. While the present work was in progress, no listing or cataloguing of the material was available, so that its exact scope could not be gauged. Generally speaking these archives consist of some 900 files containing protocols of meetings of the Central Committee and of party congresses and council sessions, as well as of meetings of local groups abroad. It also includes correspondence between the Central Committee and SRs in Russia, between the Foreign Committee (*Zagranichnyi Komitet*) and the various local SR groups throughout Europe, considerable material from the commissions of inquiry into the cases of provocation in the SR party, reports on the situation of the groups in Russia, particularly prior to 1907, and various local broadsheets. Some of the documents of the SR party's commission of inquiry into the issue of provocation are to be found in the Nicolaevsky Collection, together with the complete or partial archives of various revolutionaries, including a good many unpublished letters and manuscripts.

To further our understanding of the characteristic methods employed by the police agents, we assembled the names and biographical details of as many agents as possible from the most diverse sources available: from the archives, the revolutionary press – which published names of exposed agents from other parties as well – and from memoirs of revolutionaries and of police officers who served as the case officers of secret agents. The Okhrana Archives contain the names of all the agents who operated under its directives abroad as well as the names of other agents whose details were transferred to Paris from the centre in St Petersburg. In addition, mention must be made of the Nicolaevsky Collection, which contains clippings from the post-revolutionary press of lists of police agents whose identities were exposed after the Okhrana's files fell into the hands of the new régime. All told, these number roughly 600, and many of them were not party members but operated in various public sectors. Thus, in processing the data we only took into account secret agents with clear organizational affiliation to the SRs, the Social Democrats or the anarchists, a total of 215 agents. The data cover their period of service, its duration, their party activity, and arrests that were made. The agents' names were classified according to organization, and where the relevant information was available an effort was made to understand the ties which might provide clues to their motives for wishing to serve the police, and to understand the policy and approach adopted by the police. The tables are based on these archival data. Specific reference is made whenever other sources are consulted.

Manifestly the group of 215 secret agents is not a random sample, though its similarity to the statistics on certain aspects of the SRs and Social Democrats as well as the nature of the sources suggest it is not biased. However since no published statistics exist regarding the deployment of secret agents, only further research will verify to what degree the group is representative and how valid the consequent observations are. Nevertheless an effort has been made to cross-check the data against other documentary sources. With respect to the SR party as the agents' field of activity, their influence was examined in relation to the party's unique traits.

Since it is so well known, the Azef affair is not dealt with in full detail; the emphasis, rather, is on its effect as a major element in the overall part played by secret agents in the history of the SR party.

A definite conflict exists between the attitude of the police toward the use of secret agents as a means in the anti-revolutionary struggle, and the attitude of the revolutionary parties to this method. The contrasting attitudes are well reflected in the terminology: the police used the name *Internal Agency* while to the revolutionaries the system was known as *provocation*. The book makes use of both terms, depending on which side is being represented.

Single dates in the book refer to the Julian calendar; where two dates are given, the later one refers to the Gregorian calendar, which in this century postdates the Julian by thirteen days.

Every document that exists in print or stencil form and bears a title is referred to by that heading, along with the place and date of publication. Letters are annotated by the names of the sender and addressee, the date, and where necessary also by the sender's address and destination. Material from the archives of the Okhrana's Foreign Agency is designated as 'Okhrana Archives', followed by a Roman numeral to indicate the subject unit, as determined by the repository, and numbers specifying the file. Documents from the Nicolaevsky Collection are designated by that name, followed by the unit and file numbers. The SR archives are designated 'PS-R Archives' followed by the number of the file in which the document was located at the time the study was undertaken. The transliteration system used in the body of the book is that of the Library of Congress with the exception of names which are common in other languages. In the notes, however, the rules of transliteration have been applied throughout.

Acknowledgements

I am deeply indebted to many friends and colleagues who assisted me in the preparation of this book. First and foremost to Professor Michael Confino who introduced me to Russian history and was always unsparing of his time and support. From his scholarship and experience I have greatly benefited. I am also grateful to Dr Zvi Razi for his help and advice in matters concerning the quantitative aspects of the research and to Ralph Mandel whose outstanding linguistic skill was of the utmost importance in preparing the English text. Nelly Plocker assisted with the work throughout, Dr Gabriel Gorodetsky read various parts of the manuscript, and Ann Usishkin read the final version. For their helpful remarks I am very grateful.

Special thanks are due to the School of History and the Russian and East European Research Centre of Tel-Aviv University for their financial support. Without the Centre's assistance and the help of my colleagues this work could not have been accomplished. I should like also to express my appreciation for the help I received from the staffs of the Hoover Institution on War, Revolution and Peace at Stanford, California, and the International Institute of Social History in Amsterdam, and particularly to Dr Boris Sapir, Dr Marc Jansen and Mieke Yzermans for their friendly assistance.

Last but not least my thanks go to my family and close friends who for a long period of time bore with patience and love the burden of provocation.

Chronological Framework

14 December 1825	Decembrist Uprising
3 July 1826	Third Section Established
Summer 1879	Narodnaia Volia founded
6 August 1880	Police Department replaces Third Section
1 March 1881	Alexander II assassinated
March 1898	Russian Social Democratic Labour Party (RSDRP) founded
January 1902	SR party founded
April 1902	Battle Organization established; Sipiagin assassinated
Spring 1903	Emergence of first anarchist groups
15 July 1904	Plehve assassinated
9 January 1905	'Bloody Sunday' triggering revolutionary tide
4 February 1905	Grand Duke Sergei Alexandrovich assassinated
17 October 1905	October Manifesto on civil rights and the establishment of the Duma
January 1906	Secession of the Maximalists
27 April–8 July 1906	First Duma
20 February–3 June 1907	Second Duma
1 November 1907–9 June 1912	Third Duma
December 1908	Exposure of Azef
4 April 1912	Lena goldfield massacre triggering a wave of strikes
14 November 1912–6 October 1917	Fourth Duma

Introduction

The hypothesis underlying this study is that the interplay between two primary factors was instrumental in determining the influence exerted by the secret agent on the Russian revolutionary movement. These two factors were firstly the police assessment of the movement and of the threat it posed to the authorities and, secondly, the characteristics which distinguished those various elements in the movement which were receptive and responsive to police infiltration. In other words, the phenomenon as a whole was marked by the dynamic interaction between the perception of the Police Department on the one hand, and the specific socio-political foundations of each revolutionary party on the other hand. Several aspects of the SR party's ideological roots and the circumstances surrounding its establishment continued to be central factors in its political and social role.

The SR party evolved from the gradual unification of heterogeneous social-revolutionary groups which were formed in the 1890s in Russia and among the *émigrés*. These groups regarded themselves as representing the continuation, to a greater or lesser degree, of the populist tradition which marked the 1870s and 1880s. The concept of 'populism' in this connection requires elucidation.

As Richard Pipes has shown, the term can be defined in the narrow historical sense adopted by the *Zemlia i Volia* (Land and Liberty) between 1875 and 1878, or according to the broad but self-contradictory interpretation it acquired since then.[1] In the 1890s, the Socialist Revolutionaries inclined to the latter approach. Originally, the term was used to describe the lessons learned from the 'Going to the People' movement including the abandonment of the attempt to educate the peasants to socialism through the preaching of abstract doctrines. It also meant recognition of the basic misconception in the Bakuninist belief that the peasants were potential revolutionaries, whose revolutionary spirit would be kindled by a mere spark touching off a conflagration that would spread throughout Russia. The new definition implied curtailing the hegemony of the educated revolutionary élite and of its conceptions, and an acceptance of the interests and aspiration of the people as a guideline for revolutionary activity. In practical terms this meant foregoing the maximalist notion of a socialist revolution. Hence the comment of one of the leading exponents of this school of thought: 'The common and indispensable foundation of Narodnichestvo was undoubtedly democratism . . . the most ordinary universal one so to say'.[2] According to Pipes, populism in this sense had an anti-political, anti-intellectual and even anti-socialist character.

When the new path of *Zemlia i Volia* also proved disappointing, internal disputes surfaced, eventually causing a split within the movement. In the course of the debates the term assumed new nuances. These changed its basic meaning, and tactics for the furtherance of the limited revolution were adopted, including terrorism as a means of revolutionary political struggle. The shift from apoliticism to political revolutionism split the movement into two factions: the *Chernyi Peredel* (Black Partition) and the *Narodnaia Volia* (People's Will). The former regarded themselves as the *de facto* continuers of the previous line. The founders of the *Narodnaia Volia* party, on the other hand, advocates of political terrorism, and conscious of the historical meaning of 'populism' yet wishing to underscore their own innovative emphasis, somewhat hesitatingly termed themselves 'socialist-populists'. Confronted by the contradiction between a popular democratic peasants' revolution, and a struggle marked by the use of political terror with its concomitant centralist-conspiratorial form of organization, they sought to resolve the problem by dividing their platform and presenting both a minimum and a maximum programme. The minimum programme called on the party to seize power and guarantee political freedoms. This was to be achieved through a struggle marked by terrorism and directed against the centre of power, climaxing in the assassination of the Tsar. Once power was seized, the maximum programme would be implemented; it pledged the transfer of sovereignty to the poeple, who alone would determine the kind of régime they desired. The party was certain that an extensive propaganda campaign, to be conducted prior to its seizure of power and thereafter, would guarantee its election.

The political terrorism was directed by a special, highly centralized body, the Executive Committee of the *Narodnaia Volia*. In March 1881 its agents finally succeeded in assassinating Alexander II. However, the *dénouement* proved disappointing. Not only did the régime remain in power but the accession to the throne of Alexander III ushered in a period of severe reaction, and in its wake a protracted nadir in revolutionary activity lasting into the 1890s. Although the *Narodnaia Volia* did not regard its new tactics as constituting a substantive change in the ideological content of populism, in practice it was now infused with political terrorism and the kind of centralist, conspiratorial, élitist organization which is the polar opposite of democratism in its most ordinary and universal sense.

In the 1890s, as the debate over the direction of Russia's development raged, the concept took on a different emphasis. In contrast to the Marxists, who maintained that socialism in Russia had to evolve through the stage of capitalism, others rejected Marxist determinism and, citing the advantage of Russia's socio-economic backwardness, argued that the formation of a socialist régime could bypass the stage of industrialization. The advocates of the latter view came to be known as 'populists' even when their other arguments were inconsistent with previous attitudes classified under that definition.

As a result of these conceptual developments, the Socialist Revolutionaries of the mid-1890s claimed to be the torch-bearers of a term marked by the constant addition of diverse and contradictory meanings throughout the previous decade. These included a belief in agrarian socialism based on the communal institutions of the peasantry; a perception of the peasants as imbued with certain socialist tendencies which would transform them into a potential mass revolutionary force, as opposed to a certain scepticism *vis-à-vis* that approach, and faith in the urban industrial workers and a struggle based on political terrorism. Adherence to principles of democracy and federalism contrasted with the outlook which called for the creation of a conspiratorial, centralist, élitist organization that would seize power in the state.

It is essential to comprehend the shifts in the form and content of populism since the 1870s in order to understand how the Socialist Revolutionary groups of the mid-1890s perceived the concept they claimed to inherit, and to comprehend its contradictory facets. This is particularly important as the SR groups of the 1890s were formed after a lengthy period marked by the absence of a clear and generally accepted organizational and ideological framework. The divergent approaches of the 1890s derived from differing assessments of the revolutionary potential of the peasantry as compared with the potential of the urban industrial workers, of the use of terror in a revolutionary struggle, and of the party's organizational makeup.

In the years 1901–3 the chief components of the SR party were the regional organizations, created in the latter part of the 1890s. These included the 'Northern Union of the Socialist Revolutionaries', which was established in 1896 in Saratov and moved its headquarters to Moscow a year later; the 'Southern Party of the Socialist Revolutionaries', formed from various groups in southern Russia and the

Ukraine; and the 'Agrarian Socialist League', whose members – many of them veterans of the *Narodnaia Volia* – were *émigrés*. Smaller groups also joined, notably the 'Workers' Party for the Political Liberation of Russia', whose activity was concentrated in Jewish regions in western Russia. The sense of being associated with the populist tradition, which was common to all of these groups, was intensified and reinforced with the release from prison and exile of many veterans of the populist movement and their return to western Russia. Many of them resumed their revolutionary activity at once, becoming a focus for the organization and the object of admiration on the part of the younger generation.

Each of the groups emphasized different elements, which it regarded as the genuine heritage of populism. The platform of the Northern Union, entitled *Our Tasks* and written by Andrei Argunov, founder of the organization and a future SR leader, asserted categorically that the Union was the direct successor of the *Narodnaia Volia*. In emulation of the latter, the Northern Union also described itself as 'socialist-populist', autocracy was seen as the chief obstacle on the road to the realization of socialism in Russia, and terrorism as the sole effective tool in the struggle against it. However, unlike the original *Narodnaia Volia* platform, *Our Tasks* showed an awareness of the capitalist-oriented developments which had taken place in Russia both in industry and in agriculture; hence its assertion that the two main forces which the organization had to rely on in its struggle to attain political freedom were the socialist intelligentsia and the industrial proletariat. Although the peasants were also earmarked to participate in the revolution, their integration into the revolutionary political struggle was deferred to a future stage due to their unenlightened state and dispersion over vast areas. Due to these factors the Northern Union found it impossible to approach the peasants, and the author of its platform was confident that the victory over autocracy could be achieved without their help.

In contrast, the Southern Party rejected this argument as well as the glorification of terrorist acts. Its programmatic approach was presented in the *Manifesto of the Socialist Revolutionaries*, which pointedly refrained from so much as mentioning terrorism. Although the *Manifesto* also posited the industrial workers as the preferred objective of revolutionary propaganda, it laid stress on the economic rather than the political aspect of the struggle – not of the industrial workers alone, but of the working class as a whole. The authors of the *Manifesto* rejected the Northern Union's contention that there was no urgent need for the peasantry to participate in the struggle for political freedoms. They strongly believed that among the peasantry there were many who were no less interested than the proletariat in social and political change. In any event, without the support of the peasantry, the working class would be incapable of undermining the foundations of the Tsarist régime and thereby of transforming the face of Russian society. Summing up the blatant differences between the two approaches, the Southern Party's Stepan Sletov, who was also to become a prominent SR leader, argued that *Our Tasks* parroted the *Narodnaia Volia* platform but without adopting the latter's belief in the possibility of fomenting a popular uprising and without any attempt to implement it in practice. Thus the tactic of terrorism lost its legitimacy.

The Southern Party's stance *vis-à-vis* the peasantry and its role in the revolutionary struggle lay somewhere between the views of the Northern Union and of the Agrarian Socialist League. The League saw the peasantry as its principal target, and its chief task as helping those who worked in the Russian village. Its activity was to be based on the dissemination of propaganda material suitable to the peasants: the use of socialist propaganda tactics among the rural working sector, and the spread of the agrarian class struggles in the village, utilizing its existing forms of social organization. Strong emphasis was laid on the ability of the peasantry to participate actively in the revolutionary movement. On this point the League's platform assailed the Marxists' view of the peasantry as an anti-revolutionary element and their stand that only through proletarization could the peasants be transformed into a revolutionary socialist force. This position was based on an analysis of the changes that had occurred in the Russian village since the 1870s, and were affected by parallel shifts in revolutionary thought. In the League's view, the populists' hopes of the peasantry in the 1870s had been wholly exaggerated. Imbued now with a more down-to-earth approach, they became aware of the need to develop a graduated cultural and educational programme in order to prepare cadres for revolutionary leadership from among the peasantry itself. This leadership would form the bridgehead between village and city. The League's programme constituted a partial return to the early positions espoused by *Zemlia i Volia*, and their integration into a new perception of reality.

The Agrarian Socialist league was the last important organization to merge with the SR party, and insisted on preserving its organizational autonomy within the framework of the united party.

Its attitude towards terrorism was not the inevitable result of its basic stand *vis-à-vis* the peasantry; unlike the Southern Party, the League as a whole supported terrorism due to its roots in the *Narodnaia Volia*. In its adherence to the principles of organizational autonomy and its advocacy of terrorism, the League had close affinities with the Workers' Party for the Political Liberation of Russia, founded in Minsk in 1895. It, too, advocated political terrorism as a key tool in the struggle against the autocracy, which it regarded as the main prop of capitalism, a position reminiscent of the orientation of the Northern Union towards the views of the *Narodnaia Volia*. On the other hand, the Worker's Party believed strongly in the importance of an anti-centralist organization: the party should be structured as a federation of autonomous groups, unfettered by intervention of any kind from a central authority.

Thus questions of principle, which were sometimes inconsistent, divided the regional organizations both in Russia and among the *émigrés*. It seems that the main cohesive force that bound these groups together was a sense of possessing a common heritage, intensified by the presence of veteran revolutionaries, comrades of the earlier struggle, who now held positions of leadership in the new organizations.

Attempts to form a unified party were greatly hampered by the ideological differences. Eventually, after five years of deliberations and negotiations, both external factors and individual efforts finally led to the creation of the new party. Notable was a peasants' uprising which lent *prima facie* support to the proponents of the peasants' immediate participation in revolutionary activity, and the efforts of respected and influential figures such as Ekaterina Breshkovskaia, whose revolutionary career extended back to 'Going to the People', and Grigorii Gershuni, 20 years her junior, who already had a reputation as an extraordinary organizer and leader. Both were members of the Workers' Party for the Political Liberation of Russia. Four more years were required before the new party was able to hold its founding conference and adopt a platform acceptable to all its members. The repeated deferments of the conference were due to the differences among the participating groups. The programme eventually adopted barely papered over the divisions, and even after the founding conference – held in December 1905 on the Imatra Islands in Finland – they remained unresolved.

In theory, the principles of the SR organization were designed to tie all the diverse threads together. Viktor Chernov, a member of the

Agrarian Socialist League and a prominent SR leader, regarded the constitution that was adopted as an expression of the 'synthesizing approach' that fused democracy and federalism on the one side, and conspiracy and centralism on the other. Actually, the new party's organizational structure was not substantially different from the democratic centralism of the Social Democracts. The constitution was based on the principle of two-way supervision both from above and from below. The latter principle was embodied in the supreme standing of the Party Congress (*S'ezd*) at which all the constituent organizations were represented and which was to elect the central institutions. The supervision from above found expression in the subordination of the SR committees at all levels to the elected institutions and to party discipline.

A hierarchy was established based on the local committees in the cities and the villages. The committees operated among various groups – workers, peasants, students and soldiers. Each committee included specialists in its particular spheres of activity: for example, an 'agitator', a 'propagandist', a typesetter if the committee had a printing press, and a 'chemist' if it operated a terrorist group. A number of such committees together formed a broader organization headed by an elected rural or urban committee. These organizations, in turn, elected district committees, out of which 15 regional committees were formed. These committees were under the authority of the all-party institutions, whose members, as noted above, were elected at the annual Party Congress. To deal with ongoing affairs between congresses, a party council (*sovet*) was chosen; this smaller forum included the party leadership, namely, the members of the Central Committee and its subcommittees, and representatives of the regional committees. A second smaller body was the so-called 'Conference', whose membership and meetings were determined by the Party Council.

The organization's constitution, then, provided for the election of the party's institutions at every level. However, as in all underground parties the committees also possessed the right of co-opting new members – in order to forestall the creating of a vacuum in the leading ranks as a result of arrests.

The principle of federalism was expressed in the independence granted to each committee to conduct its affairs autonomously, as long as its activity did not conflict with the party's constitution or with party discipline. Terrorist acts were categorized as autonomous activity; to this end a so-called 'battle squad' (*boevaia druzhina*) was formed under the aegis of the local committee. The 'Battle Organization' (*boevaia organizatsia*) was attached to the Central Committee and engaged in 'central terrorism'. The latter term denoted both terrorism conducted on behalf of and in the name of the party's central body, and terrorist acts directed against the government. At this level these required preparations and resources which only a central party body could handle and involved political decisions which only a central authority was authorized to make. 'Central and peripheral' terrorism also represent two aspects of the prevailing attitude towards the significance and the role of terrorism in general. Peripheral terrorism was directed against local government institutions or representatives and was meant to reflect the people's spirit of revolt, the revolutionary frame of mind of the masses, and as such to serve as an instrument for local propaganda. Central terrorism, besides its propaganda effect, was designed to undermine the centre of government, sow confusion and disorganization within the régime, and thereby accelerate the entire revolutionary process.

On questions of organization and those relating to terrorism and the nature of revolutionary activity, the basic differences of opinion remained unresolved. Chernov's 'synthesizing approach', which reformulated the party's official theories, was widely regarded as a euphemism for 'eclecticism'.[3] Surfacing at various periods in the party's history, these conflicting viewpoints caused splits on the right and the left alike. Even after the breakaway of dissident factions, differences of opinion continued to exist. At times the ferment was latent, but it could also erupt fiercely into the open. In line with the initial hypothesis presented above, this dynamic was generated to no small extent by the phenomenon of betrayal and its impact, although other factors also played a part.

The nature of the anti-revolutionary struggle conducted by the Russian political police was also dependent on historic, structural and organizational elements. Police tasks in Russia were divided among diverse authorities which were created in response to the needs of time and circumstance. In the absence of any comprehensive definition of the roles and spheres of activity of a general, centralized police force, different periods saw the formation of criminal and political police, city and district police, industrial, port and border police and others – all of which, however, continued to operate congruently.[4] The Ministry of the Interior, working through the Police Department, was in charge of all investigations, political and criminal alike. The history of the political police – the key organization where the present study is concerned – provides a striking illustration of the process and consequences of the haphazard creation of police units.

The urgent need to create a permanent political police force was recognized immediately after the Decembrists uprising in 1825. No such force had existed in Russia until Nicholas I established the 'Third Section' as part of his private bureau. The Third Section, which remained in existence until 1880, was granted broad and rather vague powers. Charged with supervising all areas of life, it was not only to arrest and interrogate criminals who engaged in anti-state activity, but also to take preventive action. No less important was the Third Section's task of representing the 'generous autocracy' in the eyes of the people.[5] The Separate Corps of Gendarmes was established as the Third Section's operational arm; it recruited its officers from the army and employed a limited number of secret agents.

Sidney Monas, the historian of the Third Section, points out that initially the organization's administrative channels were informal and irregular. This state of affairs vividly reflected the emergency conditions under which the Section had been established. However those conditions grew more acute rather than diminished with the passage of time. Mileposts on the road toward radicalization in Russia were the reverberations of the 1848 revolutions among the Russian intelligentsia, the reactions to the liberation of the peasants in 1861, and the ensuing rapid growth of the revolutionary movement in the 1880s. It was clearly necessary to restructure the Third Section, and then later to abolish it and transfer its tasks to the 'Special Section' of the Police Department, which was responsible to the Ministry of the Interior. Finally, additional bodies had to be created to help the government grapple with the growing threat of revolution. Even before the initial changes were made in the Third Section, competition for commendations and state awards had developed between the Ministry of the Interior and the Third Section during the mid-1840s. The upshot of this rivalry was the involvement of the regular police, who were responsible to the Minister of the Interior, in political matters. When, for the sake of efficiency, the Third Section as such was abolished in 1880 and effectively amalgamated with the regular police apparatus under the Ministry of the Interior, the Corps of Gendarmes remained as the political arm of the police force. In the course of its existence the Corps had developed its own self-image and acquired institutional interests. Moreover, both the Minister of the Interior and the Director of the Police Department, who were civilians, frequently encountered proud and stubborn resistance from officers of the Corps of Gendarmes, disciples of the military tradition. Laws granting the Commander of the Corps of Gendarmes far-reaching autonomy naturally restricted the authority of the Ministry of the Interior to intervene in the Corps' affairs; moreover, the Corps came under the budgetary aegis of the Ministry of War, which provided the funds for its maintenance. Hence, even though on paper the Corps was responsible to the Minister of the Interior, his department found it difficult to exercise this authority – a problem which was exacerbated by the remoteness from St Petersburg of the Corps' areas of activity.

The growth of the revolutionary movement toward the end of the 1870s only reinforced the need for a more effective response by the authorities, specifically a centralized anti-revolutionary struggle led by the Police Department. It soon became apparent that more was required than the mere abolition of the Third Section and the transfer of its tasks to the Special Section in the Police Department while preserving the autonomy of the Corps of Gendarmes. The next step was the creation of the 'Sections for the Protection of Public Security and Order' (*Otdeleniia po okhraneniiu obshchestvennoi bezopastnosti i poriadka*). These came to be known, simply, as the 'Okhrana sections', and their activity was also co-ordinated by the Special Section. Their establishment proceeded in stages, beginning in 1880 in the industrial centres of St Petersburg, Moscow and Warsaw, because of the major importance which the authorities attached to developments among the urban workers. As a result of the accelerated industrialization the growing number of urban workers became a target for revolutionary propaganda.

The Moscow regional department, although responsible primarily for the city itself and for the surrounding province, was also in charge of 12 adjacent provinces. From 1884 it was headed by Rotmister Berdiaev; one of his most infamous agents was Sergei Zubatov. In 1885 the Foreign Agency, which was to become a key Okhrana department, was established in the Russian embassy in Paris, on the basis that underground conditions forced most party centres to operate outside Russia. Party conferences were for the most part held abroad, and party organs were generally published in western Europe and then smuggled into Russia, along with banned literature and weapons. A good many revolutionaries fled from Russia, either to avoid arrest or after they were caught and came to terms with the police. Hence the police gave high priority to the surveillance of

Russian revolutionary circles in western Europe. Okhrana sections were opened in new areas in the wake of the spreading revolutionary movement.

It should be stressed that the Corps of Gendarmes also continued to fulfil its function as a political force. This duplication led to the formal division of police operations: the Okhrana was given the task of exposing political crimes before they were committed, while the Corps of Gendarmes would investigate those crimes that were perpetrated.[6] However, this division of authority remained purely theoretical. Competition and friction had previously characterized relations between the Ministry of the Interior and the Third Section, and now relations between the Okhrana and the Gendarmerie rapidly deteriorated to the level of fierce rivalry and at times of outright enmity. Nor could the division of responsibility prevent considerable overlap between the spheres of activity of the two bodies. Many cases are known in which both Okhrana and Gendarmerie agents operated within the same revolutionary organization. Worse than this, the two departments did not balk at making use of their agents in order to scuttle each other's achievements. Nevertheless, the Okhrana sections and their agents had become the paramount arm of the police, and unlike the Corps of Gendarmes the Okhrana was directly and solely responsible to its superior. The rivalry among bodies and personalities within the political police were to have their impact on the deployment of the police in the anti-revolutionary struggle and on the formulation of a uniform conception of policy.

1 The Challenge to the Police

(i) IN SEARCH OF MEANS

The planting of secret police agents in Russian revolutionary movements commenced on a systematic basis with the accession of Alexander III in Russia, following his father's assassination by the *Narodnaia Volia*. The assassination confronted Alexander III's régime with a severe challenge, for which he sought a suitable response, aided by the French police, who were already using secret agents as a matter of course.[1]

In Russia, too, the political police had occasionally employed agents to gather information about groups under investigation;[2] the difference from the early 1880s lay in the increasing frequency and consistency with which the method was employed until the Revolution of 1917. The impact of the system, as well as its duration, not only lends it a uniquely Russian character, but also poses a number of questions. How did senior police officers in different periods view the use of secret agents as a means of anti-revolutionary struggle? Do we find a common or similar line of thought which could attest to the uniform conceptualization of the problem by the police throughout the entire period or at different and distinct stages? Finally, can the answers to these questions account, wholly or in part, for the use of this method for some 40 years?

A striking illustration of the change that began in the early 1880s emerges from a comparison between the approaches of two senior police officials who were active in different periods: Count Benckendorff, founder of the Separate Corps of Gendarmes, and Alexander Martynov, who began his career as an outstanding officer of the Gendarmes and later served as Head of the Okhrana Section at Saratov (1908) and in Moscow (1912).

Count Benckendorff was a German of Baltic extraction who, although not from an upper class background, sported an aristocratic manner and a strong sense of honour. Annoyed that society women tended to regard him as a mere 'gendarme' or as a 'spy', he set out to make the political police force respectable, to imbue it with a chivalric code consistent with its role as the representative of an autocracy that strove for the good of the people.[3] Martynov, in his memoirs, describes the process by which the Corps of Gendarmes was established, quoting Benckendorff's memorandum to Nicholas I on the need for the formation of an efficient political police force. For this force to excel and to encompass the entire empire, Benckendorff believed that it should be centralized and that the moral qualities of its Director should command respect. Only the title of Minister of Police and Inspector of the Gendarmes would gain him the sympathy of all the decent people who might want to warn the government about conspiracies or pass on relevant items of interest.

For Martynov, however, Benckendorff's ideas are mere 'visions of fantasy' (*manilovism*) which could only raise a smile:

> Count Benckendorff naively supposed that the new Minister . . . and for that matter the police force itself, would require the sympathy and services of 'decent folk' who would warn [them] about conspiracies [against the state]. It never even occurred to Count Benckendorff that it would be more efficient and more convenient to obtain the requisite information for money, through persons who are in one way or another close to the 'plotters', or that the 'decent folk', or well-intentioned citizens, of whom he speaks, all their decency and good will notwithstanding, usually know absolutely nothing about conspiracies.

Martynov pointed out that when the Corps of Gendarmes commenced its operations it had not the slightest idea about any ongoing secret conspiracies, and that it waited in vain for the help of 'the decent people'.[4]

Thus, in Martynov's opinion, secret agents who had been no more than an auxiliary tool of the police became a vital instrument. Police officers before him had held a similar view. Aleksei Lopukhin, who headed the Police Department from 1902 to 1904 saw the agents as nothing less than the very foundation stone and *sine qua non* of the entire activity of the political police. In Lopukhin's conception, the police had two tasks: to uncover criminal actions still in the planning stage and to investigate them if they were nevertheless perpetrated. Where criminal deeds of a general nature were concerned, Lopukhin hypothesized, this division was merely formal, since criminal intentions could hardly be uncovered. In contrast, political crimes were marked by 'intellectual characteristics' and by long-term clandestine planning – enabling the police to take steps not only to investigate such crimes *post factum*, but also to expose them in advance. For that purpose 'the police should enter or infiltrate the spheres of the intellectual life of suspected criminals, and to ensure their success should assume a guise of sympathy and agreement, or adopt measures which infringe on the freedom of the individual and are consequently, only appropriate for crimes which have already been uncovered'.[5]

The buying of informers, with access to the conspirators, as depicted by Martynov, or the police infiltration of the intellectual life of criminal suspects, as described by Lopukhin, were dubbed the 'Internal Agency' by police circles. In the revolutionary lexicon, however, such methods were known, pejoratively, as *Degaevshchina*, after Sergei Degaev, of the *Norodnaia Volia*, who had been the agent, and subsequently the assassin of the Head of the Special Section of the Police Department, Georgii Sudeikin. This early example anticipated many future cases, and because Sudeikin's role in it reflected a fairly clear cut concept of the potential use of the Internal Agency it deserves to be recounted briefly.

Sergei Degaev was a loyal and devoted party member; nothing in the testimonies about him presages his future betrayal of his comrades. Intelligent and gifted, he used his personal qualities and his contacts to further party interests. His only apparent flaw as a revolutionary at that time was his fierce desire to be a member of the Executive Committee. he complained repeatedly to his party colleagues that despite all his efforts on behalf of the revolutionary cause, the Executive Committee did not see fit to co-opt him. Complaints of this sort were rarely voiced, and they generated a certain antagonism.

In January 1881 Nikolai Kletochnikov, of the *Narodnaia Volia*, was arrested. Having infiltrated the St Petersburg Police Department, for the last two years he had provided his revolutionary friends with detailed lists of police agents in their ranks. Kletochnikov's arrest was a severe setback for the party. Rumours of his activities were widespread in St Petersburg among radical youth, many of whom dreamed of following in his footsteps. Thus, when Sergei Degaev's younger brother, Volodia, was arrested while in the possession of revolutionary leaflets, he agreed to Sudeikin's request to serve as his agent, in the hope that he could become the successor of the legendary Kletochnikov. Volodia Degaev took this step with the knowledge and approval of his brother, Sergei, and of the representative of the Executive Committee in St Petersburg. However, the collaboration seems to have benefited neither side.

In the meantime, the party, jolted by a wave of arrests, concluded that its survival depended on Sudeikin's liquidation. Sergei Degaev decided to take advantage of his younger brother's acquaintance with the police commander in order to get closer to him and put him under surveillance – again with the knowledge and approval of the representative of the Executive Committee in St Petersburg. With his brother acting as a go-between, Sergei Degaev found a job as a draughtsman in the Police Department. However, even this move proved unavailing: the assassination plan had to be called off due to operational difficulties.

However, if Sergei Degaev's acquaintance with Sudeikin did not further party interests, it did prove beneficial to Degaev himself when he was arrested in December 1882. Hoping for a speedy release from imprisonment and the threat of hard labour, Degaev got in touch with Sudeikin, who appeared on the scene to interrogate him personally. During their conversation, Sudeikin was able to convince Degaev that he, Sudeikin, was actually a secret revolutionary seeking to attain a position of influence in the government in order to realize the aims of the revolution at a later stage. If Degaev co-operated in order to enhance Sudeikin's standing, they could share power in the future, Sudeikin as Minister of the Interior, and Degaev as his deputy.

In his subsequent confession Degaev related that he had hoped to achieve his ends with the smallest possible loss of human life, but that the relentless pressure of the police and his intense fear of forfeiting their trust gradually forced him into revealing everything he knew. During his year-long contacts with Sudeikin, Degaev began to realize that he had fallen into a double trap: on the one hand Sudeikin had already milked him to the last drop and might therefore try to dump him; on the other hand the revolutionaries, sensing betrayal, were determined to expose it whatever the cost. Degaev, therefore, decided to flee to Paris, where he would confess all the details to the party representatives there.

The Executive Committee's statement on the case described the dilemma it faced. As the representative of a political party, the committee claimed it could not behave like a private person and base its decision exclusively on its feeling of moral revulsion or the claims of justice against Degaev. The committee felt obliged to attain a number of cardinal goals: to save the activists who were still at large, even though the police had already been informed about them; to free the party's institutions from the police scrutiny; to extract detailed information about the secret agents and police collaborators from Degaev; and finally, to execute Sudeikin, so that he himself would fall into the trap he had dug for others and his death would be an eternal warning to anyone who saw betrayal as a way of achieving his aim.[6]

Degaev was sent back to St Petersburg and instructed to provide assistance in the assassination of Sudeikin. He was assured that if he fulfilled all the conditions set by the Executive Committee, he would be brought back alive and well to Europe. The assassination was carried out on 16 December 1883. Degaev invited Sudeikin to his flat, where members of the *Narodnaia Volia*, armed with bayonets, laid an ambush for him. Sudeikin, who arrived together with a relative, was killed, and his companion seriously wounded. Degaev was smuggled across the border that same night. He emigrated to the United States, where under the name of Dr Pell, he held a university chair of mathematics until his death in 1921.[7]

It appears that Sudeikin believed that in a régime which feared terrorism and posited its eradication as a paramount aim, the standing of those responsible for security hung in a delicate balance between the extent of the government's apprehension and the degree of police success. On the one hand, the more the régime feared the danger facing it, the more it relied on the political police; on the other hand, while police prestige was enhanced by its success in striking at and suppressing terrorism, this very success was liable to diminish the government's feeling of dependence. It was this dual perception that led Sudeikin to use Degaev in order to undermine the *Narodnaia Volia* and paralyse its activity, but at the same time – in order to underscore the threat posed by the revolutionaries – he plotted to employ Degaev to assassinate the Minister of the Interior and earlier he even staged an attack on his own life. This plan, which aimed at enhancing Sudeikin's credibility, called for Degaev to waylay the former in a public garden, wound him in the left arm, and escape, using horses provided by Sudeikin in advance. The means Sudeikin chose to demonstrate his value to the government may have been unusually extreme. However, the problem the police faced in emphasizing their importance to the régime was to recur in various ways at different times – as, for example, over the question of the nature and style of the operational report.

In parallel to Sudeikin's activity in St Petersburg, the Okhrana in Moscow employed similar, if less imaginative, methods. Its commander, Berdiaev, spread his network of agents throughout the entire central region and he was able to nip in the bud most of the sporadic organizational attempts that characterized the 1880s and the first half of the 1890s. However, unlike Sudeikin's system of personal manipulation, Berdiaev's approach led him to employ a simpler method of collecting information for the immediate liquidation of revolutionary groups.[8] His successes, and the severe blow dealt to the *Narodnaia Volia*, instilled a sense of confidence of being in control in both police and government circles. Credit for this feeling was attributed to the Internal Agency, whose efficiency also reinforced the tendency to view the revolutionaries as merely a few energetic conspirators, rather than as a movement possessing deeper social roots. Indeed, this was the view held by most police officers until 1905.[9] Naturally, the deployment of the political police was consistent with this outlook. The Corps of Gendarmes was dispersed across the entire empire, while the Okhrana sections, designed to upgrade the anti-revolutionary struggle, were established in a limited number of industrial centres (*see* Preface).

However, the Social Revolutionaries launched their activities precisely in those provinces which lacked proficient investigative institutions. The SR's Battle Organization carried out its first assassination on 2 April 1902. Perpetrated by organization member Stepan Balmashev against the Minister of the Interior, Sipiagin, the attack stunned the government: 'The impact generated by Balmashev's shot was one of total bewilderment. The authorities simply did not understand what or how it had happened or from where it had come.'[10]

As in the past, this blow to the government from an unforeseen direction led to urgent calls for reorganization. In April 1902 Viacheslav Plehve, Director of the Police Department, was appointed Minister of the Interior. As his successor in the Police Department, he chose Alexei Lopukhin, a young lawyer from the district attorney's office in Kharkov. Sergei Zubatov was appointed as the new head of the Special Section. Following his tenure as a secret agent under Berdiaev, Zubatov had risen in the Police hierarchy, becoming the leading expert in political investigations. To help cope with the new situation, additional Okhrana sections were established in Russia's main cities, based on networks of secret agents (*sekretnye sotrudniki*). According to police official Alexander Spiridovich, the changes led to a series of arrests as early as the autumn of 1902. The most important of these took place in Odessa, Ekaterinoslav and Tambov.

However, it was only the events of 1905 which finally drove home the fact that revolutionary activity was more deeply rooted than the authorities had believed, and the concomitant realization that a more effective response was required. This led to the issue of guidelines emphasizing additional aspects of the Internal Agency's activity and administrative reorganization. In several instances a more penetrating study of the long-term influence of the Internal Agency was initiated.

A circular from the Police Department to the officers of the Gendarmes stressed that it was not enough to collect information aimed at the immediate liquidation of underground organizations; in addition, comprehension of the reports conveyed to the officers of the Gendarmes in the provinces was imperative. A close acquaintance with the nature, goals and methods of the secret organizations must unquestionably be the first duty of officers of the Separate Corps of Gendarmes who had to fight against them. This was because only such complete knowledge could provide the government's investigative bodies with a correct picture of the situation and assist them in developing suitable methods. Otherwise all that will be accomplished is the temporary, and sometimes chance disposal of individual representatives of the offenders, or the seizure of some of their propaganda material.[11]

The need to clarify the new developments, and assist the police who were groping in the dark, is also implied in the term employed to describe the task of the secret agents: 'illumination' (*osveshchenie*). It had broader ramifications than the mere collection of information solely for purposes of liquidation, which had been the aim in the 1880s and 1890s. Despite the more perceptive approach discernible in this circular, the reforms introduced in 1907 were quantitative rather than qualitative. For this reason the change in outlook demonstrated in it was more apparent than real.

In the spirit of the improvements introduced in 1902 following the appointment of Plehve and Lopukhin, the number of Okhrana sections was increased and the system of districts (*raiony*) was instituted. These district sections, which concentrated on investigations in specific regions, replaced the Okhrana section which had existed until then and had been directly responsible to the Police Department in St Petersburg. The establishment of the *raiony* followed the spread of the revolutionary movement: wherever a district committee of the SR or the SD operated, a district Okhrana section was also set up in order to guide the investigative activity in the area.[12]

A secret circular to the provincial and the city governors signed by the President of the Council of Ministers and of the Interior Stolypin, and the Director of the Police Department Trusevich, spelled out the lessons learned from the strikes of October 1905, and enumerated the guidelines for future police policy. The memorandum laid emphasis on the efforts of all the socialist parties to agitate among the peasantry, and to exploit the rural agrarian movement for revolutionary objectives. To counter this, the memorandum recommended not only the introduction of pacifying measures, but the waging of a vigorous struggle against the agitation; thus, every effort should be made to ensure that the police possessed as complete a dossier as possible on the agitators. The latter was to be achieved with the help of the estate owners and the peasants themselves. Moreover, identical measures were to be taken with respect to revolutionary elements operating in the army, the trade unions, the high schools and the institutions of higher education. All this information was to be forwarded to the 'supreme administrative authorities' – the *raiony* – which alone were familiar with the views of the central government and the significance of the various political streams.[13]

On 10 February 1907 the Police Department circulated instructions concerning the internal detective activity and how to organize it among the directors of the *raiony*. The linchpin of these 188 items – which came to be known as the 'Stolypin Directives' – was the secret agent: 'the only absolutely reliable means which can guarantee the information possessed by the investigative institution'.[14] This laid the foundations for the infiltration of secret agents not only into the revolutionary movements but into all public strata, and at the request of all government bodies, including city and provincial governors, not only those engaged in political investigation. In response to the revolutionary escalation from the 1880s until 1907, the authorities constantly expanded the Okhrana sections, basing their operations on the secret agent, whose presence became legion in all public sectors in Russia.

No one questioned either the effectiveness of or the need for the method. At various times, some senior police officers even stressed its deeper, long-range advantages. Already in the 1880s Sudeikin had circulated a memorandum in the Special Section, expressing his view that the activity of the agents who had infiltrated the organizations, along with the correct use of the information they provided, would generate suspicion and demoralization, thereby greatly retarding possible revolutionary activity. Sudeikin's recommendations included the cultivation of quarrels and clashes among the revolutionary groups; the spreading of false rumours to intimidate the revolutionaries and instil a fear of betrayal and espionage; and the discrediting of revolutionary leaflets and organs by attributing them to police provocation.[15]

Summing up the results of the 1902 reform, Spiridovich wrote:

> The blow dealt to the [SR] party was a severe one. Its leading activists were removed from the party's ranks. The seizure of typesetting equipment and of shipments of banned literature deprived the party of its chief means of conducting propaganda and agitation. Contacts were severed, secret flats were uncovered, and the connection between the local organizations and the centre abroad, which had been established with so much effort, was disrupted. These developments could not but leave their mark on the condition of the party. It suspended its activity, the operation of several organizations had to be halted; even though this activity was subsequently resumed, the new corpus of activists was in general far weaker than its predecessor and its operations were less successful.[16]

Like Spiridovich, Martynov also perceived the Internal Agency primarily as a preventive body. Furthermore, both men assumed that the correct use of the information produced by the secret agents had a cumulative effect. Spiridovich believed that the liquidations caused the party's constant debilitation, and likewise Martynov claimed that well-timed liquidations could keep the underground in a constant state of collapse or could actually eliminate it, by repeatedly thwarting all attempts to establish new contacts.[17]

Sudeikin, Spiridovich and Martynov were unanimous in their appreciation of the Internal Agency's long-term as well as its immediate importance. Nevertheless, the difference between Sudeikin and his two colleagues lay in their underlying premises: whereas Sudeikin believed that the psychological impact would prove to be the disintegrative force, Spiridovich and Martynov held that the organizations would fail because they lacked the resiliency to recover from successive setbacks.

Both the Police Department circular to the officers of the Corps of Gendarmes and the directive establishing the *raiony* authorities indicate that despite a certain tendency toward decentralization in the structure of the political police, the Police Department nevertheless strove to remain in the vanguard of the anti-revolutionary struggle. The department considered its task to be the development of appropriate tactics on the basis of the information received from the *raiony*.

The growing infiltration of the illegal organizations by secret agents had in fact presented the Police Department with additional and more sophisticated possibilities, enabling them to influence intra-party developments. For example, in 1914 the Police Department received information concerning tendencies toward reunification among the Social Democrats. This information was taken very seriously. The Director of the Police Department and the Head of the Special Section despatched a circular to the directors of all the investigative institutions ordering them to deploy all the secret agents under their command without delay, with instructions that while participating in various party consultations they must firmly reject any notion of organizational unity within these streams (the SD), and particularly between the Bolsheviks and the Mensheviks.[18] The comments on this subject by Stepan Beletskii, Director of the Police Department from December 1912 to January 1914, are well known. He admitted to having employed Roman Malinovskii, his agent among the Bolsheviks, to widen the split between the branches of the Social Democratic faction, based on the principle of *divide et impera*.[19] Beletskii's point of departure was that the threat posed by a revolutionary organization was in direct proportion to its size. The police also arrested Bolshevik leaders who were seeking to reunite the RSDRP in the wake of resolutions adopted at the plenum of the Central Committee in January 1910.[20]

The SR party was also the target in an attempt at political manipulation as a result of the information that Mark Natanson, one of the party's senior leaders, was about to empower Vasilii Sukhomlin to operate in Russia. The Police Department viewed this eventuality as 'entirely undesirable', given the fact that it regarded Sukhomlin as a dedicated exponent of terrorism on the most extensive scale possible, and its fear that he would use this authority and Natanson's connections in Russia to put his ideas into practice. To prevent these developments, the Police Department directed the Head of the Foreign Agency to cause Natanson and Sukhomlin to fall out to the point of a complete break.[21] This was only one instance of the earlier attempts to besmirch SR leaders.[22]

A substantial difference exists between attempted political manipulation, as depicted in the circular instructing case officers to order their agents to deepen the rift within the RSDRP and the description of Beletskii's method of operation and attempt to set SR leaders at one another's throats. In the latter instances the desired result was to be achieved through the activation of one agent, or at most several agents, by a single officer. In contrast, the former cases were marked by an effort to transform quantity into quality: to take advantage of the plethora of agents in order to promote, or in this case to thwart, a development which was of paramount interest to the police. To exploit the growing number of agents qualitatively, guidance from the centre was needed, namely the centralized organization of the investigative institutions. However, the Police Department was wholly unprepared. Not only was it fragmented between rival bodies such as the Okhrana and the Gendarmes, but by its own doing it made the formulation and enforcing of a coherent policy impossible. In practice it encouraged the heads of the investigative bodies to work exclusively toward gathering information for the purpose of liquidation, and to regard this as their ultimate aim. Commanders or chiefs (*nachal'niki*) who excelled in major liquidation operations were awarded special prizes and their prestige rose with every success of this kind.[23] The capture of a battle squad, the seizure of a laboratory which manufactured explosives or the discovery of a printing press were regarded as especially noteworthy achievements.[24] The prizes, moreover, were not restricted solely to commanders who arrested revolutionaries or scuttled major operations; their agents, those whose work had facilitated advance knowledge of revolutionary activity, were also suitably rewarded.[25] The upshot was that instead of a bond being formed between the Okhrana commanders and the Police Department, a common interest developed between the commanders and their agents. This may also be inferred from Martynov's remark that without a good agent it was impossible 'to make a career': a gendarme could only excel with the aid of a serious secret agent. Moreover, even the degree of a Commander's authoritativeness was measured by the 'seriousness' of the secret agents in his service. Commanders who at a given moment found themselves without one did not, it is true, lose their status formally, but in practice the outcome was as it used to be in the past: the impoverished feudal prince had to yield to the rule of his neighbour whose fortune had risen higher than his own, and who imposed his will on the prince's patrimony.[26]

Because of this state of affairs, many police officers were distinctly disinclined to co-operate with one another; on the contrary, the personal rivalry sometimes led to failure. Martynov tells about his contacts with the Okhrana commander in Penza. He aimed to confiscate a large consignment of banned literature without compromising the agent who had conveyed the information. However, the local commander, disobeying orders, operated on his own, endangering the secret agent. For Martynov, this incident demonstrated the entire weakness of the police apparatus. Once the consignment was seized, the Penza commander could immediately cable St Petersburg that he had captured a quantity of illegal literature, which would have had a greater psychological impact on the police commander than was justified.[27]

There appear to have been even more serious cases, in which the actions of one Okhrana commander led to the exposure of another's agent. This, at least, is the impact of Mikhail Bakai's wrongly attributing the anonymous letter of 1905, which warned the SR party against Azef and Nikolai Tatarov, to police officer Leonid Kremenetskii, whose alleged motive was his desire to dispose of Peter Rachkovskii, his rival.[28] The very fact that such a thought could cross the mind of a former Okhrana official shows that an occurrence of this kind was not impossible.

Obviously, under these conditions it was virtually impossible to exploit the numerical strength of the secret agents in order to effect a clear-cut political line. This would have required co-ordination and collegiality among the police commanders in the different localities, and would have called for the sacrifice of any prospects of immediate personal distinction in order to further a political aim with results which were not always clear and where the effort invested was not always repaid. In fact, the circular of September 1914, which sought to prevent the unification of the Bolsheviks and the Mensheviks was an exception rather than the rule.

Even where it was possible to use an influential individual agent to attain a certain political goal, the procedure depended primarily on the case officer's estimate of the police interest. Apparently, priority was given to assembling the information. This was the practice in 1901 and again in 1913, under Beletskii, despite his specific views on Police Department policy and the deployment of secret agents. In 1901 Azef, who was working for the Okhrana commander, Zubatov, helped bring about the unification of the two major Socialist-Revolutionary groupings: the Southern Party and the Northern Union, which he represented. As he explained to his superior: 'I believe that for us this is very important, particularly under the conditions in which it all took place – because now almost everything is open to us.[29] This is no more than Azef's own interpretation of the police interest, but it does indicate that the Okhrana was aware of his efforts at unification and that at least he received no orders to the contrary.

Another example concerns Alexander Mass, the librarian of the Paris group for the SR party. Mass had to take a stand in the debate between the orthodox faction, which advocated the traditional terrorist line, and the members of the *Pochin* (Initiative) group, who favoured moderate, legal methods in order to preserve the party's strength. Both groups were anxious to win him over because he had declared his intention of making a large contribution to the party out of an inheritance (probably Okhrana money) that had come his way. Although it might be thought that the police interest would be to reinforce the moderate, anti-terrorist group, Mass in fact lent his support to the exponents of uncompromising terrorrism.[30]

As these cases show, when it came to internal political questions in which the Police Department had a direct interest, it did not always try to exert an influence in line with its explicit official policy. Evidently, the Heads of the Department had no clear operational conception, and they too viewed the achievements of the anti-revolutionary struggle exclusively in terms of liquidation.

The overriding desire to obtain information also called for untiring efforts to gain access to its sources and to those centres where important operational decisions were made and which were assumed to receive a constant influx of data from the periphery. This central information was meant to add to the individual, sometimes incomplete, reports received from agents in the local groups or, in Martynov's words, was supposed to 'clarify the true physiognomy of the underground'.[31] The provider of this information was the 'trump card' of which Martynov spoke – the index of prestige and authority. At the end of 1911 the acting Deputy Director of the Police Department, Sergei Vissarionov, expressed his disappointment at the performance of Alexander Krasil'nikov, Head of the Foreign Agency. He contended that Krasil'nikov could do more to improve the agent's standing among the parties, and that none of them were moving up in the party hierarchy.[32]

There were various ways to ensure the promotion of an agent. Martynov relates that in order to enhance the prestige of an agent in the eyes of his party colleagues, he would first involve him in a discussion on concrete questions of party theory. To this end Martynov would pick out a pamphlet from the vast library of revolutionary material which he had accumulated over the years, and choose one or two of its tenets. The agent would study the material, and then use what he had learned to attack the proponents of the opposing views, thereby gaining prestige as an authority on theoretical issues.[33]

A far more accepted practice was to provide an agent with funds to further a certain party goal. Cases are known in which the Okhrana financed revolutionary journals via its agents, who played an active role in their publication.[34] Another method – successfully used to ensure the election of Roman Malinovskii as a Duma representative on behalf of the Bolsheviks – was to falsify documents in order to provide an agent with a clean past, and to arrest anyone who stood in his way.[35]

In 1917 Beletskii was asked by the committee investigating the illegal activities of the old régime how it was that the Internal Agency was considered moral and acceptable in civilian life while at a certain stage an order had been issued banning its use in the army. 'The military society possesses a completely different character', Beletskii replied, and went on to elaborate:

> It is a family united by its ties, in which unique relations exist among the officers, the soldiers, the senior and junior commanders. Both ethics and the military oath place these relations beyond the realm of such activity, because the presence of secret agents within a cohesive group framework weakens the cohesiveness and the sense of family.[36]

As noted above, the police annals include a number of instances of senior officers who recognized the immense potential latent in the very presence of the Agency within the revolutionary organizations, where cohesiveness and a sense of family were also a *sine qua non* for survival. Nevertheless, the basic conception of the Agency's goal as being primarily to accumulate information for liquidation purposes superseded all other considerations and left no room for a re-examination which might have led to operative conclusions. Moreover, it also prevented the integrated use of the detailed peripheral data together with the interpretive information from the centre, as depicted idealistically by Martynov. Since the Agency was regarded as the linchpin of police activity, from the moment its usage became systematic, no one could conceive of anti-revolutionary police activity without it. This enabled it to endure for so long despite the many changes during that period.

(ii) THE SECRET AGENT: HOPES AND RISKS

The underlying conception of the Internal Agency called for the maximum involvement of the secret agent in the illegal activity which he ultimately was supposed to prevent. Only such intense involvement could gain him access to the relevant information. We have already emphasized the police aim to advance their agents in the party hierarchy in order to gain a foothold in the revolutionary centres. An agent who wished to move up the party ladder had to excel in party activity, as Beletskii in fact admitted during his interrogation in 1917.[37] Hence, the more an agent was involved in matters that were considered criminal in nature, the more useful he became to the police. The Police Department found itself caught up in an incongruous situation. It could never be entirely certain that encouraging the agent to take part in the most dangerous work from its point of view was not promoting the very actions it sought to combat.

Article 8 of the *Directives for the Administration of the Internal Agency* states:

> The efforts of political investigation must be directed at shedding light on the revolutionary centres and at eliminating them the moment their activity peaks. Thus, an investigation must not be sabotaged merely for the sake of uncovering an underground printing press, or an arms cache which has long been unused. It must be remembered that such steps are meaningful only if they bring about the exposure of key revolutionary activists and the liquidation of the organization.[38]

Article 8 in fact epitomized the internal contradiction faced by the police. Police agents were permitted, even encouraged, to intensify their activity to the utmost, thus running the risk of letting the optimal moment for liquidation slip by. Worse still, there was no certainty that their activity was not furthering revolutionary aims without either the agents or the police having any control over the course of events. Did the termination of the revolutionary process occur at the particular moment which the police considered as 'liquidation'? In the wake of various contacts of which the agent notified the police, new connections developed which, due to the clandestine nature of the activity were unknown to the agent, despite his central position. Furthermore, there were cases in which police officers themselves conducted terrorist actions through their agents, either with the intention of excelling at any price, or in the naïve belief that the deed would serve as a magnet for revolutionaries in the field, who would be ensnared in the final liquidation.[39] Therefore the inherent incongruity in all cases where agents are used can be described as a contradiction between the chances of immediate gain as against the risk of long-term losses. This is all the more so where secret agents became the very foundation of the police work.

Alexander Gerasimov, who was Okhrana Commander in St Petersburg from 1905 to 1909, explains, for example, that according to Zubatov's method the role of the police was to identify all the members of a revolutionary organization and to liquidate them in one blow. Gerasimov disagreed with this approach, maintaining that since every liquidation of a revolutionary organization also meant the exposure of the agent who had operated within it, the result was a net loss to the secret police. Therefore, if Gerasimov had a reliable, responsible agent in an organization, he preferred to keep the organization as a whole under constant careful supervision, and to concentrate on individual arrests.[40] The Azef affair did not alter this conception – Gerasimov was convinced to his dying day of Azef's loyalty. He accused the Police Department of having taken insufficient measures after receiving advance information from Azef about the plot to assassinate Plehve organized by Egor Sazonov, a member of the Battle Organization.[41] Thus, the police could pay a heavy price in the wake of a top agent's revolutionary activity, the more so when the problem of the contradiction between long- and short-term interests was compounded by the question of trust.

If, nevertheless, an agent found himself compelled to participate actively, he had to obtain prior authorization from his superior officer as in the case of Zinaida Zhuchenko. Commencing her career as a secret agent for the SR party in Moscow in 1905, within a year she was already among the prominent figures on the Regional Committee.[42] She herself both proposed and took part in a number of terrorist acts and expropriations. In the winter of 1906 Zhuchenko informed her case officer that her organization was planning to assassinate Pavel Kurlov, the governor of Minsk, and that she had been entrusted with the task of delivering the bomb to the assassins. Following consultations she was allowed to proceed with her part in the plot, with the aim of apprehending the perpetrators red-handed. However, to prevent the actual murder of Kurlov, Zhuchenko first passed the bomb on to the police, whose experts defused it; only afterwards delivering it to the revolutionaries. The attack went off as planned. Kurlov sustained only a slight head wound and the would-be assassin who actually threw the bomb was caught and subsequently hanged.[43]

This case could serve as a model for a successful police operation. However, the success of the police in this case was primarily due to unusual circumstances. When she commenced her service in Moscow Zinaida Zhuchenko was on intimate personal terms with her case officer, Evgenii Klimovich, the Commander of the Okhrana in Moscow, and the Head of the Special Section at the time of the assassination attempt on Kurlov.[44] This factor enabled the police to act with confidence. More often, however, commanders were not on terms of personal friendship with their agents, and they frequently viewed them with deep mistrust. They regarded the very system of the Internal Agency as an unavoidable necessity, citing examples from various lands and historical periods in which the authorities had employed identical methods, as proof that this was the only system the government could adopt against its opponents.[45]

In their memoirs, police officers described at length the considerable proficiency which was required for the successful administration of the Internal Agency. However, many would have agreed with Alexei Vasil'ev, the last Director of the Police Department: 'When all is said and done, every secret agent is a traitor to his comrades.'[46] He also stressed that many of the agents were Jews, adding that they in particular were ready to sell their comrades for money – often for a pitiful sum.[47] Vladimir Dzhunkovskii, the Deputy Minister of the Interior, so strongly opposed the system that he suggested it would be preferable if civilians maintained the contacts with the agents, since these were dishonourable for an officer.[48] However, despite his blatant mistrust of the secret agents and his dislike of the policy, he was unwilling to dispense with it completely. This negative attitude is part of the Christian ethos which regards treason as the basest of sins; it is no mere coincidence that the lowest circle of Dante's Inferno, devoured by the jaws of Lucifer, are three persons who have become symbols for the most heinous acts of treason in history: Judas Iscariot, Brutus and Cassius. Indeed, the image of Judas Iscariot recurs countless times in the writings of the betrayed revolutionaries. Police officers, too, seem to have continually reminded one another about the type of people they were dealing with.[49] This emotion-laden attitude may have generated part of the constant apprehension felt by many senior chiefs that the participation of their agents in underground activity did not always serve police interests alone. Okhrana files are replete with Police Department memoranda warning chief investigators against agents 'who are unworthy of trust and who have a tendency towards provocation and extortion'.[50] There were in fact agents (the Maximalist Semen Ryss and others) who attempted to utilize the system for revolutionary purposes by trying to extort money from the Police Department, which for its part issued repeated warnings against them.

The revolutionaries themselves stressed a second contradiction which marked the Internal Agency's method of operation. In contrast to the police view which ignored the essential contradiction in the system, the revolutionaries emphasized its formal aspect. To besmirch the police and underscore their baseness, they contended that the Agency's activity violated the law by encouraging people to join illegal organizations and take part in actions which the law deemed subversive. This problem was of absolutely no concern to the police.[51] Yet it is in this dual contradiction – between the interests of the police on the one hand and the law on the other hand that the difference between the concepts of 'provocation' and the *agent provocateur* are rooted. Whereas for the police a *provocateur* can only be a person whose loyalty is not exclusively to them, for the revolutionaries an *agent provocateur* is a person who knowingly and deliberately breaks the law in order to hand over other law-breakers to the authorities.[52] Zinaida Zhuchenko was considered to be such a loyal and successful agent that even after her exposure in 1909 she was paid 200 roubles a month – less than her income prior to her exposure, but still considered quite a respectable sum.[53] In striking contrast, for the revolutionaries Zinaida Zhuchenko symbolized provocation at its basest. Vladimir Burtsev, who for years was engaged in exposing agents in the ranks of the revolution and was known as an expert on matters relating to provocation, was once asked to enumerate its chief manifestations: he listed the Zhuchenko affair as second only to the Azef case.[54]

From the revolutionaries' point of view, then, there were two distinct categories of secret agents: the informers (*osvedomiteli*), who provided the authorities with information about illegal activities and organizations – without themselves taking part in them – and the *agents provocateurs*, who were members of those organizations, encouraged others to act, and who themselves played an active role. The latter were also frequently termed 'traitors' (*predateli*).

The terminological distinction used by the revolutionaries reflected differences which also existed in practice. The informers, who for the most part were not party members, did not pass on information regularly and systematically, but reported on matters which had come to their knowledge indirectly. They might be workers who heard on the job about the time and place of a workers' meeting, or persons considered sympathetic to a certain revolutionary circle, who were surreptitiously informed about revolutionary activities. These persons, whom the police termed 'auxiliary agents' (*vspomogatel'nye sotrudniki*), were poorly and irregularly paid – usually piecemeal and according to the value of each item of information.

On the other hand, party members who maintained permanent and regular contact with the police, reporting on their organization and its ongoing activity, were known as 'secret agents' (*sekretnye sotrudniki*); they usually received a steady salary, supplemented at times by special bonuses for information of particular value. In some cases the auxiliary agents were promoted and became secret agents. Bentsion Dolin, for example, who was known as one of the most important Okhrana agents among the anarchists – if not the most important – started out as an auxiliary agent who reported chiefly on the Bund. Having excelled in that capacity, in 1904 he became a secret agent, initially within the Bund in Zhitomir. However, after he came under suspicion, he moved to Ekaterinoslav, where he joined the Communist-Anarchists, working in their ranks until the Revolution.[55] On the other hand, there were also instances in which the police sought to utilize the contacts of agents who had already been exposed, at least as auxiliary agents.[56]

Cases are known of secret agents who, while not affiliated with any specific party, enjoyed a special standing among revolutionary circles which gave them access to abundant valuable information. Berko Batushanskii, for example, was a dentist, who did not belong to any revolutionary organization. However, he was so popular among the revolutionaries that his clinic became a kind of political centre, and the incoming information enabled him to report to the police about the local intelligentsia, the Social Democrats and the SR.[57] Because he reported on a number of organizations simultaneously, Batushanskii belonged to the category of agents which Valerian Agafonor labelled *encyclopedists*. One of the most striking figures among them was Ignat Kokochinskii, who filed detailed reports not only about the Social Democrats, but also about the Bund, the Zionists and the PPS.[58] All told, however, this was a relatively small group.

At the very bottom of the scale were the detectives – the *filery*, or as the revolutionaries called them, the *shpiki*. This category of person was collectively known by the Police Department as the *External Agency* since, in contrast to the Internal Agency, they acquired the information during the assigned external surveillance missions and not from within the revolutionary organization. The task of the *filery* was purely technical: to trail suspects on the streets, in cafés, theatres, trains, public squares – in short, everywhere – in order to discover who made up their circle of acquaintances and with whom they came in contact.[59] When a suspect was placed under surveillance for the first time, he was assigned a code-name, which was the only appellation known to the *filer*. The *filer* was not allowed to know the suspect's identity or why he was important or sometimes even to which organization he belonged.

Until 1907 political police work relied primarily on the External Agency. However, due to growing dependence on the Internal Agency, its role declined, and gradually it became an auxiliary tool for authenticating reports originating in the Internal Agency, an instrument for checking on secret agents, or a means used to supplement the agents' activity. Strict care was taken to ensure that the identity of the secret agents remained unknown to the members of the External Agency.

The qualifications demanded of the *filery* were extraordinary. Article 2 of the External Agency's regulations stated that the *filer* must be politically reliable, firm in his views, a man of honour, courageous, crafty, cultured, patient, cautious, truthful, honest, concise, disciplined and self-controlled; moreover, he must have strong legs, good eyesight, be generally healthy, and be inconspicuous.[60] Indeed, the *filery* required a capacity to endure suffering, hunger and cold. Not infrequently they were called on to stand for hours at a time on a street corner, day or night, in all weathers, while waiting for the subject under surveillance to appear. They needed a good memory for details of buildings and street plans.[61] However, due to the low ranks of the position in the police hierarchy, combined with poor wages, the candidates for the External Agency were uneducated and virtually illiterate.[62]

The basic mistrust with which many police officers viewed the secret agents partly depended on the reasons that had led the agents to join the service in the first place. It was this motive that influenced the agents' determination to execute the missions assigned, their loyalty to their superiors and the reliability of their reports. From the police point of view, the most reliable agent was the non-party type, who rose gradually in the ranks of the organization and who in the course of his service in the Okhrana became dedicated to its interests.[63] Evidently such agents constituted only a small group in comparison to the numbers coerced into co-operating in the course of their imprisonment. When dealing with detainees, the police sought to utilize to their own advantage the fear felt by prisoners under interrogation. They found it more productive not to concentrate on the highly experienced, veteran revolutionaries who fell into their hands, but on those who had not yet been hardened by daring revolutionary acts. The police would confront them with the extensive data collected and then intimidate them with the threat of exile or forced labour. Nearly all the prisoners who did become collaborators were coerced into joining the Agency during their initial arrest. Details are available concerning the arrest of 48 secret agents. In 34 cases (71 per cent) a clear connection exists between the date of their imprisonment, release or escape from prison and their recruitment to police service. In 14 cases (29 per cent) such a connection could not be definitely established. 29 of the detainees became secret agents following their first arrest, four following their second and only one following his third arrest.

However, since it is obvious that only a minority of the political prisoners did in fact become collaborators, a further inquiry into the detainees' susceptibility to police pressure is necessary. Clearly this question, by its very nature, admits of only a partial answer, as various personal aspects unique to each separate case are involved. Yet an examination of the group's features, compared with those of the overall party make-up, can also be indicative regarding their motives to co-operate with the police. Thus Tables 1 and 2 deal with the secret agents' occupational structure, while Tables 3 and 4 refer to their national composition.

Details about occupational distribution are available concerning 96 of the secret agents: 44 SRs and 53 Social Democrats. In order to check the validity and significance of these data, they have been collated with the occupational analyses of Hildermeir and Lane.

The professional profile of the secret agents among the SRs and among the Social Democrats is generally similar to that of their respective parties, with the exception of two categories: workers among the former and members of the intelligentsia, notably students (nine out of 16) among the latter. Since greed is hardly a trait confined to workers or students exclusively, their over-representation among the SRs and Social Democrats is explicable by the differential wage rates that the police were willing to pay agents of each party.

Table 1 Occupational structure of the secret agents within the SR party compared to the general SR population, 1902–14

	Secret agents		SR general population[1]	
Professional party activists	1	(2.27%)	24	(2.8%)
Professors, journalists, men of letters	1	(2.27%)	38	(4.43%)
Students	10	(22.7%)	206	(24.06%)
Employees, lower intelligentsia	7	(15.9%)	130	(15.18%)
Higher intelligentsia	6	(13.63%)	101	(11.79%)
Teachers	—		63	(7.35%)
Officers	—		16	(1.86%)
Unskilled workers	7	(15.9%) }	215	(25.11%)
Skilled workers, craftsmen	10	(22.7%) }		
Peasants	1	(2.27%)	37	(4.32%)
Soldiers, sailors	1	(2.27%)	13	(1.51%)
Small traders	—		13	(1.51%)
TOTAL	44	(100%)*	856	(100%)*

Source:
[1]Hildermeier, *Die sozialrevolutionäre Partei*, p. 295. The categories chosen were those of Hildermeier, to provide a basis for comparison. The percentage was calculated of the sum total of the 'known' only.
*Due to rounding, the total sum does not always amount to 100%.

The high salaries offered to the SR detainees for co-operation served the workers among them as a further incentive to surrender to police pressure in view of their low income (see Table 8). In contrast, the meagre salaries the police paid to Social Democrat agents could not act as a similar incentive, all the more so since it was rarely possible for them to emigrate to western Europe, where police rates of payments for Social Democrat agents were higher (see Table 7). Students on the other hand, who constituted a similar needy social category seem to have taken advantage of their greater mobility. However, financial compensation was not enough to induce members of other professional groups to follow suit. We find then that financial reasons served as a secondary motive only, and that fear was after all the more powerful one.

To draw a comparison between the agents' national composition and that of their respective party is complicated due to the absence of relevant data and the substantial differences between the Bolsheviks and the Mensheviks in this sphere in particular. This was demonstrated in Lane's data. Furthermore, faction affiliation was specified

Table 2 Occupational structure of the secret agents among the Social Democrats compared to the general SD population[1]

	Secret agents	General SD population
Professionals, intelligentsia	16 (30.2%)	90 (14.1%)
Teachers	2 (3.8%)	25 (3.9%)
Officials (*sluzhashchie*)	3 (5.7%)	51 (8.0%)
Teachers, landlords, clergymen	—	7 (1.1%)
Workers	2 (3.8%)	78 (12.2%)
Factory, mill workers	15 (28.3%)	198 (31.1%)
Handicraftsmen	9 (17.0%)	110 (17.3%)
Printing, railway workers	5 (9.4%)	45 (7.1%)
Lower medical, others	1 (1.9%)	33 (5.2%)
TOTAL	53 (100%)*	637 (100%)*

Source:
[1]D. Lane, *The Roots of Russian Communism*, p. 22. While Lane divides his population into three groups: 'Bolsheviks', 'Mensheviks' and 'Unknown faction', no data are available as far as the factional affiliation of the secret agents is concerned. In order to provide a basis for comparison, in this study all the SDs were grouped together.
*Due to rounding, the total sum does not always amount to 100%.

Table 3 National composition of the secret agents within the SR party compared to the general SR population

	Secret agents	General SR population[1]
Russians, Ukrainians	55 (67.0%)	794 (77.5%)
Jews	18 (21.9%)	138 (13.5%)
Polish	4 (4.9%)	22 (2.1%)
Others	5 (6.1%)	70 (6.8%)
TOTAL	82 (100%)*	1024 (100%)*

Source:
[1]M. Perrie, 'The Social Composition and Structure of the Socialist-Revolutionary Party before 1917', *Soviet Studies*, XXIV, 2 (October 1972) 232.
*Due to rounding, the total sum does not always amount to 100%.

Table 4 National composition of the secret agents within the Social Democrats compared to the general SD population

	Secret agents		Bolsheviks[1]		Mensheviks[1]	
Russians	52	(67.5%)	82	(78.3%)	33	(34.0%)
Jews	19	(24.7%)	12	(11.4%)	22	(22.7%)
Others	6	(7.8%)	11	(10.3%)	41	(42.3%)
TOTAL	77	(100%)*	105	(100%)*	96	(100%)*

Source:
[1]D. Lane, *The Roots of Russian Communism*, p. 44.
*Due to rounding, the total sum does not always amount to 100%.

only in 14 cases of the 77 Social Democrat agents. However it enables us to infer that the overall number of agents among the Bolsheviks was higher than among the Mensheviks, a deduction in line with the general policy of the Police Department.

Where an agent's nationality was not explicitly specified classification was determined according to his name. This method is deficient as a tool especially for distinguishing between Russians and Ukrainians, though it is more reliable as far as Jews are concerned. Even if we bear in mind the shortcomings of the examination, the figures in Tables 1 and 2 show that whereas the proportion of secret agents among the Russians is lower than the Russian share in the general SD population it is considerable higher among the Jews. This is true both within the SRs and the Social Democrats, given the agents' differential distribution between the Bolshevik and the Menshevik overall population. As far as the Polish are concerned the numbers are too low to serve as an indication. However we may still infer that police intimidation was especially effective on members of weak groups, economically or nationally, which were more vulnerable and succumbed more easily to police pressure, although they were certainly not the only ones to do so.

Dr Arseny Bel'skii was arrested in Moscow on 9 January 1909. Three weeks later he was brought for interrogation before the Commander of the Okhrana unit. Bel'skii expressed his astonishment at having been detained, since at that time he had abandoned his revolutionary activity and was preoccupied with matters of professional interest. Nevertheless, the Okhrana Commander informed Bel'skii that his office was in possession of detailed reports about revolutionary activity which were sufficient to have him placed under the supervision of the Procurator General or at least exiled to the Iakutsk region. Actually, the facts enumerated by the Commander consisted of no more than a report about a meeting Bel'skii once had held with an SR leader and several other underground figures, along with the fact that he had recommended several potential recruits for the Battle Organization. Naming all of Bel'skii's acquaintances, and describing some of them in the process, the Commander concluded: 'You can see for yourself that we have enough facts to have you placed under the supervision of the Procurator General. But you yourself can prevent this and carry on with your professional work.'[64] If the prisoner hesitated, the interrogator would strike a softer note, assuring the detainee that he would not be required to turn in his friends, but only to provide general information of no great value.

Besides the natural fear experienced by revolutionaries who were ensnared by the Okhrana, many of them were overwhelmed when they learned just how extensive the Okhrana's information actually was. One such revolutionary, Mikhail Rips, describes his detention and interrogation in February 1909. After he had refused to answer a battery of questions, the interrogating officer 'began to tell me about the defeat of the revolutionary forces, and that he had information about all the revolutionary initiatives. Even before the revolutionaries act he already knows about it. So self-satisfied did he appear that upon hearing his tales, I, who had hitherto been perfectly tranquil having in the meantime managed to calm down, became very upset, because I remembered Azef. At that moment I understood that this was no mere boasting.'[65]

Repeatedly, the testimonies of revolutionaries describe the sense of shock and helplessness they felt in the face of what seemed to them, at the time, to be the Okhrana's unassailable omnipotence. Under the impact of the shock and fear, some of them were convinced that any further resistance would be futile, and simply gave up. 'Regarding ex-revolutionaries such as these,' Martynov relates, 'we would jokingly quote Franz Moor's remark in Schiller's *Die Räuber*: "The poor man was not born to be a martyr for his faith". There were, of course, many martyrs for the Marxist and the SR faith in the annals of the Russian revolutionary movement,' Martynov continues, 'but there were also many poor people who were not attracted by martyrdom, and it was they who filled the ranks of the Okhrana's secret collaborators.'[66] Gerasimov, the Okhrana Commander in St Petersburg, claimed he had at least 150–200 agents of this kind in his service, scattered among the different revolutionary and opposition parties.[67]

A prisoner who expressed his readiness to become a paid secret agent, was handed over to Okhrana personnel, who took down his confession and his statement of repentance. The prisoner was then pardoned and released. The confession served as a guarantee that the revolutionary who had just been recruited by the Agency, would not change his mind.[68] To dispel the possible suspicion of party comrades outside or of other prisoners, the usual gambit was to stage an escape. This was the method used, for example, in the case of Bel'skii,[69] and in that of the Maximalist Semen Ryss, whose flight was staged so convincingly that a policeman and a warder were tried in its wake and sentenced to hard labour.[70]

Fear and shock may be ruled out as the exclusive rationale. Seemingly, then, additional conditions were required to tip the scales – 'characteristics permitting a deal', in Beletskii's words.[71] In an attempt to define the personalities of those who were seduced into becoming informers, Agafonov describes them as being of weak character and insufficiently resolute faith, individuals who felt that they had been wronged and persons who sought an easy life.[72] In some cases the Okhrana could coerce people into co-operating even without threatening them with prolonged imprisonment or exile. For example, it might refuse to provide a detainee with the certificate of good conduct which was required for acceptance to institutions of higher learning – as in the case of Mikhail Obnovlenskii, whose contacts in the students association interested the Okhrana.[73]

The police also kept an eye on persons, who, according to available information, might, for one reason or another, agree to serve in return for payment. The files of the Okhrana's Foreign Agency contain letters concerning the economic situation of such potential recruits.[74]

It must not be inferred, however, that all police agents were recruited by coercion. Azef, for example, was only the most famous of those who applied on their own initiative. Another important applicant was Iakov Zhitomirskii, who served as a secret agent in the ranks of the Bolsheviks from 1902 until the Revolution, fulfilling several key missions abroad for the party during these years. Among the others who offered their services were Dolin and Zhuchenko; considered the finest of the Okhrana's agents, they remained in service for many years. Personal motivation clearly played a decisive role in these instances, although it differed in each individual case.

The police were well aware of the connection between the manner in which an agent was recruited and the quality of the service he subsequently provided. Beletskii maintained that most of the prisoners whose previous revolutionary activity had been marked by a deep commitment rarely provided information of any value, because their new role as secret agents weighed heavily upon them.[75] It is in this category that we must also, evidently, place those agents who ended by attempting to assassinate their superiors, among them Alexander Petrov and Mikhail Rips.[76].

In his account of the conversation during which it was suggested that he collaborate with the Okhrana, Rips describes the feelings that overcame him:

> A strange anger, hatred, dominated my entire being, I experienced one of those moments in which a person is capable of committing the most unbalanced acts. I wanted to attack him with my bare hands and strangle, strangle, strangle him to death. To avenge the insult, all the loathsome actions, the provocation, everything. . . . On the one hand I felt disgust and repulsion, but on the other I wanted to show them, come what may, what could happen to them if they made similar proposals to revolutionaries who possessed some self-respect.[77]

Rips became an agent. Given the code-name 'Tarasov', he was sent to Paris and placed under the command of Mikhail von Koten. At one of their first meetings, held to finalize the terms of employment, Rips shot and seriously wounded von Koten. However, he served only a brief prison term because the French courts regarded the incident as a political matter. After his release Rips again began to frequent revolutionary circles, even though his standing among the SRs had been compromised, and many comrades would not even shake hands with him.[78]

Vasil'ev regarded the entire affair as signifying nothing more than the psychological pressure generated by the treachery of secret collaborators, and a sudden attack of conscience.[79] Martynov, on the other hand, thought that the explanation for such incidents lay in the high tension which was an inherent part of the agent's activity and made it imperative for the case officers to provide them with sober, intelligent instructions. If these guidelines were not heeded, the absolute trust between the agent and his case officer was violated, and desperate acts like Rip's were almost inevitable.[80] Yet neither in the case of Rips nor of Petrov was there anything to suggest a breakdown of the officer-agent relationship. Both men claimed that they had agreed to co-operate with the Okhrana in order to expose its secrets and to take revenge on it for the provocation. However besides the fact that these contentions were *post factum* rationalizations, the party itself had a clear and unequivocal policy, opposing any contact with the Okhrana, even for revolutionary purposes. Moreover, the party generally placed no trust in secrets that were exposed with the aid of police sources. Certainly a veteran revolutionary like Petrov should have been aware of this attitude, and taken it into account. More probably the sense of shock and the feeling of impotence in the face of what seemed, following the arrest, to be the Okhrana's monstrous, all-pervasive power, combined with the despairing recognition that the party was riddled with traitors, led the prisoner to accept the Okhrana's offer. He believed that once released he would be able to extricate himself in one way or another. Rips himself notes that during his conversation with the Okhrana official he was wracked by 'conflicting emotions'. Trying to collect his thoughts, and assuming a calm expression, he asked: 'Tell me, what guarantee do you have that after I join I won't take advantage of it for revolutionary purposes?' In his subsequent explanations to an SR commission of inquiry, Rips maintained that even though he knew the question was liable to arouse suspicion, he wanted to understand why the Okhrana official had no apprehensions about making such an offer.[81] Rip's dual description of his feelings – shock and inner turmoil on the one hand, tranquility and a desire to understand on the other hand – is self-contradictory. Nevertheless, whether in reply to Rip's query or out of a wish to set things straight from the start, the Okhrana official responded (though perhaps not in these exact words), 'In the first place, as far as your betraying us is concerned, we have no fear because eventually he [the revolutionary agent] will encounter one of our agents. Besides, this had never happened with anyone who accepted our offer. After all, you know, it is hazardous and they simply do not dare.' It was true, the commander acknowledged, that one person did take the money and try to flee – 'But one does not mean two!'[82]

The revolutionary's release from prison and his renewed encounter with his comrades allowed him to gain a different perspective. The shock and the fear subsided. Now, all that was left was the deed itself: the forbidden deal with the Okhrana, the irrevocable deal for which there could be no expiation save through revolutionary terrorism, even possibly at the cost of one's life. The members of the SR party's Central Committee to whom Petrov confessed quote his remarks and then explain his feelings in their own words: '"What I had previously believed to be absolutely justified, appropriate and essential, now seemed to be a profound, incomprehensible illusion, even a terrible mistake." He [Petrov] understood that his actions were totally unacceptable and forbidden. He realized that after all this he could no longer be active in the party. He only asked us to believe in his sincerity, to leave him to his own devices, and give him the opportunity to atone for his sin and prove the purity of his intentions by assassinating General Gerasimov.'[83] In the eyes of many, however, even revolutionary activity could no longer redeem Petrov.

Rips and Petrov represent isolated instances out of a large group of revolutionaries who were coerced into betraying their cause. However, it is precisely these examples that attest to the intensity of the internal pressure which was wielded against such revolutionaries, both while they were under detention and following their release. Nor does it matter whether or not we believe the explanations offered by Rips and Petrov for their deals with the Okhrana. It is true that their cases are extreme examples of the sense of shame experienced by revolutionaries and of the conclusions that necessarily followed. However, a less radical solution was just not available. Defection, as the Okhrana Commander explained to Rips, was for them hazardous in the extreme. A leak by the police was all that was required to endanger their lives or at least to cause them, and at times also their families, to be ostracized. The party's attitude toward collaboration motivated by revolutionary ideals is discussed in greater detail below.[84] For the present it suffices to note that for treason there were no extenuating circumstances. A case in point is the experience of Nikolai Metal'nikov, a member of the Paris group for the SR party. Arrested in Perm in April 1911, Metal'nikov agreed to the offer of the local Gendarmes' Commander, was sent to Paris, and for some months maintained ties with him, until their contacts came to light at the beginning of 1912. In his defence, Metal'nikov insisted that he had acted out of revolutionary motives and that he had not provided the police with information. However, even though his story was not refuted, he was expelled from the party. The expulsion was publicized in the party's organ.[85] Metal'nikov himself was not the only one to suffer ostracism – his wife, Yuza, was also expelled from the group following a debate as to whether their many years of living together and the fact that she had borne his children should override the loathing she could not help but feel for him. In the debate one of the comrades declared, 'I would kill even my own father if I knew he was a *provocateur*!'[86]

Two years later Metal'nikov sent an emotional letter to the SR party's leadership abroad requesting them to discuss his case and issue a final ruling:

> All I have been through and everything that passed through my mind during these past two years, had led me to the difficult but final conclusion that my attempts to form ties with the world of the Okhrana were a terrible mistake and dealt a severe moral blow to the organization I belonged to and had served for ten years with all my strength. However, a mistake, an error, even a crime is still not treason, is still not the act of a *provocateur*. I find myself in a situation in which everyone feels himself entitled to brand me a traitor and a *provocateur*. It is as though such a judgment had already been passed solely on the basis of my connections with the Okhrana and before a final ruling has been issued by the commission of inquiry. They condemn me, in the full sense of that word, to death, and do grave harm to my family, that after all, is too severe a punishment, one that is unjust and unmerited.[87]

Beletskii, therefore, seems to be correct when he observes that many of the committed revolutionaries who were coerced into serving as agents while under arrest were deeply distressed by the role they had been forced into, even if this did not lead them to confess and atone through self-sacrifice – the only way open to them. Thus, they had no choice but to maintain their ties with the Okhrana while doing only the bare minimum that would ensure their safety. This would also seem to account for Beletskii's remark about the limited value these agents had for the police. As we have seen, however, some of the recruits constituted a real danger for the police, which evidently lead to Beletskii's directive only to recruit prisoners who confessed voluntarily for the Internal Agency and not those who only agreed to co-operate under threat.[88] The directive was reissued by the Deputy Minister of the Interior Dzhunkovskii, after he came across many cases of forced recruitment, in defiance of Beletskii's order[89] but there is no indication that this widespread practice was actually terminated.

Many police officers did not trust the secret agents, fearing the unreliability of those who had been coerced into service and of others who offered their services for reasons which the Okhrana could not fully fathom. The police lived in constant fear of counter-provocation and of the consequences of their own operations, and all these factors obliged them to be cautious and to examine meticulously the information the agents provided. As mentioned above the officer who recruited Rips commented that he was not worried about the possibility that an agent might deceive the police, because sooner or later he would be bound to run up against another police agent. As a rule the police always tried to verify information they received by cross-checking it against parallel information from elsewhere. The police termed this method of operation the 'cross-checking agency' (*perekrestnaiia agentura*),[90] and to ensure its effectiveness they used as many agents as they could in a given area. Martynov, who took over as Okhrana commander in Moscow in 1912, relates in his memoirs that during this period the agency was particularly effective among the Bolsheviks in Moscow. He points out that the cross-checking reports enabled him to read about all the affairs of the Bolshevik underground, as well as allowing him to verify information submitted by one agent against that of others.[91] This efficacious operation was evidently the result of the infiltration of 21 agents into Bolshevik cells in Moscow during the years 1910–14 alone: seven agents in 1910, four in 1911, three in 1912, four in 1913 and three in 1914. Although eight agents ceased their services during this years, 11 others continued to function until 1917; three were members of the Moscow Regional Committee (Aleksei Lobov, Andrei Romanov, Alexander Golubev). The police were interested chiefly in the broad-based activity originating in the centre, such as the smuggling of banned books or arms, or the organizing of strikes, and the presence of one or two agents in the centre – in this case on the Moscow Regional Committee – along with a few in the other peripheral organizations in the city, constituted a cross-checking agency which was able to cover Bolshevik activity in the city and surrounding area.

Another illustration of a cross-checking agency within a single group is the planting of 14 agents between 1910 and 1914 in the Paris group of the SR party. This was the most important of the SR groups abroad, and perhaps also in Russia itself, both because of its size – some 120 registered members – and because of its ties with the party leaders, the majority of whom resided in Paris. Several of the 14 were eventually exposed while others filed no reports at all. Nevertheless, throughout this period extensive information from several parallel sources reached the Foreign Agency and was passed on from there to the centre in St Petersburg.

The cross-checking agency was not confined to local settings. For instance, the Okhrana mission abroad functioned as such an agency for the Police Department in St Petersburg with respect to the Department's sources throughout Russia; the Foreign Agency was often instructed to check and clarify information the Police Department had received from its local agents. This situation was the result of the high concentration of revolutionary leaders in western Europe. Indeed, the *émigrés* provided a wealth of information on what was afoot within the groups and local organizations in Russia itself, thanks to the constant to-ing and fro-ing of revolutionaries, and because the contents of letters from Russia quickly made the rounds among the exiles, who were hungry for news from the homeland. A considerable part of the information which the Foreign Agency passed on to St Petersburg derived from such sources. Examples are a report about an 'expropriation' conducted near Warsaw, whose participants arrived in Paris;[92] a survey of the situation of the local SR committees following the visit of Sletov to Kiev, Smolensk, Moscow, St Petersburg and Helsinki;[93] and information regarding the meeting of SR committees in southern Russia, which reached party members in St Petersburg and from there was apparently forwarded by mail to Paris.[94]

Many commanders were also aware of the importance of the *émigrés* in this respect, and this lead them to dispatch agents to western Europe on their own initiative, in order to obtain information about political investigations in their areas of jurisdiction. This state of affairs induced several agents to attempt to extort double payment for their services, both from their superiors in Russia, and from the Foreign Agency in Paris, to which most of the *émigré* agents were attached. It was considered a grave offence to conceal one's connection with the Okhrana in Russia from the Foreign Agency; if discovered, the agent in question was classified as unreliable and an extortionist, and could be dismissed.

The External Agency provided additional vital tools for scrutinizing the actions of the secret agents. The detective was not confined to trailing suspects on foot. They were also expected to collect information from various service personnel with whom they came into contact: doormen of apartment buildings, hotel staff, postal workers, and so forth. This information combined to give a full picture of the life and deeds of a suspect.

When Protopopov, an unknown figure, contacted the Foreign Agency to say that he was a Socialist Revolutionary in charge of a laboratory for the training of demolition experts, and that due to a basic change of outlook he was now ready to co-operate with the authorities, his case was referred for examination to the External Agency. The first step was to compare the description, received from the officer who met him, with other information in the agency files. Protopopov, it emerged, was none other than 'Eniseiskii' or Vasilii Blokhin, an agent of the Okhrana commander in Perm, who had been dispatched to Paris to report on the Communist Anarchists but was dismissed because all his reports proved false. Nevertheless, fearing to lose information which might in retrospect turn out to be of utmost importance on a subject of vital interest to the police, the authorities decided to pursue their contacts. Employed for a salary of 300 francs per month, he was sent to Geneva where, he claimed, the laboratory was to be set up. Detectives of the External Agency followed every step. 'Eniseiskii' sent lengthy reports to Paris about his meetings with a contact who had arrived in Geneva in order to set up the laboratory, and about another meeting he had held on the same subject with an anonymous Caucasian. However, the detectives of the External Agency, who trailed him day and night, reported that he rarely met with anyone but spent most of his time in his hotel room or sitting in a restaurant, and had no callers. Once 'Eniseiskii' related that while taking off his coat during a lakefront stroll his wallet, containing his own money, plus party funds, had fallen into the water. Claiming that this would place him in an unpleasant situation *vis-à-vis* the revolutionaries, and would naturally imperil his position as an agent, he requested sufficient funds to allow him to reimburse the organization. A comparison of his reports with those provided by the External Agency revealed that on the day he had supposedly lost his wallet he had not taken any such stroll, and indeed that all his reports were pure fabrications.

The Police Department, convinced that he was engaged in preparing some sort of provocation against it, ordered that he should be continuously followed. However, since no connection was discovered between 'Eniseiskii' and the revolutionary circle, the Foreign Agency lost all interest in him, but to be on the safe side would continue the surveillance via the External Agency.[95] In line with regular procedures, the Police Department distributed a circular to all its units containing a detailed description of Blokhin and warning against any contact with the 'dangerous extortionist'.[96]

Even in cases where the police had positive proof of an agent's unreliability, their unassailable conception that their purpose was only served by information which could lead to liquidations caused them to flinch at the possibility of missing out any information at all. The upshot was that they were not always in a position to dismiss a doubtful agent or to act against him. As the 'Eniseiskii' affair demonstrates, the closer an agent was to what the police regarded as a vital interest, the more difficult it became to drop him. Only after the Foreign Agency was convinced beyond any doubt that 'Eniseiskii' had no ties with revolutionary circles was he finally dismissed.

In instances where the agent was actually involved in party activity, the police were far more loath to lose him. Such was the case with Baruch Rabinovitch, or 'Sasha', who commenced his career as a secret agent in Berlin early in 1906, at a salary of 200 roubles a month – a sum which indicates his importance in the eyes of the police. Berlin was a key point on the route to and from Russia, chiefly for the smuggling of arms or banned books. Okhrana surveillance showed that while Rabinovitch did in fact file reports, he did so on a selective basis. Actually, he was engaged in raising funds for arms purchases. Only in 1907, with the seizure of an arms ship which he had dispatched, was he finally dismissed. He had been employed for nearly two years, and though the Okhrana was on to him from the start, the authorities feared to lose sources of information and hoped to make use of him somehow. A similar case was that of Miron Segal – 'Vladimir' – who arrived in Paris in May 1909 and contacted the Foreign Agency, even though he was already attached to the Okhrana office in Bialystok. He was evidently in touch with Burtsev. Segal was also engaged in arms smuggling; the examination of his doubtful identity lasted three years.

These are a few examples out of many which could also be cited to show the basic weakness that marked the attitude of the police towards the secret agents and their tasks. From the moment the internal agency was perceived as the basis for political police work, it became indispensable even when it did not prove itself. In some ways the department was no less in the hands of its agents than vice versa.

(iii) THE INTERNAL AGENCY IN ACTION

The establishment of the Okhrana sections and their dispersion throughout Russia created a direct police hierarchy, extending from the periphery to the centre in St Petersburg. Its existence facilitates an examination of the functioning of the system that made the secret agent the linchpin of political police work, through an analysis of

(a) the structure and working arrangements of the Okhrana sections, (b) the transmission of the new data to the centre, and (c) the drawing of the requisite operational conclusions. Each Okhrana section was headed by a Commander who had under him several case officers; each case officer was in charge of directing a number of secret agents. The case officer was their contact man; it was to him that they conveyed their information, and it was he who dealt with their personal problems.[97] Only the most important agents were in direct contact with the chief, and operated under his personal directives. In large Okhrana sections, such as the one in Moscow, the agents were divided according to the organizations for which they operated. Thus, agents reporting on SR circles were under the command of one officer, while agents who were members of Social Democratic organizations were directed by a different case officer.

The External Agency was divided into several groups. The largest group consisted of detectives who trailed revolutionaries on the basis of daily directives. In addition, there was a group of 'supervisors' (*nadzirateli*) – top detectives who, although they sometimes went on street patrols in rotation with their colleagues, usually supervised events in a specific region. They examined the passports of suspects, and assigned special surveillance units as required. They kept an eye on people who frequently hosted strangers in their homes, and watched all apartments in which students or workers resided.

In the St Petersburg Okhrana, there were special groups of detectives which were not to be found elsewhere, such as the 'Okhrana Unit' (*Okhrannaia komanda*). Housed in a separate building, this Unit was responsible for protecting the Imperial family and for the safety of ministers and other ranking figures. Operating in close contact with them were the detectives of the 'Central Detachment' (*Tsentral'nyi otriad*), whose task it was to recognize and identify important revolutionaries by sight. From time to time these detectives were sent abroad in groups, so that they could learn to spot these revolutionaries – who moved around freely – under the guidance of the Okhrana's Foreign Agency in Paris.

In addition to the detectives of these two groups, the Okhrana in St Petersburg also employed other detectives, whose task was to locate strangers who were staying in hotels or in furnished rooms in the capital without having registered with the police, as required by law.

Each Okhrana section included a bureau and archives. In St Petersburg there were a general bureau and archives, which dealt with all the attendant aspects of the department's activity, and a secret bureau and archives which covered all clandestine matters relating to the revolutionaries and secret agents. The archives collected anthropometric data on revolutionaries, while their library amassed illegal revolutionary books and journals.[98]

In 1917, the total number of personnel in the St Petersburg Okhrana stood at about 600 (excluding secret agents): 250–300 detectives in the Okhrana Unit, about 80 in the Central Detachment, 70 supervisors, 40 registration detectives and about 100 regular detectives. To these we must add at least 150–200 secret agents, according to Gerasimov's report which refers to 1909.[99] In 1912, the Moscow Okhrana was, according to its chief, comprised of 12 case officers, 25 clerks, 100 detectives, 60 supervisors, 10 watchmen, messengers and the like, and about 100 secret agents[100] – a total of approximately 300 personnel. The large number of detectives was due to the fact that every surveillance operation required at least two men, and sometimes even more.[101] In the provincial towns the External Agency tended to be employed less, and more cautiously, since the small number of people on the streets and the detectives' distinctive appearance attracted attention, which sometimes led to the exposure of the secret agent in a group once the external surveillance was discovered.[102] No exact data exist on the overall size of the Internal Agency, although it is generally thought that the number of agents ran into the thousands. Maurice LaPorte, who wrote a history of the Okhrana in 1935, based on police archives to which he had access in Leningrad, maintains that the number of agents was constantly on the increase, reaching its peak in 1912. According to LaPorte, at the beginning of 1904 the Police Department had 12 000 secret agents, two years later the number had risen to approximately 19 500, and in 1912 it stood at 26 000. However, LaPorte himself notes that for the great majority the term 'secret agent' was a misnomer, since they were not members of a party or other organizations and did not receive a steady monthly salary; rather, they were adventurers of various sorts who offered the police information that they happened to come by, in return for certain benefits. Indeed, LaPorte goes on to quote a report by Vissarionov, dated 6 April 1912, stating that the Moscow Okhrana at that time had 159 secret agents who were members of political organizations and who received regular salaries. Of this total 24 were in the SR party, 20 in the SD organizations and three had infiltrated the anarchists.[103] Thus, of all the agents in various public sectors fewer than one-third were involved with the revolutionary movements which are discussed in this study.

Nor do the facts and figures which we collected lend credence to estimates of tens of thousands of secret agents, and certainly not where the revolutionary camp was concerned. As mentioned above, Gerasimov, the chief of the St Petersburg Okhrana, reports that in 1909 he had 150–200 agents; Vasil'ev cites an even lower figure, about 100.[104] It should be stressed that these figures, like those cited by Vissarionov, refer to the two largest and most important Okhrana sections in all of Russia, sections which, as we noted earlier, had under their jurisdiction not only the capitals but extensive outlying areas as well. In his memoirs Vasil'ev contends that the public's estimates of the number of police agents in Russia was vastly exaggerated, and that in fact there were no more than one thousand agents under the Okhrana's command.[105] Pavel Zavarzin concurs, pointing out that in the pre-revolutionary period there were no more than a few hundred agents in all of the empire's investigative institutions.[106] To sum up, it appears that the numbers cited by LaPorte are a gross overestimate. Everything points to the conclusion that at its peak the number of salaried secret agents active in the revolutionary movements hardly exceeded a few thousand.

While the working conditions of the Okhrana's Foreign Agency differed from those inside Russia, its basic organization and working arrangements were similar to those in the other sections. The Head of the Foreign Agency was the only person in direct contact with the Police Department in St Petersburg, and it was to him that all instructions, questions and directives were addressed. From time to time, he was summoned to the Police Department for clarifications or to make direct reports. Contact with the agents was maintained by the officers under his command. Until 1912 some agents were in direct contact with the head of the Foreign Agency, but after his identity was discovered by revolutionaries, he was urgently ordered by St Petersburg to transfer all the agents under his control to another case officer at once and to take strict precautions to ensure that the identity of this case officer was not exposed in the wake of their meetings.[107] Besides the case officers in Paris, the Foreign Agency also had agents in key centres outside France, such as London or Berlin which, since it served as a transit route for revolutionaries travelling to or from Russia, was considered especially important by the Police Department.[108]

In common with all the other Okhrana sections, the Foreign Agency had a bureau which assembled information about revolutionary organizations, along with personal details about revolutionaries under surveillance. Letters from the Police Department in St Petersburg were immediately filed under 'incoming mail,' and the Foreign Agency's bureau would at once supply all the relevant material: personal details about those concerned (*spravki*), previous correspondence, and so forth. Except for matters which necessitated co-operation with the local police or required the use of the External Agency, everything was handled by the Internal Agency. The Head of the Foreign Agency would convene the case officers, brief them on the suggestions or questions which had arrived from the Police Department, and discuss with them how best to proceed. The case officers would then meet with the appropriate agents and report back to the Agency head. If the information was unsatisfactory, or contradicted previous data, the case officers were told to make further inquiries, or the Commander would try to authenticate the information through the External Agency. Reports of sufficient clarity were transferred to the bureau, where the agency head redrafted them for the chief of the Police Department; the original manuscripts were kept in a safe in the bureau.[109]

Like all the Okhrana sections in Russia, the Foreign Agency had an External Agency at its disposal. It was largely made up of French detectives and was headed by a French national. He alone maintained direct contact with the detectives, on the one hand, and with the Head of the Agency, on the other. Besides their surveillance of revolutionaries or secret agents, the External Agency's detectives were often given the task of trailing revolutionaries on their way to Russia. When the Foreign Agency or the Police Department learned that a revolutionary whom they wished to arrest was about to leave for Russia, detectives were dispatched to follow him secretly, and the moment he crossed the border into Russia they identified him so that the Russian border police could hold him. The revolutionary was not always detained on crossing the border; often Russian detectives would pick up the trail at that point with the aim of discovering his contacts.[110]

In addition to trailing revolutionaries to the Russian border, from 1906 to 1907, the detectives of the External Agency abroad were engaged in observing and monitoring arms smuggling from Europe to Russia. Special detectives who were stationed in European ports in England, France, Belgium, Holland, and particularly in

Copenhagen, reported by telegraph directly to the Police Department in St Petersburg on the departure of any arms-bearing ships. However, these reports were not always useful, as the weapons were generally packed in crates which were thrown into the sea at prearranged points, where they were picked up by fishermen who then transferred them to the revolutionaries. It emerged that scrutiny of the Finnish coast and the Baltic ports was not sufficiently stringent, and this, according to the heads of the Foreign Agency, proved extremely vexatious to the detectives engaged in anti-smuggling activity in European ports.[111]

The External Agency was the Okhrana's most vulnerable point in its operations abroad. Because surveillance was more overt, and because of the frequent defection of detectives to the ranks of the revolutionaries, the External Agency was more easily exposed. The External Agency's subordination to the Okhrana's Paris representatives was viewed as an infringement of the host nation's sovereignty. For the most part, co-operation between the French and the Russian police was based on an affinity of outlook.[112] When these relations were exposed, however, they served the Socialist opposition as an instrument with which to excoriate the government.[113] The need thus arose to conceal and camouflage this activity, so that formally it would not conflict with French law. The solution, which was put forward in 1913, was to organize the Foreign Agency under the guise of a private detective agency, run by the two agency heads as partners. Only the most reliable of the detectives were given new contracts to sign; the others received severance pay and were dismissed. The Foreign Agency in Paris was listed as the new office's chief client. Naturally, financing originated entirely in the Police Department in St Petersburg.[114]

Each Okhrana section in Russia had several secret retreats, where case officers could meet with their agents. Apartments for this purpose were usually leased in several neighbourhoods. Quiet areas with a largely stable population were sought, so that the Okhrana could feel safe from suspicious elements who might move in nearby and stake out the agents. Those leasing the flats and responsible for their maintenance were employees of the section. Indeed, they had to be particularly reliable, since they met with the agents and knew some of them personally. They were barred from maintaining social relations with anyone outside the section, and certainly from inviting anyone to their homes. The meetings themselves took place in the guest room. The tenant had to receive the agent and his case officer, and then leave when they began their talk.[115] Martynov, who gave much thought to his agents' psychological needs, was meticulous in selecting tenants whose appearance and demeanour could instil a sense of security in the secret agent who was always fearful of discovery.[116]

Cautiousness led the Okhrana to change apartments as often as was feasible. The longer one had apartments in use, the less safe it was considered. The discovery of such a flat, followed by the observation of those entering and leaving it, could lead to the exposure of all the agents for whom it served as a meeting place. The apartments were therefore divided into three types. Those which had been in service the longest were used for meetings with new agents, or agents whose qualifications were still in doubt, so that the damage in case of disclosure would be minimal. Apartments of the second type, which had already been in use for some time, were used for meetings with experienced but not especially important agents; while those of the third type, which had been newly leased, were reserved for meetings with the most serious and important agents.[117]

As an added precaution the agents were always invited to meetings at different times, to preclude the possibility of consistent schedules or habits which could be easily monitored, and special care was taken to ensure that incoming and outgoing agents did not meet. There were occasions when the rules of caution were not followed and this facilitated matters for agents who sought to assassinate their case officers.[118]

Most of the meetings took the form of a discussion although some agents submitted written reports. The case officer had to provide a written summary of the information he had been given, noting the code name of the agent, the date on which the information had been conveyed and the movement or organization with which it dealt. These reports were transferred to the commanders who used them as the basis of reviews which they passed on to the police or to senior administrative authorities.[119] Since the Police Department depended on these reports and surveys for its view of reality, the procedural aspects of report-writing assumed considerable importance.

Until 1906, it was the local commanders who determined what was and was not to be passed on to the St Petersburg centre. The agents were considered as their exclusive assets, and were known to the Special Section personnel only by their code names. The result was that the Police Department had no control over the quality and reliability of the agents, and was, in addition, dependent on the degree of political savvy of the investigators in the outlying districts –

few of whom had read much of the revolutionary literature deposited in the archives.[120] Since their reports dealt mainly with descriptions of liquidations, The Police Department's picture of the ongoing operations of the Okhrana sections on the one hand, and of the activity of the revolutionary organizations on the other, was coloured by these details.

In 1908, the method of reporting changed. The investigators now had to submit a verbatim report of the agent's remarks on a special form, which contained a separate space for their own notes.[121] However, if previously the Police Department had been deprived of a wealth of material which might be essential for an appraisal of the situation it was now flooded with protracted, detailed reports which made no distinction between correct and incorrect or substantive and insubstantive information. The Police Department buckled under the burden of sifting through and classifying the mass of material. Hence it was decreed that the fewer the details the better, or as Klimovich, who served as Director of the Police Department from March to September 1916, put it: 'Our ideal is this: the less you write, the better! There is nothing worse than excessive chatter.'[122] Krasil'nikov, the head of the Foreign Agency, who failed to meet these standards, was reprimanded by the Police Department in St Petersburg for indulging in excessive verbiage. Attached to the letter of reprimand was an example, in the form of a cable of 35 words of which 13 were superfluous in the view of the Police Department's Director.[123] Although the explanation adduced for the reprimand was the need for economy, Krasil'nikov was, according to Klimovich, known for his unnecessarily wordy reports.[124] Krasil'nikov was also reprimanded because only five of 51 letters attached to his reports were relevant to the investigation in hand; all the rest dealt with purely social or family matters. In the light of this, Krasil'nikov was requested to pass on documents of practical interest only.[125] While the Foreign Agency's reports were not submitted on special forms, but as reviews, these too were forwarded with only minuscule changes to the agents' remarks, and the reviews consistently refrained from drawing any operational conclusions.

Thus, the procedures and quantity of the Okhrana reports, as well as its organization and its working arrangements, were the direct result of the prevailing view that the paramount task of the police was to forestall or prevent revolutionary activity by gathering data for the purpose of liquidation. These data were therefore given top priority in appraisals both of the situation and the investigator. Subjects not directly related to the immediate operational activity of the police were liable to be considered 'unnecessary chatter,' or at least of secondary import, as was explicitly stated in a Police Department directive to the Foreign Agency: 'Send me without delay all the agency's information about terrorist plots and expropriations. At this moment I am not interested in anything else.'[126] Although this blunt directive was issued in 1907, when the government's primary interest lay in the suppression and elimination of the terrorist upsurge, the following years saw no change of attitude. Thus there was a certain incongruity between the intensity of revolutionary activity with its practical ramifications and the threat it posed to the régime, and the deployment of the police to combat that activity. The degree of the secret agents' penetration of the revolutionary movement was not always consistent with the fluctuations in the movement's development. This trend is confirmed by the available data presented in Table 5. The table shows the number of agents active in the revolutionary movement annually from 1902 to 1914. The numbers were derived by subtracting the number of agents who terminated their role in the police from the accumulated number of those who had been recruited by the year in question. Only agents whose dates at recruitment are known (166) were included in the table. Where details concerning the termination of service were missing (22), the underlying assumption was that their annual distribution was random and thus did not affect the overall picture. Due to the scarcity of data concerning the anarchists, they were studied separately. Unlike the SRs and the Social Democrats, names of exposed agents were not systematically published in the anarchist press. It is assumed that due to the nature of their organization, more secret agents did actually operate in small groups which did not maintain regular contact with anarchist journals and did not report on their activity.

When considering the number of active agents in Table 5 each year, one should bear in mind that the years from 1902 to 1904 were a period of crystallization for the SR party, which until then even lacked a common platform for all its constituent elements. The anarchists appear on the revolutionary stage in 1903, but began to make their mark in the following two years. The Social Democrats were preoccupied with their own internal wrangling. Revolutionary manifestations only reached their zenith in the 1905–7 uprising. Until then, most Police Department personnel, following Plehve's lead, did not perceive them as a wide-spread phenomenon which called for reinforced police preparedness. By 1907–8 the revolutionary camp

Table 5 Distribution of secret agents, 1902–14

	1902	1903	1904	1905	1906	1907	1908	1909	1910	1911	1912	1913	1914
SR	5	5	11	15	22	22	23	20	25	29	32	27	23
SD	7	10	11	14	18	20	15	19	29	32	37	37	42
Total	12	15	22	29	40	42	38	39	54	61	69	64	65
Anarchists	2	2	2	3	8	8	7	7	7	3	2	3	2
TOTAL	14	17	24	32	48	50	45	46	61	64	71	67	67

	Size of parties in 1907	*Number of agents per party in 1907*	*1:1000*
SD	80 000[1]	20	0.25
SR	45 000[2]	22	0.48
Anarchists	5 000[3]	8	1.6

Sources:
[1]M. Hildermeier, *Die sozialrevolutionäre Partei*, p. 267.
[2]D. Lane, *The Roots of Russian Communism*, p. 13.
[3]P. Avrich, *The Russian Anarchists* (Princeton, 1967) pp. 68–9.

was already expressing deep disappointment at the ebbing tide of upheaval. This nadir in the history of the revolutionary movement also affected the SR party, and the Azef affair which erupted in its full fury at the end of 1908 dealt it a blow which was only 'the final nail in the party's coffin'.[127] In fact, from 1908 to 1911 the activity of the entire revolutionary movement was at a low ebb. Only in 1912 could a certain resurgence be discerned, following the bloody suppression of the miners' demonstration at the Lena goldmines, which generated a mounting wave of solidarity and protest strikes in industry. Yet, as Table 5 shows, throughout this period of sharp fluctuations in revolutionary activity secret agents infiltrated the ranks of the revolutionary movement in growing numbers, a development which would seem to be inexplicable in objective terms.

There are two possible reasons for this phenomenon, though a single rationale – the inability of the police to adapt to changing circumstances. The police may well have believed that their apparent success in suppressing the revolutionary wave was the direct result of their methods of operation. For if organizing for revolutionary activity actually reflected a revolutionary situation and its complications, then by the same token the reduction of that activity to a minimum must be attributed to the soundness of the method and of its underlying conception. The effort to prevent the recurrence of revolutionary outbreaks could point to the conclusion that the recruitment of secret agents should be stepped up. By contrast, the second explanation could be found in the police assessment that underground activity had not actually diminished but was merely being carried out in greater secrecy; from this point of view, failure to expose that activity was due to a dearth of information. If this assumption was true, it implied that despite certain police successes in the struggle against the revolutionary movement, the system of the Internal Agency and its underlying concept distorted the Police Department's perception of the situation with which it had to cope.

The Police Department's assessment was that the success of each Commander in his sphere of responsibility was measured by the number of liquidations he carried out. When that number declined, some Commanders, apprehensive that this was due to a lack of information, initiated efforts to increase the number of secret agents. This explanation is corroborated by several testimonies. For example, when Klimovich, Commander of Moscow in 1915, accused the Okhrana chief there of having failed to expose SR activities solely because his sources of information had dried up, Klimovich rejected all explanations that the SR party had been quiescent for years and was incapable of organizing any meaningful terrorist action.[128] Moreover, the dominant role of liquidations in determining success led many police officers to lose all interest in an investigation once a liquidation had been carried out.[129] As a result, any preparation for an isolated revolutionary act was inordinately inflated, not only beyond its general party framework but at times in total contradiction to it, leading the police to attach far more significance to the act than was warranted. This exaggerated the influence of certain facts, even when the Police Department was in possession of different information, which could have balanced the overall picture. For example, the Police Department, aware in general of the crisis afflicting the SRs, learned that Savinkov, a prominent member of the Battle Organization who had been Azef's deputy, was about to leave for Russia to perpetrate a spectacular act of terrorism. The Foreign Agency was immediately alerted. Eight of its 12 detectives in Paris were stationed around Savinkov's house day and night. Additional detectives were recruited and dispatched to every border point that Savinkov might cross en route to Russia, and the Head of the Foreign Agency himself visited the site several times to ensure that all was proceeding properly. Uncertain, however, that these measures were sufficient, he also asked for the Internal Agency to be reinforced and requested an advance of 5,000 roubles for the entire operation.[130]

The profound crisis affecting the SRs was repeatedly and unequivocally reflected in reports reaching the Police Department:

> According to the telling definition of several members of the SR, the party is currently in 'desperate' straits because the crisis they are now undergoing has long since become obvious to all, and the more time that passes the more intense it becomes. As far back as a year ago, many representatives of the party were convinced that the crisis was a temporary one, that the day of 'decisive combat operations' was not far off, and that all the complex organizational problems would be resolved in one way or another. Now it is clear to every party activist that the present situation will continue. The fact that the party lacks serious and active organizations in Russia is no longer a secret. The few remaining members in the country are trying to step up activity among the urban workers, the peasantry and the army. They are also trying to solve their propaganda problem and to revivify the 'operational issue'. Simultaneously, however, reports are coming in from all sides about a lack of manpower and of material resources. The result is that they are in a depressed frame of mind. Only the heads of the party hope for a revival soon, whereas the young activists are sceptical. The central committee, which is now engaged in mobilizing material resources, is getting negative replies wherever it turns and is incapable of initiating anything.[131]

At the same time, the Foreign Agency informed the Police Department in St Petersburg of the deep differences within the party regarding the future of terrorism, noting also that very few aspired to renew it for demonstrative purposes.[132] None the less, the Police Department cabled its representatives abroad not only to place under surveillance every terrorist group that maintained ties with Savinkov and Nataliia Klimova (both of whom the police regarded as salient and extremely dangerous proponents of terrorism), but also all the other important SR members. The order obliged the head of the Foreign Agency to increase both the Internal and the External Agency considerably.[133] This is yet another illustration of how the

Agency's apparatus was inflated, precisely at a time of almost negligible activity, due to a distorted assessment of the situation in the field. Manifestly, the appraisal of the police should have posited a correlation between the party's resources and the ability of its members, even on an individual basis, to execute acts calling for means which all reports insisted were then unavailable. The Police Department perhaps fell victim to its own basic misconception, apart from the need of every organization to demonstrate that its own activity is essential. It was this pressure that led it, consciously or not, to exaggerate the importance of the matters it dealt with, *vis-à-vis* its superiors, and finally to itself.

As suggested above, it is arguable that the intensified recruitment of secret agents stemmed from the Police Department's sense of success following the suppression of the revolutionary wave. It is also noteworthy, in this connection, that Savinkov's plans came to naught due to the involvement in the affair of the agent, Ivan Kiriukhin, who informed the police and caused their cancellation. In retrospect, however, senior police personnel, such as Martynov and Gerasimov, expressed their opinion *post factum* that the Azef exposure was one of the major factors that ended the SRs' role as a party threatening the government. For this reason the years between the exposure and the revolution were the calmest in the annals of the anti-revolutionary struggle since the beginning of the century.[134] Even if one can object that this assumption was made long after the actual events, the massive infiltration of secret agents into the revolutionary movement during a period of relative quiet must nevertheless be seen as a reflection of the Police Department's failure to adapt to the new reality. It continued to rely on outdated means which had not been re-examined and had not been tailored to suit the new conditions. This defect is all the more glaring given the internal changes that were effected in the SR party following the Azef affair.[135]

This failure to adapt is apparent even if we accept the second explanation, namely the distorted interpretation of the revolutionary situation. In that case the Internal Agency's heightened infiltration of the revolutionary movement must be seen as a tendency to react to an increasingly complex situation by simply extending the old means already in use. Qualitative changes were dealt with by quantitative means, a reaction stemming from a reductionist approach. Since the individual terrorist act and its prevention were the focus of the police interest and their criterion for success, they tended to view reality in terms of 'actions' (*vystuplenii*). This being so, the police concentrated on the operation itself, ignoring additional characteristics – its morale, organizational and general party aspects. Instead of considering the entire party fabric, into which individual plans were woven, the police formed a world picture by a mere arithmetical computation of such plans. This reductionist method of thought led them to grasp the revolutionary peril in terms of 'the assassination of the Tsar' or 'expropriations', irrespective of whether the year happened to be 1906 or 1910. The reinforcement of the Internal Agency among the SRs following the Azef exposure bears testimony to this approach.

The underlying police conception which dictated its concentration on the individual act of terrorism and prevented its operational adaptation to the new conditions, led to another assumption which was also to prove mistaken. The police supposed that the larger the revolutionary organization, the greater was its menace, since to perpetrate a major terrorist act, material and human resources were required, which were beyond the reach of a small group. As far as the Police Department was concerned, the danger latent in a united Social Democratic party, even one which contained rival factions such as the Bolsheviks and the Mensheviks, was immeasurably greater than the threat posed by a small but monolithic Bolshevik party. Beletskii expressed this viewpoint when he characterized his policy as based on the principle of *divide et impera*.[136] The same approach typified the Police Department in 1905 when the rift emerged between the SRs and the Maximalists. The head of the Foreign Agency assured the Director of the Police Department that despite the temporary quiescence in the SR Party, 'We shall once again try to sow discord among them.'[137] It should be stressed that because of the breakaway from the SRs of a small but cohesive group, the police faced difficulties in infiltrating the party with their own men. At that time, the police were still feeling confident because of Azef's presence at the very heart of the SRs, whereas with respect to the Maximalists they were at a loss.

It was only in 1906 that the police managed to recruit Semen Ryss, who agreed to join their ranks after being arrested in Kiev on a charge of participating in an expropriation. His prison break was staged with the connivance of the Director of the Police Department, Trusevich.[138] Since only a small group was involved, along with an agent whom the Department's Director thought had a ranking position within the group, he immediately ordered a halt to the detention and surveillance of the Maximalists, believing that come what may he had everything under control. Then came the explosion in Stolypin's house, on the Aptekar Islands in which 27 persons were killed, according to the official communiqué. Ryss was in fact a loyal Maximalist who misled the Okhrana, as was subsequently discovered with the help of the Agency's cross-verification procedures. Following Ryss's arrest, Gerasimov found a replacement who became the confidant of the Maximalist leader Mikhail Sokolov, thanks to special services he performed for him with the Okhrana's approval.[139] This was apparently the agent Ivanov. On the surface the Okhrana had been deceived by Ryss because it had trusted him, but had it taken the danger posed by the small Maximalist group more seriously it might not have relied on Ryss alone but instituted additional supervisory measures, as it did in other cases.[140]

The attitude of the police toward the various movements was influenced by its grasp of reality. Its approach dictated the infiltration of the Internal Agency into the entire opposition camp, including the Cadets.[141] But its conception also led it to adopt sharply divergent approaches to the various components of the revolutionary camp and to evaluate differently the dangers posed by each group. This in turn affected the degree of the Agency's infiltration of each revolutionary movement, as was shown in Table 5.

Three factors had a bearing on the Internal Agency's infiltration of a movement: the degree of interest evinced by the police in the movement's activity during a specific period, the size of the movement and the nature of its organization. No data exist on membership in the SR party prior to 1905. According to figures compiled for the party's Second Congress at the beginning of 1907, it then numbered 60 000 members – as already mentioned, though Hildermeier puts the upper limit at 45 000. As for the Social Democrats (Bolsheviks and Mensheviks), their membership is put at 3250 in 1904, 16 800 the following year, and 81 000 by the end of 1906.[142]

Given this earlier numerical discrepancy between the two parties, along with the fact that the RSDRP was founded several years before the SR and had been the focus of police attention, it should come as no surprise that the absolute – though not the relative – number of police agents within the SDs party had exceeded the number in the SR party in the early years. The stepped-up recruitment of SR agents is discernible in 1904, and increases continuously until 1909. The beginning of this period is marked also by the emerging prominence of terrorist tactics as the SR party's principal form of self-expression, with its assassination attacks on Plehve in 1904 and on the Grand Duke Sergei the following year. In contrast to the first three years of the party's existence, when it perpetrated a total of six acts of terrorism, in 1905 alone it carried out 44 attacks.[143] Once terrorism became unmistakably the SR's chief means of revolutionary struggle, this emphasized the absolute discrepancy between police infiltration of the SR and SD parties. Significantly, the authorities attached greater importance to terrorist activity than to the revolutionary activity in the industrial sector that was attributed to the Social Democrats. 'In my view,' the Okhrana chief in St Petersburg wrote, 'the most dangerous of all the revolutionary groups at that time were the Socialist Revolutionaries.' His major concern, he noted, was to get his agents as close to that group as possible and thereby obtain information about the plans of the Battle Organization.[144] His sense of urgency was shared by Dmitrii Trepov, the Governor-General of St Petersburg. In his memoirs, Gerasimov relates that he was visiting Trepov when the news was received of the assassination of the Grand Duke Sergei. He goes on to quote his host:

> It turns out that a new terrorist group, recently arrived from abroad, is operating in St Petersburg. They are plotting to assassinate the Grand Duke Vladimir and who knows who else. Now listen! Your primary task is to liquidate this group! Do not worry about large expenses – catch these people at any cost. Do you hear: at any cost![145]

The high concentration of secret agents among the anarchists in 1907 shown in Table 5 is yet another indication of the tremendous importance attributed by the police to the issue of terrorism. However the scope of the infiltration did not in itself indicate the importance the police attached to a specific organization as a target for intelligence gathering. This was because the number of agents in its ranks at any given moment was not dependent solely on this factor. Therefore the wages the police were willing to pay its agents should be considered in the light of their organizational affiliation.

Tables 6 and 7 examine police payments to its secret agents both in Russia and abroad, in roubles and francs, respectively. Table 8 provides data concerning the level of wages current in Russia at the beginning of the century. Considering Tables 6, 7, and 8, the tremendous gap between the normal wage levels at the time and the police salaries to secret agents is most striking. This testifies to the importance attached by the police to the Internal Agency as the basis of its political activity. At the same time, it also provides an indication

Table 6 Distribution of agents' wage levels according to party affiliation, 1902–14 (in roubles)

Monthly salary in roubles	*Social Democrats*	*Anarchists*	*SRs*	*Total*
10–25	11	—	—	11
26–50	9	—	—	9
51–100	2	2	8	12
101–300	1	—	4	5
301–1000	—	—	2	2
TOTAL KNOWN	23	2	14	39

Table 7 Distribution of agents' wage levels according to party affiliation, 1902–14 (in francs)

Monthly salary in francs	*Social Democrats*	*Anarchists*	*SRs*	*Total*
10–150	—	3	—	3
151–450	5	8	9	22
451–1000	1	—	9	10
1000+	—	—	2	2
2000+	1	—	1	2
TOTAL KNOWN	7	11	21	39

of the low level of motivation for co-operation with the police which consequently necessitated such extraordinary financial incentives.

Tables 6 and 7 also point to a considerable gap between the salaries paid in Russia to agents in the two largest revolutionary parties. Agents in the SR party earned three times the amount earned by their Social Democrat counterparts. Indeed, the latter's salary in Russia was about 45 per cent lower than that of anarchist agents. That the Police Department had a higher regard for agents close to the centre and leadership of the party emerges from the comparison of wages in francs. The gap between the SRs and the Social Democrats is small, whereas due to the absence of anarchist centres directing the movement from abroad, the importance of anarchist agents outside Russia diminished, and as a result their wages were far lower than those of their counterparts among the SRs or even the

Table 8 Example of wage levels in Russia at the beginning of the twentieth century (in roubles p.a.)

Bureaucracy[1]			*Police*[1]			*Workers*[2]
Senior ranks						
Directors of ministerial departments	7000	(250–583.3 monthly)	Police chiefs (*politsmeister*)	4000	(166.6–333.3 monthly)	
Chiefs of sections	3000		Assistant to Police chiefs	2000		
Middle ranks						
Heads of bureaux (*stolonachal'niki*)	2000	(100–166.6 monthly)	Chiefs of police stations	300	(75–108.5 monthly)	Average wage 187.6 (15.6 monthly)
Assistants	1200		Assistants to chiefs of police stations	900		
Low ranks						
Clerks	360	(15–30 monthly)	police officers (*okolotochnye nadzirateli*)		(150–400; 12.5–33.3 monthly)	
Accountants	180					

Sources:
[1]P. A. Zaionchkovskii, *Pravitel'stvennyi apparat samoderzhavnoi Rossii v XIX v.* (Moscow, 1978) pp. 86–9.
[2]L. Schapiro, *The Communist Party of the Soviet Union* (London, 1970) p. 20.

Social Democrats. Thus the high correlation between the number of agents and the number of anarchists as shown in Table 5, and in contrast, the agents' low pay as compared with their SR counterparts, show that the agency's massive infiltration of the anarchist movement was due primarily to their organizational structure, and only secondarily to the nature of their activity. A secret agent in a key position, such as Azef, was able to turn in all the members of Karl's Flying Detachment, the terrorist arm of the Northern Organization, and the members of Lev Zil'berberg's Battle Organization which was set up in St Petersburg in 1906, without the police having even one agent among them. He was able to accomplish this because of the vantage point he had gained thanks to his senior standing in the centralized SR Party. Where the anarchists were concerned, however, there was no possibility of planting agents in an organizational centre. There were indeed a few agents of high party repute, such as Dolin, whose personal standing enabled them to amass more information than was usual in anarchist groups. However, the absence of central institutions among the anarchists and the failure of their efforts to create some form of federative structure compelled the police to infiltrate their ranks in far higher concentration than was the case with the centralized parties, in order to ward off the threat of local terrorist acts.

As evident from Table 5 the gap began to close in 1910, due to the dissolution of most of the SR organizations in Russia. Yet the continuing importance the police attached to exposing SR activity is still reflected in Table 9 in the rate of recruitment in 1910 and 1911, despite the nadir in the party's activity.

In 1912, for the first time, the police directed their full attention to what was happening in industry, and hence to the Social Democrats. A top secret circular sent by the Director of the Police Department to the local and regional Sections of the Okhrana casts light on the gravity of the strikes that followed the Lena events. Stressing the fact that the Internal Agency had had no advance knowledge of the preparations for the strikes and demonstrations, the circular urged greater efforts to recruit serious agents, who would be able to expose the persons behind this activity.[146] While the circular called on the Internal Agency to infiltrate the ranks of the SR and the Social Democrats, the fact was, as Martynov noted, that hardly any meaningful SR organizations existed. The only groups showing more or less vigorous activity were the Social Democrats and the agency was, as a result, particularly strong among them.[147] Inevitably, there was a

Table 9 Annual recruitment

Party	1902	1903	1904	1905	1906	1907	1908	1909	1910	1911	1912	1913	1914	Unknown	Total
SRs	4	2	6	4	9	5	7	7	10	9	5	2	—	20	90
SDs	7	4	2	3	4	4	2	4	12	10	9	5	6	10	82
Total	11	6	8	7	13	9	9	11	22	19	14	7	6	30	172
Anarchists	2	—	—	2	7	6	4	1	1	—	1	2	1	16	43
TOTAL	13	6	8	9	20	15	13	12	23	19	15	9	7	16	215

Note: The figures refer to new agents recruited and not to the total number of agents active in each year.

decline in the number of SR agents as is apparent from Table 5, and a concomitant rise in the number of secret agents among the ranks of the Social Democrats. The objectives of the police were to direct agents to industrial centres such as St Petersburg or Moscow, to infiltrate workers' circles in large plants, and to collect information about the atmosphere among revolutionary workers.[148] This was to be effected both through the recruitment of SD members as in the past, and through the recruitment of workers both at their places of employment and in workers' organizations. The tendency to recruit agents in the so-called 'labour movement' – in contrast to party organizations – was discernible parallel to the increase in the rate of recruitment within the SD from 1910 onwards. A new concept of police activity was now evident:

> No more liquidation by means of searches and arrests in the wake of insufficiently processed reports, but following a thorough and absolutely secret study of the strikes being staged in two or three of the largest plants. In addition, we must make it our sole aim to spotlight the movement's intellectual leaders and activists, using the method noted above, so that we can try to recruit agents from among them even without liquidation.[149]

Thus, something of a shift had occurred not only with respect to the targets of infiltration but also concerning methods of operation. Undoubtedly this change was influenced by the respite provided by the apparent cessation of terrorist activity, even though the police did not dare drop the surveillance of the SR party. Indeed, until the Revolution, SR agents continued to make up the majority of the highest paid secret agents.

The incipient trends in Russia did not reflect the situation abroad. In contrast to the state of affairs inside Russia, where a large number of agents was needed, the Agency abroad concentrated chiefly on party centres or on groups close to the centres. The apprehension of the police that a major terrorist operation might be organized from abroad never diminished, and this was also reflected in their concentration of agents in party centres abroad. In 1914, its 22 agents in France were divided as follows:

12 SR (9 in Paris, 3 elsewhere)
6 SD (3 in Paris, 3 elsewhere)
3 Communist-Anarchists (all outside Paris)
1 Bund (location not specified).[150]

In summary, between 1905 and 1912 the Agency's value for the police was measured in terms of its connection with terrorist activity in general and central terrorism in particular, and in terms of how close it was to the centre of organizational revolutionary activity. For this reason the police directed most of their material and human resources toward penetrating the ranks of the SR and the anarchist groups. It was only at the beginning and end of the period under discussion, prior to 1904 and towards 1912, when the SR threat had not yet been revealed in its full force, and subsequently when despite the constant fear of its activity virtually no targets remained for infiltration by the Internal Agency, that the police were able to give deeper thought to revolutionary activity in industry. In this period indications emerged of an incipient shift in the objectives set for the agency. It is hardly surprising that precisely at this time Malinovskii had his dazzling career as a secret agent in the ranks of the Bolsheviks. An attempt was made to understand the manner in which a specific reality was formed and to influence it, instead of monitoring events and revolutionaries solely for liquidation purposes. No similar attempt was made after the Internal Agency was designated the linchpin of police activity.

The part assigned by the police to liquidation in its anti-revolutionary activity, combined with its disproportionate concentration on the SR party as a centralized terrorist organization, exacted a devastatingly high price from that party. By 1907 the police had been able to arrest or to exile about 15 000 of the party's activists,[151] who accounted for one-third of its membership at the height of its operation, if we accept Hildermeier's estimate. Party gatherings in general, and its congresses in particular, afforded the police prime opportunities to trail participants and to seize them on their way to a meeting or as they made their way home afterward. Equally important, such meetings were a veritable goldmine of information, particularly the party congresses, where a comprehensive survey was offered of the party and all its branches, and decisions were made about future revolutionary trends. The police therefore made a special effort to ensure that its agents attended those congresses which it had learned about in advance, or to obtain information about the proceedings of the meetings which it heard of after the event. The files of the Foreign Agency bulge with requests from the Police Department in St Petersburg to verify reports concerning congresses which, rumour had it, were about to take place, or asking the Foreign Agency to obtain internal party reports about the proceedings of meetings that had already been held. Many of these letters are preoccupied with the problem of how to ensure the participation of secret agents as official delegates or as observers. Other letters contain orders to have the External Agency trail the participants of the congresses, particularly those from Russia, with the aim of uncovering their organizational affiliations and, ultimately, to have them liquidated. A case in point is the directive of the acting Deputy Director of the Police Department, Vissarionov, to the head of the Foreign Agency, ordering him to dispatch agents to the congress of the Ukrainian SD Workers Party in order to find out who the participants were, to investigate their activities, and to liquidate them in due course.[152] However, despite this directive, the differing attitude of the political police towards the SR and the SD parties was reflected not only in the extent of agency infiltration, but also in the limits to organizational activity the police allowed each party.

The centralist structure of the two parties meant that the party congress, as the highest instance, assumed a key organizational role. This was the forum in which programmatic and tactical questions were discussed, and in which a single course of action had to be decided on from among diverse political tendencies; the key party activists took part in the congress, which also chose the organization's central institutions. However, to organize such a congress was excruciatingly difficult in underground conditions. To fulfil the constitutional requirement and to convene a representative congress, the party had first to hold elections in all its groups and branches, and collect information on their status and activity, so that the congress agenda could be worked out. Once the items for the agenda were

Table 10 Agents' party activity

	Terrorism[1]	*Labour movement*[2]	*Political*[3] *organizational activity*	*Propaganda*[4]	*Other*[5]	*Total*
SRs	21 (36.2%)	7 (12.1%)	12 (20.7%)	6 (10.3%)	12 (20.7%)	58 (100%)
SDs	4 (7.1%)	14 (25%)	29 (51.8%)	6 (10.7%)	3 (5.4%)	56 (100%)
TOTAL	25	21	41	12	15	114

[1]Arms smuggling; preparation of explosives; participation in 'expropriations'; membership in a battle squad.
[2]Trade unions; strike organization; Party activity in factories.
[3]Membership in a regional/municipal or central committee; membership in a foreign bureau/delegation; co-ordination, special missions; membership in a commission/committee; secretary; delegate to a conference; press; Duma.
[4]Propaganda among peasants/students; *organizator*; smuggling of banned literature.
[5]Rank and file; forgery.

determined, each constituent organization had to hold discussions in order to formulate the stand to be adopted by its delegates to the congress. Finally, a venue had to be found which was beyond the reach of the police – generally abroad – and the safe arrival of the delegates had to be ensured. The upshot was that it took so long to organize a congress, and so many party members were involved, that it was virtually impossible to keep the matter secret. Irrespective of the use Lenin made of his party's congresses, it is worth recalling the description of Nadezhda Krupskaia concerning the vast importance that Lenin always attached to those congresses. She also points out that the young generation does not know what it means to be compelled to wait for years before the entire party could meet to discuss the most burning questions of policy and tactics. Therefore they are unable to imagine the difficulties entailed in convening illegal congresses in those days, and are also incapable of grasping Lenin's attitude towards those congresses[153] Available statistical data shed light on the nature of the activity assigned by the police to the agents of different party affiliation and its political consequences.

As is apparent from Table 10, 50 per cent of the secret agents among the Social Democrats were involved with purely operational activity as against 80 per cent among the SRs, where terrorism constituted the centre of gravity. In striking contrast, however, 50 per cent of the Social Democrat agents were engaged in political-organizational spheres compared to only 20 per cent among their SR counterparts. This distribution reflects the profound police interest in the Social Democrats' internal affairs, and hence its efforts to facilitate the participation of its agents in various party forums, notably congresses, and then make use of them as sources of information for future liquidation. The police evinced no similar interest *vis-à-vis* the SRs. On the contrary, the police concentration on Socialist-Revolutionary terrorist activity meant that its primary efforts were directed at immediate liquidations.

Thus the possible exposure of the party to the police while preparations for the congress were underway, and the attendant extensive risk of arrest, was difficult enough for the persecuted SRs, and it was a particularly heavy price to pay in order to put the organization's principles into practice. Although we may assume that this was not the only factor that dissuaded the party's central institutions from seeking to hold annual congresses as required by the constitution, a connection does, nevertheless, exist between the attitude adopted by the police towards the SR party from 1905 to 1910, and the fact that in this period the party was able to organize only two congresses – neither of which met the requirements of the organizational regulations. Extensive elections were not held prior to the party's founding congress of December 1905, which was to decide the platform; elections took place only at the committee level with the result that no more than 49 enfranchised delegates took part in the congress, besides the representatives of the central bodies and the members of the Foreign Committee. Only 60 delegates – again, most of them committee representatives – took part in the second congress which convened, under relatively easier conditions, at the beginning of 1907. In contrast, the Social Democrats held five congresses between 1898 and 1907. Only in the case of the founding congress of the RSDRP held in Minsk in 1898 – before the founding of the SR party – did the police attempt to intervene and thwart the meeting. Time after time the congress was postponed; finally it was convened in such haste that no platform or constitution could be adopted. Although the congress did manage to elect a central committee, two of its three members were arrested immediately after the congress dispersed.

However, in 1907, as the SR party held its hastily organized and poorly attended second congress, the SDs were holding their fifth congress. Prior to its convening, the police dispatched the important veteran Berlin-based agent, Iakov Zhitomirskii, to Russia so that he could make contacts that would ensure his election as a delegate.[154]

The congress was attended by 350 delegates. The two SR party congresses during this period were marked not only by poor attendance, but also by a lack of the necessary preparations. During the first congress the constitution and many key resolutions were drafted hastily in the corridors; and according to Argunov's evidence the same conditions prevailed at the second congress.[155]

In contrast to the difficulties entailed in convening a congress, it was a far simpler matter to hold a party council meeting. Because the council was not an elected body, no prior organization-wide elections were required, nor did the preparations involve the entire party. A council session could be organized at short notice and in relative secrecy. However, not even party councils could be convened without difficulties. Nearly all the council members who went to Saratov in 1908 in order to renew party activity in that key region were arrested after Azef informed on them.[156] The fifth party council, for example, which convened in 1909, waited abroad for two weeks in expectation of the arrival of the representatives of the regional committees. Two of them were arrested as they crossed the border. Finally, the council met without the full quorum, despite contentions that any resolutions adopted by this reduced body would not be binding.[157] Five council meetings had been held by 1914, all of them dealing with urgent questions of principle – questions which by their very nature should have been placed on the agenda of the congress. In practice, however, the council came to take the place of the congress, as no representative congresses were held and no forum was available for the comprehensive clarification of key programmatic or tactical questions. Moreover, the body responsible for implementing the organization's principles embodied in the constitution was in fact non-existent and supervision from below was not implemented. The veteran leadership was united by ties of long-time underground activity – which in some cases had preceeded the establishment of the party – as well as by bonds of personal friendship and sometimes of family as well. It was they who possessed supreme authority and they who divided the central party functions among themselves. As Hildermeier points out, far from fulfilling the principle of democracy, they embodied the principle of co-option and oligarchy.[158]

This state of affairs inevitably generated criticism, as is also clear from Argunov's allusion to it in the party organ. Police activity could not be held as the sole reason for the party's failure to convene its congresses, or for the fact that a small group of activists controlled its central institutions for many years; however, in replying to criticism of this situation, Argunov did indicate that the primary reason was the underground conditions in which the party operated. At the same time, in a party marked by deep divergences of opinion on the most basic issues, the combination of ideological conflicts and oligarchic leadership was bound to foment bitterness and resentment. Against such a background the phenomenon of the secret agents was to assume a special significance.

Zinaida Zhuchenko was one of the outstanding secret agents in police annals. Active in the SR party for years, she came to epitomize the police agent *par excellence*. It is fitting to close this discussion of the Internal Agency in action and of its value for the police, particularly as it functioned within the SR party, with a brief profile of a leading but less known agent.

Zhuchenko was recruited in 1894, 'not in the wake of an arrest, not under the pressure of threats, and not even for thirty pieces of silver', as she herself put it, but because ideologically she identified with the régime. Her recruitment came after she made the acquaintance of the Police Department's Deputy Director, Semiakin, who referred her to Zubatov.[159] Thus in the mid-1890s she became a secret agent of the Moscow police. Her name was linked with famous revolutionaries, and when she went abroad in 1898 with an impressive revolutionary past behind her, including arrest and exile as a cover, she found no difficulty in penetrating revolutionary circles in which the Okhrana evinced an interest, first in Leipzig and then in Heidelberg. Her police code name was 'Mikheev'.

In September 1905, as the need grew for police agents at home, she hastened to return to Russia, and it was then that she embarked on the career that was to make her a heroine in the eyes of the Okhrana and an abomination in the eyes of her former revolutionary comrades. She returned to Russia equipped with recommendations and secret addresses (*iavki*) which she acquired on the basis of the contacts she had made first in Moscow and then abroad, and without which it was impossible to infiltrate revolutionary circles. It was the *iavki* that paved the way for every revolutionary, hence also for every secret agent. They were a condition for acceptance to the party or group and for the maintenance of close relations with persons of influence.

As described by her colleagues, Zinaida Zhuchenko was tall and thin and had sympathetic features, a high forehead and light hair. She wore glasses, and her serious and slightly reflective eyes radiated confidence.[160] Her shoulders were extremely narrow and her shoulder-blades protruded oddly, but she carried herself well and was strict about her posture, in order to conceal her deformity. She was generally very friendly, and so pleasant an impression did she make on her interlocutors that they had no hesitations about opening their hearts to her. Undoubtedly her contacts, standing and expertise in on-going events, helped her. But it was the combination of all her traits that made her a leader in the eyes of many. Her most striking quality was her practicality, accompanied by a modesty so intense that it sometimes amounted to self-effacement. Never did she make a final decision on any problem, contending that she lacked the authority, although her standing and ties certainly belied this. Not long after she arrived in Moscow Zhuchenko took part in the revolt that broke out there in December 1905. In March 1906 her prominence brought her into the ranks of the fighting squad of the Regional Committee, where she served as secretary alongside Sladokpevtsev – 'Kazbek' – the squad leader. 'Kazbek' had the reputation of a ne'er-do-well who was incapable of carrying out an operation to its planned end. Their combination of qualities served Zhuchenko's purposes well: the failures and setbacks were imputed to him, whereas her unflagging resourcefulness and dedication enhanced her reputation and attracted the attention of the Regional Committee, who invited her to serve as its secretary.

Zhuchenko's new position gave her access to all the secrets of the entire Moscow region. The Moscow Regional Committee was one of the most important and most central institutions in the SR party, both because of the city's central location and because of its standing as the empire's second capital. It served as a transit point for comrades en route from the centre to the periphery, the place where they acquired *iavki* for party purposes. In her new role, too, Zinaida Zhuchenko demonstrated her characteristic initiative and resourcefulness. Diligently and precisely, she collected a list of addresses and secret apartments at the Regional Committee. She established new relations, sent detailed questionnaires to the local committees, and amassed data about what was taking place in the extensive area that was under the leadership of the Regional Committee. She always tried to accompany the committee members on their trips and had a hand in all events and decisions, with the result that she soon became the most knowledgeable committee member about events in the field, and thus also formed ties with the party's Central Committee.

Born into a fairly notable aristocratic family, she attended a boarding school and then studied in a women's course in Moscow. According to what she told her confidants, she first met the man who was to become her husband in Moscow, and then again in the 1890s, when she was exiled to the Caucasus. He was sick and feeble, and she married him more out of humane and compassionate feelings than out of love. After the birth of their son, she claimed that their married life became intolerable. Her husband, who was a consumptive began to show signs of mental derangement as well,and she herself was gripped by fear that her son, too, might one day suffer from these illnesses. Her agony, she stated, ended only with the death of her husband. Taking the legacy he had left her, she went abroad with her son for seven years to sort herself out.

Zhuchenko claimed that she was unable to stand aside when the events of 1905 erupted. Difficult as it was to leave her son, his poor health made it imperative that he be placed in the hands of a foster family in Berlin. There, thanks to her legacy, she was able to visit him once a year. The truth, of course, was that she financed her trips, as well as her other needs, with Okhrana funds and not with money from her husband, who was separated from her and worked as a doctor in Siberia.

No one had the slightest doubt as to Zhuchenko's reliability. Alexander Pribylev claimed that there were some who mistrusted her, but kept their suspicions to themselves since they had no proof. Zinaida Zhuchenko continued her secret activity as an agent until after the Azef affair. Only when the first rumours from abroad began to filter in concerning her ties with the Okhrana, were the police forced to liquidate the vestiges of the organizations in the Moscow region, while she herself fled abroad.

From the police point of view, Zhuchenko launched her career with a number of important assets. In the first place, she was recruited voluntarily out of an anti-revolutionary stance. In addition, she was educated and possessed a sagacity that guided her every step. She strove relentlessly to reach the centre, yet did so without showing and without expressing any ambitions liable to arouse suspicion. On the contrary, her modesty and humility were lauded, along with her serious work for and absolute dedication to the revolutionary cause. Instead of curiosity, which often made the revolutionaries suspicious, she showed a welcome initiative. Truth and fabrication were inextricably intertwined in her cover story, which was designed to arouse sympathy for her suffering. What was more important, it explained the source of her financial resources, a matter which was often one of the chief causes of suspicions directed against agents. Perhaps her key asset was her ability to position herself in a way that the liquidations which followed her reports were explicable as technical failures or as the provocations of others. In 1906, for example, a special circle engaging in propoganda work and the dissemination of literature was organized in Moscow. In the wake of repeated and incomprehensible failures, the group's members became suspicious of a woman who was close to the circle. The usual procedure was for the group to receive a go-ahead from the Regional Committee to take action against exposed agents. At that time Zhuchenko was the secretary of the Regional Committee, and all the circle's requests in this matter went through her. They were rejected one after another as being insufficiently grounded. Every time the matter came up for discussion, the woman under suspicion disappeared, only to reappear after the danger from the members of the circle had passed. In retrospect, after Zhuchenko's exposure, this affair was cited as proof that the only persons Zhuchenko spared were police agents like herself. On the other hand, the disappearance of the suspect – if indeed she had any connection with Zhuchenko – could also be explained by the fact that her continued activity close to the group deflected all suspicion to her. Likewise the failure of the Kurlov assassination attempt was no doubt explained by Sladokpevtsev's poor organizational ability, or the arrest of Fruma Frumkina – who was going to assassinate Stolypin and for whom Zhuchenko had sewn the pocket in which the gun was hidden – was attributed to Frumkina's well-known and conspicuous nervousness, which attracted the attention of the police.

Most important, the attitude of the police towards the SR party lent particular value and immediate operational significance to the type of information collected by Zhuchenko. It was agents of her mettle who enabled the police not only to undermine the party's organizational foundations and torpedo congresses and other initiatives but even to disrupt on-going connections between the centre and the periphery. The absence of such contacts, according to Hildermeier, was one of the key causes of the party's weakness.

2 The Revolutionary Response

(i) DENIAL OF THE THREAT

The fact that secret agents – *agents provocateurs* – had penetrated to the very heart of the revolutionary movement hardly came as a bolt from the blue to the SRs or to other revolutionaries. This was one of the police methods in the anti-revolutionary struggle, with which they were well acquainted, not only from everyday life, but also from the Degaev affair, a part of the tradition of the *Narodnaia Volia* with which the Socialist Revolutionaries felt a close affiliation. Their derogatory term for it – *Degaevshchina* – reflected not only their revulsion at the method itself, but also their recognition that, despite its extreme nature, the Degaev affair was a typical example of the Police Department's method of combating the underground revolutionary movements.

Given this knowledge, one might have expected them to pay particular heed to the phenomenon which served as the main instrument of the police in their efforts to curb revolutionary activity. Such attention could have been reflected on either of two levels: a stringent level which viewed provocation as the party's fundamental problem and sought to deal with it as such; or on a second, more elementary level of awareness of conspiracy, as an integral part of the overall underground struggle.

In the former case the problem of the provocation seems to have had no impact on the SRs. No records of deliberations on the subject have turned up, and there is nothing to even hint that it was perceived as a problem in any way related to the party's mode of existence or its form of organization. Presumably the exposure of every secret agent grieved and shocked his close friends, and had a certain impact on the group of which he had been a member. However, besides the publication of the names of exposed agents in the party press – a custom adopted by all the revolutionary parties and a matter over which they co-operated – there is nothing to suggest that the subject held any importance for the party or that it was deemed worthy of special attention. Indeed, not even the habit of publishing the names of the exposed agents – with the aim of warning other organizations – was strictly adhered to, and this sometimes provoked anger.[1]

For the SRs, provocation was inseparably linked to their struggle against the régime, and was perceived as further evidence of the régime's wickedness and brutality. It is in this tone that the subject is dealt with in the party organs under headings like: 'How to React to the Government's Bestiality?',[2] 'The White Terror of the Government and von Koten',[3] and 'The Bacchanalia of the Black Hundreds'.[4] Thus, the SRs' attitude towards the problem must be seen in the light of their consciousness of conspiracy in general.

To protect themselves from the régime, all the revolutionary parties adopted precautionary measures which were supervised by special conspiracy committees. The revolutionaries had certain basic rules in common: they all employed revolutionary code-names by which they were known to one another. The code-names were changed from time to time, and on special occasions, such as congresses, several different code-names might be used. Under the accepted requirements of conspiracy, each party member was allowed to be acquainted only with those who helped him fulfil his party tasks. New applicants were accepted only at the recommendation of known and reliable members. However, those basic rules alone cannot attest to the degree of conspiratorial sensitivity but rather the discrepancy between these rules and ongoing revolutionary activity: namely, how far revolutionary activities were measured in the light of the need for secrecy. From this point of view, the parties seem to have gone their own separate ways. Based on his own experience, Zavarzin averred that the Jewish Bund, the Armenian Dashnaktsiutun party, and the Polish Socialist Party (PPS) paid considerable attention to the need to preserve the conditions of conspiracy. The Mensheviks, on the other hand, tended to engage in widespread activities, thus becoming convenient targets for exposure; while the SRs took no special precautionary measures beyond their operational activity.[5]

The conspiracy question in the context of the national organizational structure can only be explained in correlation with two additional factors: national homogeneity and a strict organizational approach. The higher the proportion of a single nationality, the stronger the organizational structure, discipline and operational capability[6] – and, apparently, also the consequent conspiratorial awareness.

If we accept Zavarzin's description of the above four parties, there would appear to be a connection between the degree of homogeneity within the three national parties, the PPS, the Bund and Dashnaktsiutun. This connection is also evident in the case of the Mensheviks, who from the national composition point of view were the least homogeneous of the revolutionary parties. However, this factor is absent in the SRs. Despite a high degree of homogeneity[7] and an orthodox organizational structure, contrary to Zavarzin's impression, their conspiratorial consciousness was surprisingly low, even in the sphere of terrorist activity. This presumably was due to the fact that contrary to the other three parties, they did not constitute a national minority group.

The absence of a feeling for conspiracy is manifest at all levels: at the personal, the non-operational organization, and at the operational level, namely in the terrorist organizations. The most trenchant personal expression of this phenomenon is to be found in the letters. The revolutionaries knew that the police intercepted postal matter and copied the contents of suspicious letters in special so-called 'secret rooms' (*chernye kabinety*) in Russia's main post offices. They were well aware that special clerks were engaged in this work, and when they came across a letter written in code or with invisible ink, they would send it to the Police Department for deciphering. The revolutionaries also knew that copies of suspicious letters were sent to Okhrana sections and to the Gendarmerie in order to establish the identities of sender and addressee[8] and yet they did not refrain from sending even the most secret messages by mail. A striking illustration is provided by a letter written by the representative of the Battle Organization abroad, Mikhail Gots, which was sent from Geneva to Kiev in November 1902. It contained a message in invisible ink stating: 'In our view it is essential . . . to direct all forces against Plehve. . . .'[9] The files of the Foreign Agency contain dozens of similar letters replete with details about forged passports, and so forth, including one penned by a Paris revolutionary who writes confidently that if the Russian régime were skilful enough to seize all the letters containing secret information, it could be certain of surviving for even another hundred years.[10]

Just as the highly confidential information was revealed in letters, the most deeply guarded secrets of Zil'berberg's Battle Organization were exposed due to its bizarre methods of operation. Like the Police Department, the Battle Organization carried out its pre-operational investigations by means of 'internal detection' and 'external detection'. However, while the latter was entrusted to the members of the organization, when it came to internal detection – that is, the collection of data concerning the target of the operation – they were aided by extensive circles that bore no direct connection with the organization, and at times not even with the party.[11] This naturally provided an opening for the leakage of information about the organization's current activities and future plans. Every party member who might be in possession of any details about a projected assassination attempt was obligated to pass them on to the Battle Organization, and any member of a party organization who had connections which might prove useful in promoting current operational activity, had to place them at the disposal of the Battle Organization. The disadvantages of this method finally forced the Head of the Organization to look for a different solution. Rather than having the Organization dependent on chance information that might come its way and hampering orderly planned activity, he decided that he would approach the sources he required. The composition of the Organization was altered and the remaining core of six or seven persons was joined for special missions by others from various places and of diverse professions, some of them not even party members. 'It was obvious to them [the members of the Organization] that the ties with the periphery and the approaches for *iavki* to people who were not party members, could lead to failures, informing and provocation, but . . . they were convinced that there was no other way.'[12] These words were written by the wife of the Organization's leader in 1910, when the concepts concerning provocation as well as the attitude towards it had already undergone a radical change. Yet it is difficult to believe that a solution of this kind was acceptable, in the light of its grave significance in terms of conspiracy, not only *vis-à-vis* the Battle Organization itself, but with respect to the entire party.

In the Northern Organization, in Karl's Flying Detachment, the overwhelming majority of the activists were not party members. By January and February 1907 the situation had reached a point where only two of the unit's ten members were ideologically motivated SRs. Not one of the remaining eight was a party member. They had joined the group for a motley of reasons, ranging from an excess of youthful revolutionary ardour to a desire for personal revenge.[13] It should, of course, be borne in mind that this was a unique period of mass revolutionary agitation, a time when 'for every party member who was arrested there were ten who were eager to take his place'.[14] During a period when it was terrorism that specifically attracted thousands of young people, even the participation of outsiders in the most clandestine activity did not immediately raise the question and the degree of their political reliability, their personal loyalty or their commitment to the cause. Nevertheless the phenomenon does attest to, if not a total absence of conspiratorial consciousness, then at least to its low priority among the considerations that guided the leaders of the battle squads — such veteran, experienced revolutionaries as Zil'berberg and Karl Trauberg. However they were not alone. Most of the SR groups abroad preferred to define themselves as groups 'for the SR party', rather than as SR groups as such, thereby opening the door to persons who did not regard themselves as party members and expanding their circle of influence. In so doing, they laid themselves open to the infiltration of elements about whom they lacked sufficient information, which inevitably lowered the threshold of suspicion. In 1907, the Paris group, for example, numbered some 70 persons about whom next to nothing was known concerning their ties with the party in Russia or their activity there.[15] Years later, after the Revolution, Agafonov sought to explain the Okhrana's success in penetrating the ranks of the SRs by pointing not only to 'the recklessness and the faith of the revolutionaries', but also to the fact that 'in the last 20 years they began to adopt a more nonchalant attitude than they had previously shown to the infiltration of their ranks by persons who were alien to them in spirit'.[16]

In contrast to the crucial importance the police attached to the Internal Agency and the use to which it was put against the revolutionaries, the absence of a clear attitude towards provocation as an issue and the disregard of conspiratorial considerations are particularly astonishing. First, how can this attitude of the SRs towards an issue which, by any logic, should have been preoccupying them more than any other be accounted for. Secondly – a question relating to Sudeikin's hypothesis[17] – was the Internal Agency capable of generating such profound demoralization and evoking such terrible suspicions and fears among party members to the point where revolutionary activity would be brought to a standstill?

It is a simpler matter to account for an explicit attitude than it is to explain the disregard for a certain subject. Nevertheless, the absence of any reaction at all just where one would naturally have expected it, can in itself indicate the attitude towards the subject in question. It is quite possible that the absence of conspiratorial consciousness, or what Agafonov terms 'recklessness', was actually a defence mechanism that insulated SR activity and allowed it to take place despite the fears and suspicions that Sudeikin sought to sow among them. Revolutionary activity in general, and acts of terrorism in particular, presupposed a high level of intimacy and trust among a group's members; otherwise, such activity would not have been feasible. Well aware of this, Sudeikin attempted to undermine the interpersonal basis of this activity. But the SRs reacted unexpectedly. In order to defend themselves, they suppressed the entire issue of provocation to its most elementary formal level. The significance of their disavowal of the problem, and the danger this posed, are strikingly illustrated by Gerasimov's story. To break the spirit of the Battle Organization's members, he worked out a special plan which, as a key element, aimed at heightening the revolutionaries' consciousness that the police were constantly on their trail, that every move they made was an open book to the authorities. In order to wear them down and fray their nerves, he led them to think that the police had them under permanent surveillance – to which end he employed special experts who got a kick out of this type of activity. So closely would these agents follow the revolutionary that they would almost bump into him; only a blind person could fail to spot them. 'Such overt surveillance could not but have a lasting impact on all the fighters. . . . Initially they may have tended to view these as chance phenomena, but if they recurred constantly, and always when the organization seemed to be so close to its target, this then necessarily evoked doubts as to the whole purpose of their activity.'[18]

Sensing, in fact, that they were being watched, the members of the Battle Organization decided to disperse in order to shake off the surveillance. The organization's chief, Azef, instructed his deputy, Savinkov, to meet with him in St Petersburg three weeks later, after he had successfully covered his tracks. For three weeks Savinkov travelled the length and breadth of Russia, jumping off trains in mid-journey, or loudly ordering a hansom driver to proceed to a certain address and then suddenly changing his destination. When he saw that the manoeuvring ability of the cab following him was limited – he would abruptly change course – but the detectives never lost his trail. Returning to St Petersburg he encountered one of them face to face. 'Well, you see . . .', the detective said to him, smiling. Finally, he managed to flee to Finland without having been able to meet with Azef or to obtain any news from him. While in Finland, he learned of the anonymous letter which had been sent to the party stating that 'the engineer Azef and the former exile T. [Tatarov] are police agents'. Yet at no time – not during his futile attempts to elude the police and not even when he learned of the anonymous letter – did he suspect anything. From Finland he travelled to Geneva for a meeting with Mikhail Gots, who had now also heard about the anonymous letter. To Gots's question of what he thought about it all, Savinkov replied that he had no opinion.[19]

Although the close surveillance did force the members of the Battle Organization to disperse, it did not achieve its declared purpose. Savinkov's spirit was not broken. He entertained no suspicions despite his desperate efforts to evade his pursuers for three solid weeks and despite the anonymous letter received immediately afterwards.

This denial is also given expression in Savinkov's book *Kon' blednyi* ('The Pale Horse'),[20] written before Azef's exposure. In the book Savinkov seeks to depict the inner world of those who practice terrorism through the tale of a battle squad which is in the midst of preparations to assassinate the local governor. The book describes the personal relations among the members of the squad, their experiences and intimate feelings as they go about planning the operation, and the awareness of the danger posed by the police is explicitly expressed. The book's protagonist, the head of the squad, constantly suspects that he is being followed. Everyone who addresses him – on the street, in the railway station or in the hotel – seems to be a spy. Shortly before the scheduled date of the assassination attempt, the squad members discover that the police are on to them, and they have to disperse and postpone the operation. Yet nowhere in the entire story does any of the characters entertain even the shadow of a suspicion regarding one of his fellow conspirators. This is not because it would have been out of place within the framework of the plot – after all, the story was supposed to reflect a reality in which betrayal was a common phenomenon – but because the possibility of such an eventuality did not even occur to the author. Likewise in real life, neither his own personal experience nor the Battle Organization's rapid succession of failures led him to suspect the loyalty of any of his comrades.

The general picture of denial and disregard in the period under discussion – namely until Azef's exposure in 1909 – is filled in by other relevant data shown in Table 11, which typify the manner in which secret agents in the party's ranks were exposed.

The most glaring trend during these years is the lack of exposures, or their very low number, in all the revolutionary groups until 1906. With the ebbing of the revolutionary tide, however, the number of exposures abruptly increased among the anarchists in 1907 and among the Social Democrats the following year. No similar tendency

Table 11 Number of annual exposures compared to the number of active agents in the same year

	1902	1903	1904	1905	1906	1907	1908	1909	1910	1911	1912	1913	1914
SR													
Active agents	5	5	11	15	22	22	23	20	25	29	32	27	23
No. of exposures	—	—	—	—	2	1	3	5	4	4	1	4	2
SD													
Active agents	7	10	11	14	18	20	15	19	29	32	37	37	42
No. of exposures	1	—	—	—	—	—	7	—	—	2	1	—	—
Anarchists													
Active agents	2	2	2	3	8	8	7	7	7	3	2	3	2
No. of exposures	—	—	—	—	2	5	4	—	—	1	1	1	—

is discernible where the SRs are concerned. It is only following Azef's exposure at the end of 1908 that a continuous trend of exposures emerges, and the number of agents exposed is relatively higher than that in other parties.

It is true that an Okhrana officer, Leonid Men'shchikov, defected abroad in 1909 and provided the revolutionaries with long lists of names of secret agents who were operating in their ranks. However, a good many of the exposures were not due to him. It must be borne in mind that an Okhrana man, Bakai, had defected in the previous period as well, and his reports not only went unheeded, but they actually evoked the wrath of some Socialist Revolutionaries, who cautioned others to avoid him. At the end of 1908 a leaflet, signed 'An SR Circle', was circulated in Paris and directed at the readers of Burtsev's paper *Byloe* and the SR opposition organ *Revoliutsionnaia Mysl'* ('Revolutionary Thought'). The leaflet maintained that Bakai, who was regularly publishing details about police agents in these papers, was himself a veteran *agent provocateur* against whom the organ of the SR party had warned as early as 1903.[21] Even if this was correct, and even if the struggle over Azef's good name lay behind this warning, the leaflet affected the seriousness with which Bakai's statements were taken, and once more attests to a low awareness of the conspiracy issue and of the need for defence against the police.

It is clear that the denial of the provocation issue was not absolute. There were accepted ways to deal with suspects or with persons whose ties with the police had been proved. But the suspicion threshold was high, and to Sudeikin's chagrin the Socialist Revolutionaries were not obsessed with fears and suspicions. For this reason the harm caused by a provocation, even when it was discovered, was not critical for general party activity. Some idea regarding the purpose served by the denial from the SRs' point of view may be gleaned if it is borne in mind that they were a central target of the Okhrana and that by 1907 about one-third of their total membership had been arrested. Reports from SR groups in Russia repeatedly speak of mass arrests that temporarily put an end to the activity of entire groups, until a handful of activists assumed the task of reorganizing everything from the beginning.[22] Was this activity possible while maintaining a serious attitude towards the significance of provocation, and towards the fears and suspicions which a full awareness of the subject naturally evoked?

Just as the disregard of the provocation and of the requirements of conspiracy in the peak years of the revolution served the urge for revolutionary action, so the decline in the years that followed forced the SRs to regard the weakness of conspiracy as the cardinal reason for their failure – and as a source of hope for the future. 'It's no secret that we are defeated,' Chernov said at the party's conference in London in August 1908,

> but it is not as a mass party that we are defeated – it is as an organization. The reason for our defeat lies in the tremendous inconsistency between our enfeebled organizations and the strength of the masses, whom we want to serve, to grip and to strengthen. Hence our need for creative work. That work must take the form of the adaptation of our organizations to the conditions of police activity, by reinforcing the foundations of conspiracy and centralism.[23]

However, whether this declaration was meant to be of some consolation or the expression of hope for the future, the trauma of the Azef affair ended all hopes of change in future.

(ii) THE UNBOTTLING OF THE GENIE

'The black year of the party' was how Chernov dubbed the period that commenced immediately after Azef's exposure, 'a year of disgraceful and nightmarish revelations'.[24] Indeed, the shock and pain that followed the uncovering of the treason of one of the SR party's most important and admired leaders split all the party's organizations and affected its entire range of activities for years to come. Under the pressure of this heavy blow, for the first time the party was forced to cope with the problem of provocation comprehensively. The affair dealt a severe blow to the morale of those who had for years been Azef's comrades in the leading ranks or in the Battle Organization, and of party members everywhere. The exposure also cast doubts on several key tenets of the Socialist Revolutionaries, for example, the form of party organization, and the role of terrorism. Echoes of the affair were also heard in connection with the issue of underground revolutionary activity versus legal party activity, which developed soon afterwards. Thus, from being a matter whose existence was all but denied, the provocation became a central party topic of discussion.

Nor was the storm that broke following the exposure of the Head of the SR party's Battle Organization confined to that party alone. The entire revolutionary camp was now preoccupied with the question of police infiltration into its ranks and was forced to take a position on a phenomenon that affected every part of it. Even if the stands adopted did no more than reinforce previously held positions or outlooks, nevertheless provocation was for the first time grasped as an inherent part of the framework within which it was employed, or as influenced by it. The Azef exposure was a turning point with respect to the phenomenon of the provocation; its profound impact accounts for the significance it was to assume in the SR party history for many years to come.

Azef had a special place in the SR leadership because of his organizational ability and his rare technical gifts. Nicknamed 'Golden Hands', he was considered an irreplaceable leader. His part in planning the famous terrorist acts of the Battle Organization, and in perfecting the methods of terrorist combat, became a byword in the entire party, even if his actual deeds were known only to a small group who were privy to the secrets of the Battle Organization. His ability to exploit his role as a secret agent for his own private benefit convinced everyone that the party's operational success hinged on him and on him alone, thus rendering him the decisive and exclusive authority in all matters relating to the Battle Organization.[25] So greatly was he admired that Breshkovskaia, 'the grandmother of the Russian Revolution', who herself became a symbol for generations of Russian revolutionaries during her own lifetime, bowed before him as a mark of gratitude for the successful assassination of Plehve – an act which had run into considerable obstacles until Azef assumed responsibility for its organization.[26]

Externally his ugly and repulsive features were complemented by awkward and graceless behavior. Invariably, the initial impression he created on others was highly negative. 'What a suspicious character he is!' Chernov commented to Khaim Zhitlovskii in whose home he first met Azef. Both Chernov and Zhitlovskii's wife took a dislike to Azef. Yet Zhitlovskii overcame this reaction, saying, 'What's wrong with you – he's one of ours. He is the absolutely reliable organizer from Moscow who has been known for some time.'[27] Indeed, admiration for Azef led many who worked with him to believe that beneath the gruff exterior existed a gentle and sensitive soul, effusing warmth and sympathy. Azef played the part to the hilt. He might, for example, express quiet and bashful sympathy for a comrade who had fervently advocated a certain point during a discussion by going up to him afterward and, without speaking a word, giving a kiss and departing at once. He would embrace a comrade who had returned from a dangerous mission and kiss his hand. It was related that once, when an escaped prisoner told how he was beaten with a rod while in gaol, Azef suddenly began to weep hysterically.[28] When Osip Minor was placed at the head of a group of activists and given the task of reorganizing party activity in the Volga region, on the eve of his departure he met Azef who implored him relentlessly to forego his plan lest he, too, fall into the hands of the police and be hanged. 'It's not for you to speak like this, Ivan,' Minor replied. 'How many times have you risked your own life – yet you have never flinched from danger.' Finally Azef accompanied him home, embraced and kissed him, and left without speaking another word.[29] He then informed on him to the Okhrana.[30]

In his sleep Azef would utter deep and heart-rending sighs attesting, so his comrades thought, to the immense suffering of one who walked always in the shadow of the gallows, hazarded his own life and was responsible for the lives of others, and who was constantly compelled to engage in acts of bloodshed. All of this intensified his comrades' feelings for him and their dependence on his leadership. Once, when he sought to divest himself of responsibility for heading a Battle Organization, everyone present – 25 in number – declared that without him they would not go on and that they too were ceasing their activity.[31] Thus it is easy to imagine the extreme shock at his exposure. Even after his guilt had been proved, many refused to believe it. Fourteen of the party's key activists met in secret session to determine that the fact of Azef's treachery had been demonstrated beyond all doubt. However only four of them considered that the data provided by the former Director of the Police Department, Lophukhin, to Burtsev and to the SR representatives, were sufficient to warrant a death sentence to be effected without delay. The majority view was that such an act would generate a split in the party, particularly if the verdict was not sufficiently grounded and if Azef were not given the opportunity to defend himself properly. Some, not entirely convinced of Azef's guilt, demanded assurances that he would not be harmed, or declared they would warn him that his life was in danger.[32] Peter Karpovich of the Battle Organization threatened, 'I do not believe it! I do not believe it! And again, I do not believe it! If so much as one hair of Azef's head is harmed, I will shoot them all.'[33] Even after Azef's flight had convinced the last of the sceptics, some still could not grasp the immensity of his treachery. In his heart, Minor, who related how he had taken leave of Azef on the eve of his departure for Saratov, still refused to believe that the farewell embrace and the eyes welling with tears were no more than the pretence of a traitor. He concludes his description as follows: 'Who knows, perhaps in the heart of the human beast, the man momentarily overcame the beast'.[34] So it is hardly surprising that when the hard truth became known, many shared the feeling that

> If Ivan Nikolaevich is a *provocateur*, who can we believe in and how can we go on living? If the person we believed in as the best of friends, as a brother, turns out to be such a base traitor, does this not mean that it is no longer possible to believe in man altogether, that there is no truth in the world, that there is nothing worth living for? And if this is so, does it not mean that no moral basis lies to life?[35]

These were the questions that Vladimir Zenzinov, a member of the Battle Organization, asked himself. Zenzinov relates that he had placed absolute faith in Azef, trusting him as he trusts himself, and that he had, like many others, never for a moment hesitated to place his life and his fate in Azef's hands. These comrades were wracked by a severe inner crisis following the revelation of Azef's treachery. Some were unable to cope; one even took his own life. For years afterward they could not talk about the affair without becoming agitated, and the more they reflected on it, the more incomprehensible they found it to be.[36]

Mark Natanson, the old, experienced revolutionary leader of the SRs, who had witnessed many revolutionary disasters as well as the suppression of the 1905 Revolution, 'lost his head to the point where he was incapable of making any decision'. In those days of 'the explosion of fear', of 'the Bacchanalia of helplessness', of 'general chaos', he received a letter from his peer colleague, Egor Lazarev:

> Comrades, there are reprehensible times and there are reprehensible people. The former are depressing because of their unfathomable absence of personal involvement, while the latter wound human honour and the most intimate and sacred feelings; thus the injury they do to those who are close to them is far more painful, and they are capable of unhingeing even the most equanimous of people. In such sad circumstances, the good of the entire movement demands that in the midst of the depression and the chaos of the general bewilderment, that some remain who do not lose their heads and who recognize their awesome responsibility for the future.
>
> Personal pain, private feelings and the sense of insult must be overcome with all possible speed. Personal feelings must be subdued for the good of the whole. However great one's personal difficulties, they are nevertheless only one aspect of the overall course of events; they must be overcome and left behind, and we must march ahead . . . . The overall situation is even worse. But it must not be forgotten that the people has undergone its greatest experience, and in general we did prodigious work. There is no place for despair. Despite all the troubles and setbacks, victory is ours. Examine the chessboard coolly . . . . With a heavy heart and tear-filled eyes I send you my greetings, as a brother and a comrade, for the Russian New Year. [May you have] the courage and the tranquillity to bear this new blow of treachery and the strength to pave new paths, to erect new milestones. I can write no more . . . .[37]

The SR party had sustained serious losses in the suppression of the revolutionary wave of 1905–7; and it was not the Azef affair that led to the disintegration of most of its organizations in Russia and to the regrouping of most of its activists abroad. Of all its members and sympathizers in 15 regional organizations (*oblasty*) throughout Russia, the emissaries of the Central Committee who prepared the Council meeting in the wake of the Azef affair found substantive organizations only in the Urals, in a few places in Siberia and in Baku. Minuscule groups survived in Moscow, St Petersburg, Kharkov, Odessa and sourthern Russia. Yet it was not the organizational lassitude that most appalled them. During their years of activity the party leaders had grown inured to the relentless process of the liquidation and rebuilding of organizations. What marked the current crisis and set it apart was a nadir in morale unparalled in all the years of the party's existence. Besides withdrawal from party activity, the emissaries of the Central Committee also encountered emotional estrangement from the party. Seeking to reforge severed ties and to return dispersed activists to work, the mission members toured the length and breadth of Russia. But time and again they encountered refusals on the basis of family circumstances, examinations, ideological differences with the party, or other excuses. Alternatively, they were given a cool reception and treated with pronounced mistrust. Apartments for holding meetings, references (*iavki*), places to lodge and even addresses for simple correspondence easily obtained in the past, could now be had only with great difficulty. 'It is clearly the Azef treachery that has caused the deep crisis in the psychology of the party activities,' asserted Zenzinov, one of the mission members, adding that in all his years of public activity this had been his most trying experience.[38]

Indeed, while the personal blow suffered by Azef's close friends in the leadership and in the Battle Organization had been severe, the impact of his exposure among broader party circles was even deeper and more long-lasting, as Zenzinov's testimony indicates. Those on the periphery did not experience such an immediate emotional crisis; their coming to terms with the significance of the exposure was more gradual, but also more far reaching. For the veteran leadership the ramifications of the Azef affair were essentially on the organizational-personal plane. They believed that once the initial pain had passed and certain conclusions had been drawn, the party would recover and emerge pure and strengthened from the nightmare, without having to revise the principal tenets which had guided it since its foundation.[39] This was the line taken by Chernov when he spoke about the Azef affair to the Paris Group for the SR Party. Concluding with tears in his eyes, he called on all party members to cast away the evil that had sullied party life because of Azef, to unite and to turn over a new leaf. Many in the audience broke down in tears, including the chairman, Il'ia Fundaminskii. Others sat with bowed heads, not uttering a sound.

Yet their grief did not prevent them from asking Chernov some barbed questions. Was it true that the Central Committee had paid Azef 6000 roubles per year? Why was Azef not executed? Was there any truth in the rumour that the Central Committee had helped Azef to flee in an air balloon?[40] At another meeting Chernov was asked why one testimony had sufficed to kill the *provocateur* Tatarov, whereas all the proofs had been insufficient to have Azef done away with.[41] These questions are not only indicative of the rumours, which always flourish at a time of crisis, when the sources of information cannot keep up with demand; rather, they reflect the crisis of confidence that had begun to surface between the rank-and-file and the veteran leaders of the party.

Initially the reactions were not uniform. Certain groups, notably in Russia, forwarded the resolutions they had adopted in the wake of the exposure to the Central Committee and they were published in the party's organ. Together with an awareness of the gravity of the provocation – 'which is unexampled in the annals of the Russian revolutionary movement'[42] – all the resolutions express virtually unqualified support for the Central Committee and for its handling of the affair. Even when they demanded that the Committee should tender its resignation simply because the provocation had penetrated to its very heart and soul, the Central Committee itself was not held responsible for or considered guilty of 'the aberration, which was unusual not only because of its actual nature, but also in terms of its dimensions'. Provocation is an inherent element in every underground party, the bureau of the Northern District stated in its resolution, and as long as conditions in Russia did not permit a shift from an underground existence to open political activity, it would be impossible to put an end to the phenomenon.[43] In its communiqué, the committee of the Baku organization acknowledged that the Azef affair had caused the party incalculable harm. At the same time, the committee regarded the affair as an accidental phenomenon which could not diminish the party's moral vigour or sully its ideological purity. The committee therefore expressed its confidence in the party's ideological leaders in the Central Committee and a group of political exiles in Kholomgory did likewise.[44]

However beyond these expressions of identification members began to voice doubts and hesitations, particularly abroad, concerning the party's past and future course. Some regarded the Azef affair as an absolute moral and organizational crisis. In their view, Azef's provocation had rendered the party's continuation on the basis of its old principles impossible, since the affair had revealed serious flaws in the party's structural foundations. This being so, a fresh start had to be made. The entire party should be disbanded, if only because Azef's central position had exposed all to the police; politically, the entire party edifice was totally devastated.[45] In the Paris Group for the SR Party, for example, opinions were divided. One Section viewed the Azef affair as just a single factor in a chain of events that had driven the party to this state, as no more than an excuse for the final recognition of the party's organizational crisis and one which also involved other questions, namely activity among the peasants and the position of the Battle Organization. This approach, which was subsequently to become the majority stand, sought to defuse the Azef bombshell and to divert the organizational problems that arose in its wake to the level of a general discussion on the party's situation.

In contrast, a minority group of 14 members was formed whose resolution explicitly saw the origin of the crisis not only in the general political conditions in Russia but also in the party's organizational principles which, they claimed, had caused the *Azefshchina*. They believed that only by introducing substantive reform, to the point of reorganizing under new principles, could the party extricate itself from its present morass.[46] Although this was a minority viewpoint within the Paris Group for the SR Party, its perception of the provocation as rooted in structural problems, and its energetic demand for the party's reorganization, meant that it shared the stand of the Paris opposition group.[47] The latter would subsequently withdraw from the federation of SR groups against the background of disputes with the party leadership, *inter alia* over this very issue.

This opposition group, which was called 'The Paris Group of Socialist Revolutionaries', stressed that conclusions should be drawn from the devastating experience. They maintained that the attempt to forge a large centralized party had failed. Reality had shown that the party was led by a small group who had constituted the permanent leadership, all of whom were prey to the wiles of a police agent. The agent had bolstered up terrorism or toned it down at will, and when the blows became too harsh for the government he suspended terrorism completely. Yet it was demonstrable that even when the party, at the peak of the centralization, had been a plaything in the hands of the police, its activity had still benefited the revolution and harmed the régime, at a time when the SRs were active independently on the periphery. Only because of the centralist approach could the responsibility for terrorism fall on a police agent and thereby wreak so many disasters.[48] The lesson was a bitter one and must not be lost. What was required was reorganization, a total revamping of the party's procedures and institutions. An organisational plan had to be drawn up on a federative basis; acts of terrorism should be assigned to autonomous squads. The central functions should be divided among a large number of authorized institutions which would co-ordinate their activities and whose character and composition would ensure that no similar aberration could occur in the future.[49] If terrorist acts were perpetrated by separate autonomous squads, the group argued, and if each squad was made up of persons who knew each other well, the possibility of infiltration by a *provocateur* would be diminished; even if the police did manage to slip in a secret agent, the consequences of his treachery would be immeasurably less than if all terrorist activity was concentrated in the hands of one or several members of the Central Committee.[50]

Similar calls for the party's reorganization on the basis of democratic, federative principles were voiced by a group of SRs in St Petersburg which was founded in 1910. They urged a re-examination of all past methods of operation and a change in the nature of the ties between the periphery and the centre. While they made no explicit reference to the Azef affair or to the problem of the provocation in general, they were harshly critical of the part played by representatives of the Central Committee in the failure of party activity. The latter were primarily interested in imposing the authority of the centre, they charged, stressing that the reforms they called for were necessary in order to keep up with the times.[51] The undertones of their comments are reminiscent of criticism of the Paris opposition group and its organ, *Revoliutsionnaia Mysl'*.

Because of the bewilderment of the party leadership, apart from a brief communiqué declaring Azef an *agent provocateur*, considerable time elapsed before the Central Committee issued a formal, detailed account of the affair and its development.[52] The field was thus left open for the accusatory statements of the Paris opposition and of Burtsev, and for extensive commentaries in the Russian and foreign press, revolutionary and rightist alike. All of this could not but have a powerful impact on party members.

On 1 January the opposition Paris Group of Socialist Revolutionaries published its version of the affair. Entitled 'Concerning the Azef Provocation', this account emphasized that the consequences of the affair were extremely grave not only for the SR party but for the entire revolutionary movement. The document dwelt on the Central Committee's blind and unmitigated faith in Azef, despite all the proof that had accumulated against him since 1904. The statement went on to describe the group's actions, including the establishment of an independent commission of inquiry to clarify the source of the provocation, whose proximity to the party centre, the statement said, was manifest to all following the collapse of the Northern Organization's battle squad.[53]

> The presence of a *provocateur* in the party's central institutions for so many years, notwithstanding the most trenchant and insistent proof from diverse sources, cannot be an accidental phenomenon. The causes of this situation are deeply rooted in the entire structure of the party organization, in its procedures and in the frame of mind that prevailed from its first days – phenomena which our group never ceased to combat. The time has come when all of this must be exposed, not only to the party, but to world public opinion. A stringent investigation must be carried out, without mercy for anyone or anything.

The group claimed that it was the Central Committee which bore the greatest blame, for it had worked with Azef for so many years and had fallen under his hypnotic influence. Not only had it defended him stubbornly at all times, it had actually allowed him to escape – to Russia itself – where he could carry on with his provocationist activities. Such a committee could not and must not take part in the purging of the party. For that, a special commission was required. Finally, the statement called on all those who valued the party's continued existence to work for these ends together with the group.[54]

The Central Committee's silence seemed to confirm all the accusations and all the apprehensions, weakening the power of the SRs who were ready to launch a counter-campaign under the leadership of the party hierarchy. One such group of Socialist Revolutionary exiles in Italy fired off an angry protest to the Central Committee for its continued silence which was preventing party members from uniting to put an end to the affair.

> We have seen a detailed statement from the (opposition) Paris group concerning the Azef affair, but only a brief communiqué from the Central Committee. We believe the Central Committee has not acted properly. It should have been the first to issue a statement on the Azef affair, and should have taken public opinion into account and informed all party members about its steps at an early stage. Otherwise, the moral authority of the Central Committee will be completely undermined. The Azef affair is already undermining it.[55]

Other members also appealed to the Central Committee to seize the initiative. 'The party is silent. Until now the comrades in Paris have left us without any information. The entire Paris press is publishing reports – which may be false or tendentious – while we sit here like fools, unable to react.' The writer went on to complain that the fact that Burtsev and his accomplice, Bakai, were the source of all the information about the Azef affair, only reinforced the impression that the party was either on its last legs or desperate, an impression that was playing straight into the hands of the party's enemies.[56]

The Central Committee finally issued a statement about the affair and launched a powerful counter-offensive in its organ *Znamia Truda* ('The Labour Banner') in January. But it appears to have been too late. In its statement the Central Committee reviewed, one by one, all the reports that had reached it over the years concerning Azef's connections with the police, seeking to demonstrate that in each instance the suspicions had been rejected because of insufficient grounds, either because the facts were inaccurate or the police sources were unreliable. In conclusion, the Central Committee acknowledged the severe impact of Azef's provocation *vis-a-vis* the party and assumed responsibility for the situation that had emerged, while noting that all the previous Central Committees also shared in this responsibility. The upshot was that the Central Committee saw its duty as the presentation of a full and comprehensive report on its actions to an authorized party Congress and the convening of such a Congress at the earliest possible date.[57] In the meantime, however, this proved insufficient to stem the swelling tide of rumours. There was a need for visits and explanation to groups – such as Chernov's visit to the Paris group – as well as supplementary statements by the Central Committee. One such statement, issued in February, denied the rumours concerning the disbanding of the party and its local organizations. The statement explained that it had not proved possible for the party to bring Azef to trial formally because he had fled immediately after he was charged and interrogated for the first time. It also branded as a lie the rumour being disseminated in the press that another 'four participants in the trial – that is, leading members who defended Azef – had fled together with him'.[58]

It should appear, then, that the initial reaction of the SR remnants in Russia was to support the Central Committee and rally around the party. This trend was more marked in Russia than abroad. This may have been due to the fact that there was a large SR concentration abroad which had not lost its affinity for the party, even if it adopted a critical position. In Russia, however, the Azef crisis only emphasized the low ebb that characterized revolutionary activity as a whole. The expressions of support originated with a minority which remained loyal to the party. The majority, whose voice was not heard, left the party either because of arrests and suppression or in the wake of the Azef affair, giving expression to their negative stand by withdrawing from party activity, and even more so by their estrangement from the party and its emissaries.

Hardest of all for the party was the impact of Azef's exposure on the idea of terrorism, and in consequence on the entire appraisal of the party's past activity. The idea was so dominant and so entrenched a part of the SRs, that undermining it called into question the moral basis of all its operations. The exposure of the ties with the police of the Head of the party's Battle Organization naturally immediately provoked the question of how deeply the Okhrana was involved, and indeed who had been the beneficiary of this activity. Since terrorism was a controversial subject within the revolutionary camp, the SRs' political adversaries were quick to channel their criticism in that direction. Lopukhin was the first to reflect on the connection between police interests and revolutionary terrorism, when he heard the details about Azef's true role in the Battle Organization. The truth about Azef's revolutionary career led him to suspect that he was instrumental in curbing Lopukhin's promising career by collaborating with his rivals. This conclusion was apparently the main reason that led him to reveal the secret to the revolutionaries.

Since it was Plehve who had taken the young jurist out of the district attorney's office in Kharkov and placed him at the head of the Police Department in St Petersburg, through his assassination Lopukhin lost his political backing and along with it any prospects he had of a career. The assassinations of Plehve and of the Grand Duke Sergei undermined the standing of the Police Department and its director; concomitantly, the position of Lopukhin's adversaries was reinforced, chiefly that of Rachkovskii, who for years had headed the Okhrana abroad but had been removed from his highly influential posts about two years before the assassination. Although Rachkovskii had no influence at this time, he maintained friendly ties with powerful officers in the Police Department such as Trepov, Evstratii Mednikov and M.I. Gurevich, and it was thanks to their intervention that he was eventually restored to a respectable rank in the Okhrana. Following the assassination of the Grand Duke Sergei, Rachkovskii was appointed Okhrana Commander in St Petersburg; in parallel, the Tsar sharply expressed his dissatisfaction with the way the Police Department was functioning. Lopukhin was left with no alternative but to submit his resignation.

Theories similar to those of Lopukhin were also voiced by political groups like the Cadets and the Social Democrats. This view was a lethal blow to terrorism as a means of revolutionary struggle because it pictured the members of the Battle Organization as innocents who thought they were giving their lives for the good of the people, while in reality they were mere puppets whose strings were being pulled, through Azef, by rival factions in the Police Department.[59]

For many SRs the significance of this conclusion was that in practice terrorism was no more than an empty threat. It could only be perpetrated with the sanction of the authorities; it could only succeed with the concurrence of a *provocateur*. Plehve was murdered because that was what Rachkovskii wanted; and only due to Rachkovskii was Stolypin still alive. The police were too strong and the terrorists were incapable of standing up to them. Would it not be better to admit defeat and courageously face the hard truth? Would it not be preferable to be frankly weak rather than strong in words only? The upshot was that party circles began to raise doubts about whether terrorist activity should go on. Some demanded that terrorism be abandoned until the time it could be practised in a way that would restore its former lustre.[60]

These arguments too were fiercely resisted. An article entitled 'A Thousand and One Guesses' discusses the hypothesis in an attempt to refute it: assuming that Rachkovskii wanted to get rid of Plehve, how could this have been done, could he have told Azef? That was quite unnecessary. As at a major junction, all the paths of suppression and oppression converged on Plehve. All the suffering, all the oppression in the country cried out his name in unison. From this point of view, the Battle Organization heard only the voice of the party, while the party listened to the voice of the people. The Battle Organization executed the verdict passed by the collective conscience of the people. If so, the article asks, was it Rachkovskii who helped Azef carry out the deed? After all, he was far removed from the centre of activity. Yet even if we assume that he was able to do so, where do we see one element of the government engaged in an internal struggle with other elements cynically exploiting the Battle Organization? Where in the government was there a gang which was interested not only in Plehve's assassination but in a whole series of terrorist acts headed by Azef? What a bizarre gang this must be whose well-being coincides with that of the Russian working people. The author goes on to argue that the faction within the Police Department whose interests were allegedly furthered by Plehve's ouster in fact enjoyed the protection of the Grand Duke Sergei – who was also liquidated by the Battle Organization.[61] The article by Savinkov also seeks to puncture the theory. Reviewing the actions of the Battle Organization one by one, he finds no traces of collaboration of any kind between Azef and the Okhrana. Azef was a *provocateur* and the head of the Battle Organization, but Gapon was also a *provocateur*, and was the Russian revolution thereby sullied? Moreover, 2000 years ago Judas had turned Jesus over to the Romans, yet Christianity was still flourishing. Would anyone dare say that the sins of Judas had desecrated the doctrine of love? And was terrorism now dead? Was the revolution dead? Had Azef's sins desecrated the doctrine of socialism? Was the slogan 'By struggle shall you obtain your rights'[62] no longer valid, was Gershuni not alive, Sazonov not fighting, had Kaliaev not gone to the gallows?[63] It was not Azef who had created terrorism, nor was it he who had breathed life into it. Therefore he could not destroy the temple which his hands had not erected. Gapon had sold his soul to the devil, yet the revolution remained free of any suspicion. Azef, too, had sold his soul, yet terrorism remained as pure as it had always been.[64]

The storm that erupted following Azef's exposure, the Central Committee's announcement that it intended to tender its resignation, and the debates that broke out over questions of principle such as the form of the party's organization and the place of terrorism in its activity, all these necessitated the earliest possible convening of an authorized party forum. This body would have to deliberate these burning issues, or, as the party's official statements put it, 'eliminate the results of Azef's provocation'. Immediately after reaching its decision, the Central Committee dispatched a delegation to Russia to prepare the meeting. However, the organizational disintegration which the delegation found there made it perfectly clear to all concerned that a party Congress was out of the question. Of the 15 regional organizations which, under the party's constitution, were supposed to elect the Congress delegates, only six remained.[65] Clearly a narrower framework was required. In January 1909 the Central Committee declared that 'because of organizational considerations, and due to the lack of material resources', the idea of a special congress would have to be dropped in favour of a meeting of the party council. Given the importance of the questions to be discussed by the council, the Central Committee decided to enlarge the local representation from Russia by allowing representatives of prominent provinces to take part in the discussions – with the right to offer advisory opinion – in addition to the regional representatives. The

Central Committee would submit its resignation to the Council, and from that moment the Council would bear responsibility for choosing a new, provisional committee until such time as a permanent committee could be elected by a party Congress. In its announcement the Central Committee also proposed the establishment of a commission of inquiry, consisting of three to five Socialist Revolutionaries with impeccable credentials, to question party activities at an individual level in order to rid the party of possible vestiges of Azef's provocationist activity, and to determine which persons or institutions bore responsibility for the affair.[66] At once a debate broke out in the party concerning the planned Council's character and function, and the form of representation; and since only a few, weakened organizations remained in Russia, it was the foreign groups and notably the largest, the Paris Group for the SR Party, that took the leading role in the debate.

Opinion in the Paris group was divided between supporters and critics of the Central Committee. The former, who tended not to view the Azef affair as a reflection of deep flaws inherent in the character of the party, advocated a highly generalized formulation concerning the need 'to clarify the causes that allowed its existence for so many years', along with the need to discuss questions relating to the form of organization. They also favoured expanding the local representation, including that of the foreign groups. Further, they called for the establishment of a commission of inquiry to be composed exclusively of veteran party members. In contrast, the minority's resolution linked its demand for the convening of the Council to its perception that the origins of the current crisis afflicting the party lay in organizational defects that required fundamental reform. The minority demanded that the representation of the foreign groups should be at least equal to that of the Russian groups, and that a commission of inquiry should be formed to include non-party persons who enjoyed widespread trust. Their resolution also called for the establishment of an organizational committee, composed of the most accepted and experienced party members, to administer the party until an all-party Congress could be convened. A still more extreme stand was taken by a group of 14 that regarded Azef's provocation as stemming from the all-party centralist organization. This group also urged greater representation for the foreign groups, as well as the creation of a commission of inquiry composed of non-party participants.[67]

The dispute between the two groups, known as the 'Group of Thirty' and the 'Group of Fourteen', actually focused on the composition of and control over the proposed Council. This was against the backdrop of the Central Committee's decision to augment the representation of the Russian groups which, as we have seen, tended to support the Committee's traditionalist approach. Similarly, underlying the debate over the composition of the proposed commission of inquiry was the question of how much latitude the commission would have to determine its areas of investigation and its conclusions, independently of those who had possessed supreme authority in the party since its inception. In other words, the gist of the argument was linked to the issue of the Central Committee's continuous monopoly on party life, as a member of the Group of Fourteen explained in an attempt to account for the party's crisis by pointing to the suppression of party members by the Central Committee. For its part, the Committee tried to divert the debate to objective factors relating to the general political situation, and insisted on giving priority to the representation of Russian members.[68]

Among the Group of Thirty was George Patrik, a key figure in the Paris Group for the SR Party, who had often served as a member of its committee. He was also one of the most highly paid secret agents of the Okhrana's Foreign Agency. His police code-names were 'Never' or 'Lucy' – names which, in conformity with Police Department reporting procedures, appear on many reports concerning developments among the SRs in Paris in general, and among the Paris Group in particular. Appended to Patrik's report on the majority and minority resolutions are the texts of the two resolutions, which are identical to the wording in the party archives. Patrik's report also names the members of the two groups. For the Group of Thirty he cites 28 real names along with their revolutionary code-names – including veteran members who were close to the leadership such as Sletov, his wife Maria Seliuk, the sister of Fundaminskii, Vul'f Fabrikant, Bilit, the wife of Osip Minor and others. However, a mere six members of the Group of Fourteen are listed, and by their code-names only: 'Sergei the Worker', 'Popov the Bulgarian', 'Oskar the Worker', 'Izak the Worker', 'Count Kuzmin', and 'Ronin'. We may infer that these were two separate and contrasting groups: one was comprised of the veteran revolutionaries, the traditional leadership and their *confidants*, and the other of persons some of whom defined themselves, perhaps demonstratively, as workers, but whose identity was unknown to as prominent a member of the group as Patrik. Evidently, they had only recently joined the party and were never part of the established well-known Group of Thirty. This division of opinion may well foreshadow the dispute that was later to split the group and the party over questions relating, in one form or another, to issues of provocation; when despite this issue, the split was to be between circles of the traditional leadership and their opponents from the younger generation of activists.

Following considerable efforts the emissaries of the Central Committee were able to make contact with several local organizations in Russia to prepare the Council meeting. Subsequently, elections were held in the Northern District, the Urals region, the Ukraine, the Southern District, the Trans-Caucasus and St Petersburg. However of the delegates chosen, only six managed to go abroad;[69] two were arrested as they crossed the border,[70] and two others were known to have left their places of residence but never reached the Council session. Even in comparison with the party's Fourth Council, held in London at the end of July 1908 when party activity was at a low ebb, the current Council meeting was a particularly shabby affair. In 1908, in addition to members of the Central Committee and foreign representatives of the organization, 13 delegates from Russia participated: eight representatives of regional organizations and five attachés to those organizations on behalf of the Central Committee.[71] Under the party's constitution, delegates from the 15 regional organizations had to be represented on the Council, while a lawful quorum required the presence of half of them, namely eight. This was especially vital at the current Council which, in view of the grave problems on the agenda, was to have convened in an expanded forum. For two weeks the Council participants waited in vain for the elected delegates to turn up. After some anguished soul-searching it was decided to hold the discussions and to regard the meeting as an authorized Council session, on the assumption that its postponement by a few months was liable to spell the end of the little that still remained in Russia. Moreover, given the party's organizational straits, there was no good reason to believe that a later meeting would be attended by a larger number of delegates than were already present. A further consideration was the feeling of the Central Committee – whose authority had already been undercut by the Azef affair – that a deferral of the Council session might lead to backbiting. Reinforcing the decision to go ahead with the meeting was the opinion that there was no basis for any argument to the effect that a narrow Council lacked authority and that its resolutions were not binding. The Council meeting could be regarded as legal as over half the regions where party organizations were still active were represented. Thus the Council meeting was formally opened, and following a discussion and the transfer of mandates from absent representatives to others in their stead, the breakdown was as follows: one mandate each to the Northern District, the St Petersburg representative, the Ukraine, the Baku District, the Southern District, the Volga District, and the representative of the Kharkov committee; two mandates to the Central Committee, one to the party's representative on the Bureau of the Socialist International, and one to the organization of foreign groups. Everyone else who was present was granted the right to offer advisory opinions only. Thus all that remained of the idea of convening a special expanded Congress in order to deliberate the most severe crisis the party had ever undergone was a narrow Council that finally opened in May 1909 with merely ten official delegates.

The representative of the Central Committee submitted a report on all the Committee's activities regarding the Azef affair. Of particular interest was the manner of Azef's escape. The local reports showed that it was this issue that evoked the most intense anger, generating criticism of the Central Committee for having failed, at the critical moment, to demonstrate the necessary determination and internal consensus. At the same time, no one questioned the motives of the Central Committee's members, with the result that the Council expressed its full confidence in the Committee, although criticism was expressed about other aspects of its activity relating to the Azef affair.

As the Central Committee was about to tender its resignation, in accordance with its prior resolution, one of the representatives spoke out sharply against this step and against the election of a new committee. If the resignation were accepted, he said, it would conflict with the expression of confidence the Committee had just received from the Council. He also expressed doubts concerning the authority of this narrow Council to accept the resignation of the Central Committee and to elect a new Committee in its place. His main point, however, was that there was no other group in the party who enjoyed such broad authority as the members of the current Committee; hence those who would be chosen to replace them would come from the rank-and-file and would be incapable of providing ideological leadership. If the Council were to remove the party's best forces from the Central Committee, it would be impossible to replace them. These arguments were rejected by all the other delegates. They did not consider their acceptance of the Central Committee's resignation as tantamount to its condemnation or as an expression of non-confidence, but viewed it as a resignation for purely formal and tactical reasons, taking into consideration the Central Committee's admission that it has erred in its handling of the Azef affair and its acknowledgement that its continued service would harm the party. Failure to accept the Committee's resignation would be detrimental to both the Council and the Committee, and would inevitably lead to complaints about deception. The Central Committee's authority had been undermined by the Azef affair, so it was pointless to talk about authority for which there was no substitute. Moreover, the party was not so weak that it was impossible to elect a new Central Committee with the requisite authority. Finally, the committee's resignation would not signal the end of its members' service to the party; the party would continue to benefit from their influence, experience and authority in various spheres.[72] Thus the Central Committee tendered its resignation. Its five veteran members – Natanson, Chernov, Argunov, Nikolai Avksentiev and Nikolai Rakitnikov – were replaced by Vladimir Zenzinov, I. Kovarskii, Vasilii Pankratov, Lev Freifeld and A. Shimanovskii, none of whom was in the forefront of the party leadership. With the exception of Zenzinov, who had been a member of the Battle Organization since 1906 and had known Azef well personally, not one of the new Committee members was directly connected with Azef's activity, nor had any of them been stigmatized by stubbornly defending him. Aside from Zenzinov, not a single one of the new members was destined to play a major leadership role in the years to come. Boris Voronov – 'Lebedev' – Boris Nestrovskii and A. Khovrin were co-opted to the new Central Committee.[73]

A resolution was passed requiring all the Central Committee members to reside in Russia, while party affairs abroad were placed in the hands of a Central Committee representation known as the 'Foreign Delegation' and comprised of Natanson, Chernov, Nikolai Sletov, Argunov and Fundaminskii.[74]

Of the eight Committee members who were to reside in Russia, only five – Voronov-Lebedev, Zenzinov, Kovarskii, Khovrin and Freifeld – actually arrived at their place of operation. Nestrovskii was arrested as he crossed the border, Pankratov remained in exile, while Shimanovskii simply refused to go to Russia. The Committee members chose Kiev as their centre of activity, but shortly after their arrival the police discovered their whereabouts. Khovrin and other activists were arrested at once, and soon afterwards Zenzinov was also picked up. Once again activity ground to a halt. The Central Committee members dispersed, leaving the administration of party affairs in the hands of the Foreign Delegation, in which the elderly Mark Natanson played a key role. Thus, despite the replacement of the Central Committee, the old party leadership remained intact. Although the new Central Committee still existed, the constant fluctuations in its membership and the relatively low intra-party standing of its members meant that its existence was no more than nominal.[75]

Besides electing a new Central Committee, the Fifth Council also decided to establish a judicial commission of inquiry 'for the absolute elimination of all manifestations of Azef's provocation'; the commission members would be exclusively party members. The resolution gave the commission the right to question any party member whatsoever, whether as defendant or as witness. Its judgment would be final and could be appealed only to the Congress or the Council. Formally established on 8 September 1909, the commission members were Alexei Bakh, who had been a member of the commission of inquiry that examined the Tatarov issue, Sergei Ivanov – 'Berg', S. M. Bleklov – 'Senzharskii', and Valerian Lunkevich – 'Araratskii'. As veterans of the *Narodnaia Volia*, Bakh and Ivanov-Berg were considered to be of the same moral stature as Vera Figner and German Lopatin, who had served as judges in the Burtsev trial. Ivanov, moreover, was also a *Shlissel'burzhets* – a graduate of the Shlissel'burg prison, a mark of prestige for revolutionaries. Lunkevich was a veteran party member, whereas Bleklov had only joined officially on his appointment as a commission member.[76] Having chosen Bakh as its chairman, the commission began its work at the beginning of November; it was to take a year and a half to complete its mission.

As in the case of the composition of the Council and of the commission of inquiry, the stand on terrorism of the outgoing Central Committee was also accepted. The Council chose four discussants to take part in the deliberations on this issue: two representing the minority position advocating the suspension or total cessation of terrorist acts, and two representing the opposing majority stand. Prominent in the debate were Chernov in favour of terrorism and, on the other side, Il'ia Rubanovich, the SR party's representative to the Bureau of the Socialist International.

The most striking element in the arguments advanced by both sides was the almost total absence of any connection between the positions taken and the Azef affair – which, after all, was the reason for re-opening the debate in the first place. Indeed the opening speaker against terrorism prefaced his remarks by stressing this very point, noting that he had long since determined his stand, and had done so without any connection to the affair. He claimed that long before the exposure, he had voiced his convictions to the members of a committee in the Northern District who were about to perpetrate a major terrorist act. Influenced by his arguments, they had decided to drop their plan. He added that his co-speaker in the debate had also formed his negative opinion of terrorism well before the affair was known and irrespective of it. It did indeed seem to be the case that the six chief arguments advanced by the opponents of terrorism stemmed from an appraisal of the general political situation that had prevailed prior to the affair and were anchored in *a priori* positions; the same held true for the other side.

The harsh impact of the political situation on the party, police suppression and the party's organizational deterioration formed the background to the first argument against the employment of the SRs' terrorist tactics. According to the speaker, its aim had been to sow confusion and disorganization within the government and to generate unrest and enthusiasm among the masses. However, the question had to be asked: was it still possible to cause confusion among the targets of terrorism and could the resulting disorder be exploited by a mass movement? If so, did the party have the necessary reserve strength to launch an offensive against the régime? To both questions the speaker replied in the negative, explaining that the government had learned to react so quickly to terrorist operations that it was impossible to cause even temporary chaos. The government was well acquainted with the party's true situation, and the Azef affair had demonstrated the party's weakness to the people. Yet it was not only the SRs who were characterized by impotence. The government was well aware that in all of Russia no revolutionary organizations existed that were capable of assuming the leadership of a mass movement. In the current state of affairs, terrorist operations would have no impact, no mass movement would follow in their wake, and the government would quickly reorganise. Hence the essential basis for terrorist activity – the link with a mass movement – had been undercut, rendering a terrorist struggle impossible. Nor should any hopes be pinned on the notion that terrorism would help create an atmosphere of revival which would allow new cells to be organized. The Russian public was weary, depressed and indifferent. The speaker asked that his remarks be considered without any connection to the Azef affair – as though it had never happened. But if his audience would nevertheless bear in mind that the affair had occurred, this would only reinforce his analysis. Following the affair the party was in total chaos. It was incapable at this time of leading a mass movement, and in the near future could not even hope to establish party organizations with uniform views. In the absence of agreement, a united operation was also out of the question. However, if terrorist acts – the subject of grave doubts after the Azef affair – were to be suspended, the party would once more succeed in achieving general agreement among its members. Terrorism's good name would not be restored by means of bad terrorism which could only harm it irremediably.[77]

The second speaker also acknowledged that the prestige of terrorism had suffered but not because of the Azef affair. It had been stained even prior to that. It was 'revolutionary romanticism' that had put an end to its psychological influence, and which had also brought the 'anarchistic licentiousness' (*anarkhicheskii razgul*) of recent years. This romantic phase was now behind the party, the speaker averred, and had given way to a period of coldly objective calculations. These calculations showed that the government was now stronger than it had ever been and that it could not be intimidated by two or three acts of terrorism.[78]

A far more principled position against the terrorist tactics is implied in the remarks of the third speaker. Terrorism, he said, was a complex problem, involving political considerations. Elaborating on the political, judicial and moral considerations, the speaker pointed to the fact that the régime in Russia was currently supported by the propertied class and the industrialists, as well as by the international bourgeoisie which feared the class-ridden character of the Russian revolution. No longer was the terrorist struggle one between groups, but between classes, which was why it must be a mass and not an individual struggle. The speaker also referred to the immoral aspect of the terrorist tactics. The division of labour whereby some conceived the terrorist idea, others planned and prepared the operation, while a third group perpetrated it and were also killed in the process seemed to him immoral. This division of functions, he stated, had transformed the party's entire operational activity into a kind of business. The role of the Central Committee was negligible, while Azef's terrorist expertise and the general admiration for terrorism had made it 'contractual'. Did this not undermine the sense of morality, did this 'contractuality' not create 'military professionalism' in the revolutionary camp, and did these professionals not develop a psychology that led to a supercilious and negative view of 'civilian' spheres of activity?[79]

Chernov, the principal speaker on behalf of terrorism, represented the stand of the old Central Committee. One by one he replied to the arguments advanced by the minority position representatives and called for their rejection. He admitted that the SR terrorism was organically linked with a mass movement. But this did not mean it was necessary to follow every step of this movement. When it was powerful, there were also many acts of terrorism; when it ceased to exist, so did terrorism. In the period of Sipiagin no mass movement existed and the party believed that propaganda was insufficient in order to actualize the people's bitterness. Imbued with this belief, the party had launched terrorist activity and reality had justified its decision.

Terrorism had fulfilled expectations, and even though the party had been beset by treachery from the outset, the government had nevertheless dubbed it 'that terrible party'. The Azef affair had not adversely affected terrorism. If despite the presence of a *provocateur* at the heart of the party it was capable of dealing such harsh blows to the government, obviously under better conditions far better results could be expected. Chernov too was ready to acknowledge that the people were weary. But that one-sided weariness had been caused by the government's unilateral terrorism, which had a hypnotic effect on the people. Only counter-measures would put an end to the phenomenon. To those who feared that the party lacked the strength to follow up its successes, Chernov replied that it took a long time to reap the fruit of this labour and, secondly, if the party were to follow the rule of not launching terrorism before it possessed sufficient forces, it would never actually perpetrate any terrorist acts at all. When we began, Chernov continued, we were few and we were very weak. Were we wrong, he asked, to launch the struggle then? It was precisely activity that generated a quick growth.

Chernov admitted to the moral problems terrorism entailed. The party's terrorist activity confronted each and every member with the question of whether he was truly ready to lay down his life at any moment. However that problem was not limited to terrorist parties alone. Even in non-terrorist parties that aspired to bring about an armed uprising, every written word that advocated such an uprising was liable to cost human life – perhaps thousands of lives. Yet it was true that the dilemma was particularly acute for members of a party in which terrorism provided the tactics of the struggle. Thus every person joining such a party must clarify for himself whether he was ready to lay down his life at any moment that he might be required to do so; anyone who had not resolved that question had not solved his moral dilemma and therefore had no right to be a party member.[80]

The arguments against terrorism were actually of two kinds: the first related to a temporary situation requiring the suspension of SR terrorism for a while. In contrast, the second type of argument was marked by opposition in principle to this party method, and implied its total cessation. It was to this that Chernov referred when he remarked that these were arguments that the opponents of terrorism had always raised againts the party.

> The debate currently raging among us is of a different order. It is not a debate about whether to halt terrorism, but a debate on whether to reject it. It is the debate which we should have held when we launched our operational activity.[81]

It is clear, then, that like the debates in the Paris Group for the SR Party, the Azef affair also served the Fifth Council as the grounds for an internal debate on principles, whose connection to the affair itself was extremely loose. True, discussions of tactical issues and of ongoing questions occupied every party gathering, but this was a special Council session, held in an unusual setting. The problem of terrorism was raised following the severe allegations that were voiced by the party's membership in connection with the affair. However, the opponents of terrorism at the Council session did not reiterate even a single one of these allegations. But for the first time in an all-party meeting, an attack was launched against terrorism as a method, evidently made possible by the intensity of the crisis and the party's sensitivity in its wake. Rubanovitch's Marxist leanings were known, and had already in the past led to differences regarding activity among the peasants.[82] According to a report of the Okhrana's Foreign Agency, the position he took at the Council was influenced by the stand of the Bureau of the Socialist International, which opposed terrorism in principle.[83] The positions were greatly reinforced by being linked to an affair which had rocked the party to its very foundations.

The motion was rejected by a vote of six to one with three abstentions. The abstentions were formalistic in nature, and of the three abstainers only the representative of the Socialist International actually supported the motion. The two others, the representatives of the Central Committee and of the foreign groups, voiced their opposition. The members resolved to lift the restrictions which the party's Second Congress had imposed on the operational activity of the regional organizations, so that terrorist acts performed by battle squads attached to these organizations no longer required the approval of the Central Committee. Thus the minority motion was defeated. However, this did not put an end to the spectacle in which ideological or other questions related to the provocation issue were raised in order to obtain greater support for them, nor did it end the question of terrorism. That problem was soon to assume a new form.

The import of the resolution on terrorism was no more than the rejection of the proposal to suspend it; indeed, in another resolution, wholly unrelated to the debate, the Council asserted that the re-establishment and reinforcement of the local organizations was the cardinal task facing the party and that, given the need to conserve the party's forces, must be given supreme priority.[84] However, for some veterans of the Battle Organization, notably Savinkov, the resolution meant a green light for the establishment of a new terrorist group whose activity would purify 'the honour of the Battle Organization and the honour of its living and its dead members.[85] He submitted his proposal to the Conspiracy Committee formed by the council. Immediately upon receipt of the Committee's approval, he began to implement his plan. But for all his lengthy preparations, lasting over a year, his project never got off the ground.

The Council also affirmed the stands of the veteran leadership with regard to questions of organization. The resolution adopted stated that there was no room for changes of any kind in the party's organizational constitution as approved by the First Congress. It also asserted that the centre's ties with the periphery must be strengthened *inter alia* by means of maintaining a Central Committee representation in all the regional organizations. Furthermore, the resolution mentioned that special groups of activists, such as peasants, labourers and army personnel, could enjoy a modicum of internal autonomy, but only with the approval of the local organizations and in accordance with the party's constitution.[86]

The importance of the Fifth Council does not lie in the resolutions it adopted. With the exception of the judicial commission of inquiry it established, none of those resolutions was destined to leave a positive imprint on the party's life.[87] In no way did its resolutions deviate from the party's old, conventional principles; the arguments that sought to link these principles to the Azef affair were rejected. Nor was any significance attached to the replacement of the membership of the executive institution that headed the party. Yet the description of the events of the Council sessions does demonstrate the force of the Azef affair and indicates the first rumblings of the part that the phenomenon of provocation was to assume in the party because of that bombshell.

Even though the party rejected attempts to view its basic principles as the underlying cause of the Azef case, the dimensions of the affair and its powerful impact meant that it could not be written off as just one more provocation that the party, like other revolutionary movements, had experienced. The fact that it was termed *Azefshchina* – on the model of the *Degaevshchina* which preceded it – shows that it was also perceived as a phenomenon rather than as an isolated case. It was in that spirit that the judicial commission of inquiry appointed by the Fifth Council set about its investigation of the affair. Its point of departure was that Azef's provocationist activity was no accident. It was as a *provocateur* that Azef had joined the party. Developing and growing together with the party, his activity had reached dimensions that were unrivalled in the annals of the entire revolutionary movement. 'It is clear that conditions existed in the very way of life of the party that allowed the development of the *Azefshchina*.' This being so, the commission aimed at the most detailed clarification of these conditions that was possible both from the point of the party's principles of organization, and the activity of the responsible party institutions.[88] To that end the commission divided its investigation into three spheres: the circumstances of the founding of the party and of the Battle Organization, and the nature of the latter's connections with the Central Committee; Azef's role in the leadership; and the suspicions raised against him and the reactions they drew.[89]

The commission sat for a year and a half, holding 73 sessions and interviewing 31 persons. It also examined documents from the party's archives. In 1911 it published its findings in a pamphlet entitled 'The Conclusions of the Judicial Commission of Inquiry into the Azef Affair', which at once evoked dissatisfaction and criticism from various quarters. The commission found that the chief cause of the development of the years-long provocation by the Head of the Battle Organization lay in the inordinate importance the party's leaders attached to terrorism. This terrorist frame of mind ran like a thread through the entire history of the SR party, and had enabled Azef to advance in the leading ranks rendering him immune to all suspicion. In its conclusions the commission quotes one of the witnesses who appeared before it: 'Terrorism was sacred to us, and it was inconceivable that the Central Committee should conduct it other than through a battle comrade from its midst. If such a person existed, he had to be voted for. In the light of this, the commission chose Azef as a member of the Central Committee, thus bolstering his position even more.'[90]

The report goes on to quote the party's treasurer who told of a law that the Battle Organization was to be refused nothing. Money or no money, the means had to be procured and made available. The Battle Organization must never suffer from a lack of resources and when these were insufficient, allocations for literature and for other matters were cut down. Never were there any cutbacks in operational matters.[91] From these testimonies the commission inferred that although the party's leading circles had seen to general party activity to the best of their ability, they had regarded terrorism as the cardinal issue and had therefore skimped on other activities to ensure that terrorism did not suffer. In the commission's view, this attitude toward terrorism had caused the total isolation of the Battle Organization, which had become an obedient tool in Azef's hands. On the other hand, all this had helped create a cult of terrorism and unlimited confidence in those who perpetrated it successfully. Given this state of affairs, 'the traitor who was unexampled in the history of the revolutionary movement' could exist for years on end without anyone being the wiser.[92] The worship of terrorism and the Battle Organization's isolation also led to the emergence of a unique fighters' psychology: concentration on operational matters, contempt for ideological deliberations, and a supercilious attitude toward party activists in other spheres.[93]

The commission found that the source of the immense esteem for Azef's personality lay with two activists who played instrumental roles in the history of the SR party: Grigorii Gershuni and Mikhail Gots. It was their attitude, the commission stated, that determined Azef's standing in the party for a long time. Yet, the commission insisted on asking, how could it happen that a veteran and highly experienced revolutionary like Gots, who was knowledgeable and so clever, not only evinced unqualified esteem and trust for a reprehensible traitor, but actually showed 'unbounded love'? Gots, according to the commission, attributed vast importance to terrorism within the framework of party activity. He considered Azef a brilliant executor of the idea he held so dear, and this led him to disregard the character traits in Azef which under different circumstances would have caught his attention. Gots's attitude toward the Battle Organization and toward Azef gradually became that of the party's leading circles, and hence the isolated position of the Battle Organization failed, with only a few exceptions, to arouse any protests within the Central Committee. The exaggerated importance attached to terrorism ensured practitioners – and particularly its leading exponent, Azef – preferential treatment. In the eyes of the party leadership, Azef appeared in an aura of heroism, whose details were known to only a few who spread his reputation throughout the entire party. A further factor which greatly enhanced Azef's prestige and strengthened his position, the commission found, was the fact that the Russian intelligentsia in general, and the Russian revolutionaries in particular, were people of ideas rather than people of action. Because they held the operational aspect of the party in such high regard, they considered the people of action within the ranks of the revolutionaries to be of inestimable value. Azef was known as a man of action, possessing rare technical skills.[94]

The preferential treatment and admiration for Azef were apparent when the letter arrived from St Petersburg accusing him and Tatarov of being *provocateurs*. The Central Committee immediately launched an investigation of Tatarov, but angrily rejected the accusations against Azef. In order to resolve the contradiction implied in acceptance of the information for the one but its denial in the case of the other, the investigation committee concluded that a theory of police intrigue was conceived: the police were ready to sacrifice one agent in order to liquidate the dangerous revolutionary Azef, whom they had been unable to apprehend. Henceforth this theory was advanced time and again as rejection of all accusations against Azef.[95]

Although the commission's report implied serious charges in a definite direction, the accusing finger was pointed at an abstract term – 'frame of mind' – and not at specific persons. This was underscored when the commission stated in its concluding remarks that no blame could be imputed to any one individual, but only to the conditions and the criteria according to which the party functioned operationally. The party leaders with whom the commission met in the course of its investigation were found to be unreservedly dedicated to the cause of the party, and their mistake with respect to Azef had been made in good faith. Noting the immense service they had rendered the party, the commission asserted that their continued service was not only desirable but essential.[96] At the same time, besides laying down guiding principles for the party's terrorist activity, the commission recommended the reinforcement of collegial principles in party institutions in general and in the Central Committee in particular. It also advocated a greater emphasis on the moral demands of party members which, the commission felt, were a vital need and a *sine qua non* for the establishment of mutual trust and esteem among the comrades.[97]

Despite the cautious wording, the commission's conclusions evoked the wrath of some leaders and of certain members of the Battle Organization. The former members of the Central Committee asked to appear before the commission in order to present additional clarifications and explanations. However, the commission turned them down on several grounds: it had dealt exclusively with the objective conditions that had enabled the development of *Azefshchina* and not with personal charges or the responsibility of any specific party institution; and those who so desired had been given the opportunity to present their objections following their testimony. In addition in two joint sessions of the commission and the outgoing Central Committee the latter's members had had ample opportunity to clarify all questions that had arisen from the investigative material, and those clarifications had been taken into account when the conclusions were being drafted.[98]

Former Central Committee member Chernov angrily broke off all party activity and left for Italy.[99] His resignation generated considerable depression in party circles.[100] In an open letter to *Znamia Truda*, Peter Karpovich, a leading member of the Battle Organization, declared that even though some of the commission's harshest conclusions referred to his activity in the Battle Organization and his attitude toward the Central Committee, the commission had nevertheless not found fit to question him even once, thereby depriving him of his right to defend his revolutionary past.[101] In protest he withdrew from the staff who were preparing a pamphlet in memory of Egor Sazonov, who had taken part in the assassination of Plehve and in 1910 had committed suicide in his prison cell. Other former members of the Battle Organization – Savinkov and Maria Prokofieva – followed in Karpovich's footsteps.

> Is it possible to punish the entire party for the actions of one institution? Is it possible to boycott it because of one action carried out by a certain institution? If you think specific operations are wrong, then protest, write, shout out, demand a clarification, approach the Congress, react however you like – but don't boycott the party if you too are counted within its ranks.[102]

Thus Rakitnikova – 'Ritina' – one of the most longstanding party members, described the atmosphere of mistrust and unwillingness to act that followed the commission's judgment. 'The entire matter must not be allowed to fall apart because of this,' she warned.[103]

However not only circles connected to the leadership and the Battle Organization were infuriated by the commission's conclusions. Harsh criticism was also levelled by the independent Paris group of Socialist Revolutionaries, which for a long time had stood in opposition to the Central Committee against the backdrop of the Azef affair. Meeting on 28 April 1911, following publication of the conclusions, the group passed a resolution fiercely condemning them, and asserting that the conditions under which the commission of inquiry had been formed had preordained a tendentious and barren discussion. The commission's conclusions, the resolution continued, showed a total misunderstanding of the true factors that had brought about the development of *Azefshchina*, and its explanations were either incomplete or clearly at variance with the truth. The resolution charged that the commission, seeking to clear the party hierarchy which had accorded Azef such an important standing, had tried to attribute responsibility for the *Azefshchina* to the psychology of the fighters. The latter were actually the victims of the party leadership's severe blunders with respect to Azef. Rejecting the conclusion that an exaggerated perception of the role of terrorism within the framework of general activity had caused the *Azefshchina*, the group's resolution stated that such a conclusion could only mislead public opinion as to the true origins of the phenomenon, and constitute an obstacle to healing the party. Finally, the group charged its conspiracy committee with the task of preparing and issuing a separate report, to contain its own conclusions about the causes and consequences of the Azef affair.[104]

That same year, Iankel' Iudelevskii, one of the opposition leaders, published his conclusions in a pamphlet bearing the accusatory title 'The *Azefshchina* on Trial'.[105] Most of the pamphlet is devoted to an attack on the working methods of the commission of inquiry and an effort to demonstrate the deliberate distortion of its conclusions. Only the seventh and final chapter deals with the perpetrations of the *Azefshchina*, as Iudeleveskii sees them.

The author sees the organizational procedures that took root in the party from the very outset as the background to the phenomenon. Formed and organized from the top down, the party had assumed a saliently centralist character. From its very inception it had been built and educated in the spirit of the ideas and the philosophy of a small founding group. That in itself was natural, Iudelevskii wrote, and quite acceptable. The problem was that this founding group had come to regard the party as its own private business, a perception which had been reflected primarily in the ideological sphere. The members of the group had a monopoly on ideology, systematically stifling any criticism or independent thought that conflicted with the party's official outlook. However, the author contended, their monopoly was also organizational. The running of the party was concentrated in the hands of a clique imbued with a bureaucratic spirit and system, which it had then passed on to the committees and other official party forums. The members of this clique, who were responsible for the supreme administration of all party affairs, were bound to one another by years of joint activity, and even more by a deep recognition that they were fulfilling a unique mission within the party. The source of their prestige lay in this vital nature of their role. In their own eyes, Iudelevskii states, they were leaders by divine grace, and from this point of view Azef was not an unusual phenomenon. The party's centre saw itself as the divine embodiment of its wisdom and the seat of its reason. So great was the sense of identification among the leading members that an attack on the prestige of any one of them was perceived as a blow to the entire centre, with the result that the members zealously refrained from besmirching anyone in the group.

Like the Roman emperors, Iudelevskii writes, the members of the centre grew accustomed to regarding the party as their own private preserve, and in emulation of the emperors they doled out posts to their wives, family members and close friends. Thus a revolutionary dynasty began to develop, a 'ruling officer clique', engendering in turn sycophants and revolutionary careerism. All of this, the author averred, was what actually accounted for the *Azefshchina*: provocation was able to penetrate to the centre of the party because in the assessment of a person's character, his moral traits were not taken into account but only his potential usefulness to the party. According to Iudelevskii Azef's coarse and repulsive personality was known to many, but nevertheless he was accepted into the party and became a hero. Iudelevskii explained the different treatment of Tatarov and Azef in the wake of the anonymous letter from St Petersburg by pointing out that Tatarov had not yet been accepted in the 'holy of holies' (he was only a candidate for co-option to the Central Committee), whereas Azef had reached 'Olympus' speedily and was firmly ensconced there. The party leadership could not even imagine that provocation was taking shape within it. This would have conflicted with its entire philosophy and its self-image. The upshot was that for every suspicious manifestation in the Azef affair 'the different explanation (police intrigue) was found.[106]

Neither the conclusions of the party's judicial commission of inquiry nor those of Iudelevskii dealt with the problem of provocation in its entirety, but covered only one aspect of it: the Azef affair. Both committees concluded that provocation was an outgrowth of the struggle against the régime. At the same time, in both instances an effort was made for the first time to examine at least this one limited phenomenon within its own framework, and to seek an explanation that went beyond its own parameters. In other words, unlike the approach in the past, when provocation was perceived exclusively as the expression of the corrupt nature of the Tsarist régime and its methods, people sought explanations that were anchored in the background from which provocation had developed. For the commission of inquiry the explanation lay in a certain party frame of mind which was like a hothouse for the growth of provocations while in the view of the opposition, it was the traits of the party leadership that had allowed provocation to flourish. If hitherto the entire matter could be written off as harmful but inherent in the revolutionary struggle – as an evil that had to be lived with, like the danger of arrest, hard labour and the gallows – the deeper import of the Azef affair would no longer permit such evasion or denial. Although the new mode of perception did not necessarily entail an objective and unbiased approach, it did necessitate a clear and unequivocal attitude. And this shift of attitude in itself constituted a turning point which, as we shall see below, was to have considerable impact on the party's development.

From this point of view the SR party was in the most difficult straits: it had to seek the explanation in its own house. The party opposition had the advantage of being able to pin the blame on its rivals, while the other revolutionary parties could view the Azef affair – despite its unusual dimensions – as part of a broader phenomenon resulting from certain characteristics that were peculiar to the SR party.

For the Social Democrats, the unique characteristic that fully accounted for the provocation affair was also the focal point of one of its sharpest disputes with the SRs. This was the question of terrorist combat. In the debate over the Azef affair they pitted the SR concept of the 'initiative of the minority' and terrorism as its means of struggle, against their own approach which centred on a mass class struggle. Since they too viewed provocation as an inevitable by product of the revolution, they presented the Azef affair as the lethal result of that provocation *vis-à-vis* the SRs, while at the same time they perceived the activity of Zubatov and Gapon in the labour movement as the lethal result of provocation *vis-à-vis* the government since ultimately it had advanced the class awareness of the workers and had led to mass revolutionary manifestations. It was this difference, they averred, that was at the core of the absolute divergence between the positions and tactics of the two parties.[107] According to this view an event like the Azef affair was possible in the SR party. Since no underground organization was immune from agents and spies, the Social Democrats were also no doubt afflicted with their share; the difference was that the rôle even the most brilliant of them could play within the Social Democratic party paled into insignificance in the face of what Azef could accomplish in the SR party.

They pointed to the conclusions of the SRs' commission of inquiry to show that the infiltration of a secret agent into terrorist ranks was hardly an insurmountable problem. Azef had done it easily. To that end he had required neither any special/prowess nor a strong character, nor even any unusual powers of suggestion. It was sufficient for him to have the backing of the strength and means of the police in order to project himself to his comrades as a powerful and undefeatable figure. None of this was possible in the Social Democratic party: for an agent to achieve a ranking status there he would have to manifest extraordinary intellectual qualities 'which can't be pulled out of the bulging money-bags of the police'. Moreover, he would have to demonstrate far-ranging theoretical knowledge without which not only would he be unable to attain the status of leader – he could not even be a good soldier. In the absence of that knowledge he would be unable to work for the advancement of the workers' class awareness, and such activity, even by an agent, must always produce good results whatever its source might be. Because of this, informing or betrayal within the Social Democratic party could be damaging to one person, or at most to a group of persons. A slowdown in activity might ensue, but under no circumstances could such action affect or sidetrack the workers' movement as a whole. In contrast, in the terrorist groups an agent could become a key figure and topple the entire organization, even if he himself was intellectually inferior – as was demonstrated by the Azef affair.

The Azef affair and the commentaries it elicited provided the Social Democrats with the opportunity to re-emphasize their objection in principle to terrorism, on the ground that it harmed the interests of the revolution. It was stressed that terrorism helped foster the myth of the hero and thereby imbued the masses with an inordinate belief in the strength of the individual, arousing their hopes of liberation through heroic figures without themselves having to play a part in this process. Furthermore, despite the claims of the SRs that terrorism was just one means of struggle, historical experience proved that over time it debilitated all the other means, rendering them unimportant. This was what happened to the *Narodnaia Volia*, the Social Democrats maintained, and exactly the same thing had happened to the SRs. The Battle Organization had become the most important element in the party and had effectively taken it over. Indeed, this was only natural. What importance could the Central Committee or the party organ have, compared with warriors who performed great and wondrous deeds such as the assassination of a minister or the Grand Duke? In an organization of this kind, it was stated, the key office-holder was not necessarily the person blessed with intelligence and foresight, but the person for whom no internal or external rules existed, who was ready to throw his life away and who recognized nothing but the validity of action; in a word, the hero. Azef, they averred had conformed with both this image and the secret goals of the police. The explanation lay in the fact that while on the face of it the police were combatting terrorism, in secret some police officials actually supported it. This double game, the Social Democrats maintained, was designed to divert revolutionary activity from a path that was liable to imperil the régime far more than terrorism ever could; namely, propagandizing and stirring up the workers, who with each passing day posed an ever growing threat to the Russian government.[108]

For the anarchists, too, as for the Social Democrats, terrorism, which was one of the key areas of their dispute of principle with the SRs, also constituted a focal point for criticism and discussions of the Azef affair. The anarchists had often voiced their objections and opposition to the principle of centralized structure long before the Azef affair. Peter Kropotkin, for example, in his article 'An Organization or Free Consent', had written,

> All of them [all the centralist organizations] become, following a brief period of success, a direct obstacle to the development of the

> revolutionary cause. They interfere with the development of local and individual initiative, and they inevitably stifle the spirit of revolt. The Central Committee, knowing the degree of responsibility that falls on its shoulders as a result of an act of violence performed by any party member, begins to pull in the reins. To forestall brutal suppression – of which the leaders will undoubtedly be the first victims, followed by the entire party – it begins to pour cold water on the local strikes and the small uprisings, and more so, on every manifestation of a spirit of personal revolt. 'We are preparing something big for the capital', 'Look, don't bother us with your petty case' or 'We're preparing a revolution. When the time comes we will determine the day of the uprising, but in the meantime be careful, don't squander your energy'. . . . The success of any popular revolution depends in the first place on an infinite number of small manifestations at each and every location, [which are] imbued with the spirit of personal or popular revolt. To prepare a revolution, thousands of personal attacks are required, operations of revolt against every authority in the factory, village or town. Thousands of actions of revolt and local uprising are needed.[109]

This position now became the axis of the anarchists' stand *vis-à-vis* provocation in general and their perception of the Azef affair in particular. The criticism of the Paris opposition group as it appears in its organ *Revoliutsionnaia Mysl'*, like the similar criticism of the Maximalists in *Trudovaia Republika* ('The Working Republic'), is quoted extensively and positively. 'We too believe that the *provocateur* Azef would not have brought such a terrible disaster on the revolutionary movement if the party's central institutions had not contained extremist Jacobins who in the course of many years introduced extremely radical centralization, brought about a revolutionary bureaucracy and generated a "personality cult" that reached the point where the members of the Central Committee – the party's "holy of holies" – were transformed into a kind of revolutionary infallible popes, while those on the periphery either did not dare speak out against them or were too impotent to do anything.'

Rejecting the Social Democrats' contention that provocation was engendered by terrorism, the anarchists cited a series of examples from the days of the Paris Commune, when methods of provocation were employed against non-terrorist groups. If there was anything to be learned from the Azef affair, they said, it was hardly the lesson that the Social Democrats were stressing. The affair did not underscore the bankruptcy of terrorism, but the damage provocation could wreak in the revolutionary terrorist struggle when terrorism was subject to party scrutiny and dependent on a specific organization. Provocation was quite normal in revolutionary movements. Provocation had always existed and would always exist in the movement as long as it continued to be revolutionary and underground. There were only two ways to prevent their presence: to forgo the force that attracts them – underground activity – by abandoning the methods of revolutionary struggle and concentrating on purely cultural activities; or to remain revolutionaries but to forge conditions in which provocation could not develop and thrive. The latter task was difficult and required two conditions: the absence of revolutionary bureacracy and the determination to take steps in any situation 'to remove from circulation' *provocateurs* who had infiltrated the movement.[110]

Neither side changed its position in the debate over the factors that had abetted the emergence of provocation. The Social Democrats adhered to their position that terrorism attracted provocation and created convenient conditions for its development. The anarchists and the SRs utterly rejected this argument. But while the former insisted that only the forgoing of the principle of centralism would minimize the harm caused by provocation – which would always exist – the SRs held that precisely the strengthening of the centralist organization and the augmentation of the centre's supervision over the periphery would upgrade the conditions of secrecy which were required to protect the party organizations against similar phenomena in the future. Nor did positions change in the SR party's internal debates. They would, however, soon change, when several party leaders took part in the *Pochin* ('Initiative') group which sought semi-legal solutions for the problem of the party's existence and activities under conditions of police pressure. However, this was not necessarily directly connected with the Azef affair.

Yet despite the adherence to traditional principles, and despite the practical insignificance of the organizational changes decided on by the SR party's Fifth Council, the shock waves of the Azef affair did set in motion certain developments which were to leave their mark on the party: the subject of provocation became the main issue on the agenda, a place it would hold at least until the outbreak of the First World War. Because the Azef affair was so charged with deep and extreme feelings, it became – knowingly or unknowingly – an issue on to which it became covenient to hitch internal and inter-party disputes. Only an issue as sensitive as the Azef affair could have lent such intense reverberation to the arguments advanced by virtually anonymous SR members against the power excercised by the veteran leadership or, for example, to Rubanovich's stand against terrorism. Only a phenomenon like the Azef affair could seem a suitable means through which elements in the revolutionary camp could justify *a priori* positions of principle.

As an issue which had penetrated the SRs awareness, provocation would not lose its explosive force, and would continue to play a similar role in the internal life of the party.

3 Chain Reactions

(i) THE MORAL ISSUE

When the SR party's Fifth Council decided on the establishment of a judicial commission of inquiry to eliminate the consequences of Azef's provocation, no one imagined that those results were not yet fully evident and that precisely those most serious for the party's future would surface at a later stage, seemingly unrelated to the Azef affair, and in a sphere over which no commission of inquiry – or any other party institution, for that matter – would have any control or influence. In retrospect it emerged that despite the severe losses the party sustained due to Azef's informing on party activities to the police, his exposure was actually more devastating to the party than the information he passed on in secret. The dam that burst in the wake of the affair and its aftermath did more damage to the party than the storm that struck it during the exposure itself. From this point of view, the Azef affair is perhaps better likened to a cluster bomb which goes off in phases, each phase deadlier than the last. The final phase, which is the subject of this chapter, is less directly related to the events of the Azef affair itself than it is to the frame of mind which it engendered, a frame of mind which transformed the entire provocation issue into a cardinal socio-political question for the party. It resulted from the abrupt and dramatic passage of the provocation question from its repressed state to the very centre of party consciousness. This new awareness, following hard on the heels of the jolting experience of the Azef affair – for individual party members and for the party as a whole – meant that every manifestation of provocation became an explosive issue, and hence also a unique and powerful element in the life of the party. This made itself felt for the first time in the Petrov affair, which rocked the party less than a year after Azef's exposure.

Alexander Petrov was a veteran member of the SR party, having joined it immediately upon its founding while he was a teacher in a rural school in the Viatka province. His six years of activity in the party were marked by one arrest after another, though he was always released speedily: in 1903 and 1904 for lack of evidence, and in 1905 as part of a general amnesty; in 1906 he staged a successful prison break. Going underground, he began to engage in terrorism in

Kazan, taking part in expropriations and assassinations, while working in an explosives laboratory. One day in January 1907, while he was working with a comrade in the laboratory, a blast ripped through the room. His friend died instantly. Petrov, badly wounded in the leg, was again seized by the police and sentenced to four years' hard labour. Once again he escaped, and this time those who had assisted in the prison break smuggled him out of the country. He was hospitalized for treatment of his leg, which had to be amputated. Following a brief period of recovery he made his way back to Russia, becoming active in the group headed by Osip Minor which was helping reorganize party activity in the Volga district. The entire group, Petrov included, was arrested in November 1908. This time, however, he was set free by the police themselves, after he had signed a confession and a declaration of readiness to serve as a secret police agent within the SR party. The police had great hopes that he would fill the void created in the ranks of their agents by the loss of Azef.[1] While this is not in dispute, we find two different accounts of the manner and purpose of his recruitment. His own version, as related to the Central Committee, was accepted as reliable and published in the official party organ; the second version was that of two key police officials, Gerasimov and Martynov, each of whom published his own account in his memoirs.[2] All the accounts are identical in their first sections, but differ in their interpretations of the facts.

Petrov claims that he offered his services to the commander of the Gendarmerie and the head of the Okhrana in Saratov – Vladimir Semiganovskii and Martynov, respectively – with the aim of deceiving the police and exposing their secrets. He had reached this difficult decision, he said, because of the despair and gloom that had gripped everyone when the news of Azef's treachery reached the Saratov prison. Everyone was completely taken back. In the prison the only topic of conversation was the provocation issue. As they recalled earlier *provocateurs*, and told tales of past betrayals, they began to fear that more could be imminent. Provocation, Petrov relates, hung like a cloud over all. Under the spell of that atmosphere he began to imagine scenarios each more horrifying than the last. In his mind's eye he saw the party as ruined, and riddled with *provocateurs* from top to bottom. He concluded that it was inconceivable to resume party activity without first finding relief from this blow. If provocation were really a 'two-edged sword', as he had heard many times from every quarter, he must prove that it harmed not only the revolutionary camp but also those who used it. The upshot was that Petrov decided to become a revolutionary *provocateur*. He would become a police agent, discover the Police Department's secrets, its espionage apparatus, its agents in the SR party – and would then reveal all to the party.

Martynov, on the other hand, maintains that in March 1909 Semiganovskii told him that after much persuasion he had managed to get Petrov to provide a sincere account of his party activity. It was possible, Semiganovskii added, that Petrov might even agree to co-operate with him in the future. Thrilled with his success, Seminagovskii hurried to contact the Police Department in order to obtain confirmation and get further instructions. Within a week a positive reply had arrived from St Petersburg, but the Director of the Police Department suggested that Martynov should also talk with Petrov and then convey his impressions.

In Gerasimov's view, Petrov realized that a stiff punishment awaited him, involving many years of hard labour which for an ailing amputee would be a particularly cruel ordeal. This, Gerasimov averred, was the reason for Petrov's consent to act as a police secret agent; he, too, added that Petrov's agreement had come at a highly propitious moment because ever since the Azef affair the Police Department had been extremely anxious to rehabilitate its central agency in the SR party.

Regarding the negotiations he conducted at Saratov, Petrov relates that both sides presented conditions: he demanded that in return for his consent to serve, the comrades arrested together with him be released. Otherwise, he would be unable to bear the guilty feeling if he went free while his friends remained in prison. In addition, he argued, the members of the group would facilitate his approach to the sources of information of interest to the police. According to Petrov, Martynov and Semiganovskii agreed to release everyone with the exception of Minor, demanding in return that Petrov declare in writing his assent to act as a secret agent, and that to prove his intentions he should add an account of the most important revolutionary activity which he knew to be underway at that moment. If he did so, his freedom would be guaranteed, along with a salary of 300 roubles a month. Petrov told the Central Committee that he had made the requested declaration, and that in order to enhance his credibility in the eyes of the police he stated in his confession that his specific area of revolutionary activity was terrorism. He then went on to list a whole series of revolutionary plans, all of them fabricated, and signed the document, not in his own name – which was unknown to the police – but as Andrei Iasnenko, an officer in the Sebastopol army who had been tried and sentenced to hard labour but had fled without leaving a trace.

A different picture emerges from Martynov's memoirs. The Okhrana chief says he led Petrov to understand, above all, that he was talking with him as director of political investigation at Saratov, in order to discover whether local SR leaders were still at large, adding that in view of his agreement to co-operate with the Okhrana he expected very sincere replies. Martynov relates that Petrov spoke of his disappointment in the party's leaders following Azef's treachery: after many hesitations and much soul-searching Petrov had reached the conclusion that it was better to live free than 'to feed fleas in prison' – a fate that certainly awaited him if he failed to co-operate with his interrogators. He told about his participation in assassinations, his wound, his flight abroad, and how he joined the Minor group which had gone to the Volga district. He went into detail about how the group's members had begun to form underground contacts and had set up printing facilities in order to issue a Volga newspaper on behalf of the party. He explained how their terrorist activity had been organized. When Martynov asked him to name the activists involved, Petrov rattled off a list of persons and their functions. Since, according to Martynov, all these facts were known to him from his own agents he was convinced that Petrov might well be enlisted as a collaborator. The two went on to discuss practical possibilities of co-operation, their friendly conversation lasting until midnight. It should be emphasized that it was Martynov who had carried out the arrest of the group and that in addition to the information from Azef, the secret agent Tatiana Tseitlin was also part of the group. Martynov mentions nothing about Petrov's unknown identity, nor is this cited in Gerasimov's memoirs.

On the basis of the reports from Saratov it was decided to bring Petrov to St Petersburg, to clarify further the degree of his seriousness. The Director of the Police Department assigned Gerasimov, chief of the Okhrana in the capital, to speak to him. Petrov, who was brought under guard to the Okhrana deparment in St Petersburg, was then housed handsomely in a well appointed, spacious room, as befitted an honoured and important agent.

From this point the accounts diverge widely. Petrov says that from the outset he encountered an attitude of mistrust in St Petersburg, despite the good lodgings. His requests to have all the group's members released, including Minor, were turned down, and the motivation he offered for wanting to serve as an agent were also treated sceptically. In the course of an interrogation by Gerasimov's assistant, Ivan Dobroskok, Petrov refused to reply to questions concerning his identity. When the interrogator retorted with abusive language about Petrov and his revolutionary friends, Petrov, unable to restrain himself, threw him out of his cell. Within half an hour he was in handcuffs and en route to Sebastopol for identification. It was immediately determined that he was not Andrei Iasnenko, and he was taken back to the Saratov prison. Thus, Petrov says, his outburst put a stop to his plan and led him to a dead end. The plan 'to take up the sword' had failed. His prospects of harming the Okhrana had vanished, but because he had negotiated with its officials, the way back was also blocked. Never again would he be able to engage in party activity. Despairing, he began to contemplate suicide, when he suddenly had a brainwave: he would feign madness, be hospitalized in the prison clinic from which escape was easy, and once out would again volunteer his services. If he were not believed as a prisoner, he would certainly be believed when he repeated his offer while at liberty. Once back at Saratov, Petrov began to act like a madman. At first he failed to convince anyone. He was physically abused in prison in revenge for the disappointment he had caused the authorities. But Petrov did not give in. He persisted in his act until the prison authorities were convinced and appointed a committee to examine him. The committee decided that he should be transferred for three weeks to a mental hospital for further examination. A few days after his arrival there, Petrov slipped out through a window. From his hiding place he sent Martynov a letter offering his services as an agent. When the two met, Petrov reiterated his demand that his comrades be released. Martynov contacted Gerasimov, and another meeting was arranged between Petrov and the Okhrana chief in St Petersburg. This time Gerasimov consented to Petrov's prior conditions and went to Saratov himself to make the arrangements.

Gerasimov's account is, as we noted, totally different. He says that at his first meeting with Petrov in St Petersburg, he asked him to write out his *curriculum vitae* in detail, including all the revolutionary operations in which he had taken part. He then compared this autobiography with the files of the Okhrana and the Police Department. Gerasimov acknowledges that Petrov's account contained many details that were unknown to the police, while he was found to be telling the truth about all the points that could be authenticated.

Only then did Gerasimov enter into substantive talks with Petrov. The latter explained that his personal disappointment in the party's leaders and in the revolutionary movement as a whole had led him to agree to serve as an agent. He had considered abandoning his revolutionary activity even earlier, but only in prison made a final decision. In joining the Okhrana's secret agents, he was actively seeking to frustrate the plans of the revolutionary camp.

Satisfied with Petrov's tale, Gerasimov advocated his acceptance into service. Once the assent of the Minister of the Interior Stolypin was obtained, consideration was given to the manner of Petrov's release. According to Gerasimov, this was a major problem. The release had to be effected without arousing suspicion among his party comrades. Petrov suggested that the entire group be dispatched to Siberia under administrative expulsion; from there he would have no trouble escaping. Gerasimov rejected this idea out of hand because the group's trial was imminent, nor did he see any possibility of releasing committed and dangerous revolutionaries such as Minor. Instead, Gerasimov relates, Petrov conceived the idea of staging an escape from prison. Upon his return to Saratov he would feign madness. 'With the Okhrana's discreet help', doctors who harboured partial sympathy for the revolutionaries would have him sent to a mental institution. From there it would be 'child's play' to escape. This plan, according to Gerasimov, was also approved by the Police Department and by Stolypin. The only member of Petrov's group to be released by Gerasimov was Boris Bartold. Gerasimov relates that immediately after Petrov's escape from the hospital he met him again. It transpired that he had not had an easy time while feigning madness. Despite the assistance of the Okhrana chief at Saratov, the warders could not be let in on the secret, and it was from them that Petrov's madness in the Saratov prison was faked and that he was informed about it in advance by Semiganovskii. Moreover, he, Martynov, had been asked to place a safe apartment at Petrov's
Martynov, had been asked to place a safe apartment at Petrov's
disposal where he could hide after his escape from the hospital. Petrov arrived there and contacted Martynov. At their meeting Martynov tried to convince him to remain in the Volga district, but Petrov insisted that under his agreement with the representative of the Police Department, he was to proceed to St Petersburg.

From this point – Petrov's arrival is St Petersburg – the two accounts once more begin to converge. According to Gerasimov, Petrov needed a period of recuperation, which could best be accomplished by sending him abroad. Such a trip would be useful for the Okhrana as well, since virtually all the party's leaders were at that time residing in Paris. The Okhrana was therefore interested in having an agent there who would keep an eye of the party's key figures. Gerasimov gave Petrov precise instructions, warned him particularly against Burtsev, sent a liaison man named Dolgov with him to Paris, gave him 1500 roubles, a Browning and an address for correspondence, and took leave of him.

Petrov was hardly the first to claim that he had made contact with the Okhrana for revolutionary purposes. There had been similar instances in the past. But the party discerned the differences between each case, and determined its stand accordingly. Petrov's action could be classified as one type and the Volodia Degaev affair was an example of a second type. A third was exemplified by the case of Nikolai Kletochnikov, of the Narodnaia Volia, who at Alexander Mikhailov's advice infiltrated into the Police Department as a clerk and for two years supplied his party with names of secret agents operating in its ranks.

Of the three types, only the third was acceptable to the SR party, after it had cautiously estimated the benefit it could derive from such an agent: what was the party giving and what was it getting in return? On the one hand it was sacrificing a member whose only future revolutionary activity would consist of obtaining information. Furthermore, like the police when they employed agents among the revolutionaries, the party asked itself whether such activity, even if it was wholly passive, did not ultimately benefit the enemy. And like the police, the party's answer was unequivocal: a comrade who was assigned to spy on the police from the inside might, through the information he conveyed, enhance the revolutionary activity of the other comrades far beyond what one person could do in the operational sphere.

> Just imagine if a spy like that would help rid the party of internal treachery by exposing the network of agents and *provocateurs* that the police have spread with so many years' hard work. Just think that with a timely warning he might save a whole chain of organizations and projects from collapse. This benefit far outweighs the loss of one person, and all the more so when he is playing the passive role of a clerk.[3]

However, despite the party's awareness of its immense utility, this method of struggle against the police was extremely rare. In fact, the only known example was that of Nikolai Kletochnikov; no other instances were known in the party. Nor did the party assign anyone to such a mission, maintaining that it was due to the difficulty entailed in penetrating deep into the investigative institutions. A revolutionary who was given such a dangerous and responsible mission would necessarily be a veteran member of the movement – meaning that he would be known to the police, at least as being of doubtful reliability, and hence ruled out for service in its ranks. From the party's point of view, a person assigned such a task would have to demonstrate unreserved dedication – which would necessarily also be reflected in his entire way of life, and would, in the last analysis, be irreconcilable with the characteristics required for a police career. Rare inner qualities were required: 'Readiness and psychological ability to serve socialism and the revolution in this way.'[4] Few revolutionaries were attracted to this difficult path. On the other hand, many instances are known of persons who, in an attempt to penetrate the world of political investigation, posed as betrayers of the revolution and, with their group's knowledge and consent, offered their services to the police. Volodia Degaev was one example. Yet whereas Kletochnikov brought the *Narodnaia Volia* incalculable benefit and his exploits were related from one generation to the next as exemplary, the case of the Degaev brothers proved catastrophic for the party, entering the annals of the revolutionary movement as a despicable and notorious episode. Although the term *Degaevshchina* refers only to the treachery of the older brother, Sergei, it should be born in mind that the affair began with Volodia, who contacted Sudeikin and arranged for him to meet his elder brother.

The intentions of both Kletochnikov and Volodia Degaev were purely revolutionary. That their activity produced opposite results stemmed from one difference of principle which, as far as the party was concerned, validated the former and utterly invalidated the latter: the benefit that could be derived from connections such as Kletochnikov derived from the growing trust in the party member by his superiors in the police, without he himself having to do any 'dirty tricks'. In other words, the information obtained in this manner was the result of trust, but the revolutionary did not have to pay for it by informing on his comrades. However, when the police recruited agents from among the revolutionaries, the situation was fundamentally different. Effectively, these revolutionaries had only one alternative: not to reveal anything and risk having the police slam the door in their faces at once, as befell Volodia, or to become genuine, fully fledged informers, and play a part in sending their revolutionary comrades to the gallows, as in the case of Sergei.[5] This was because in contrast to the former affair, in which it was possible to play a perfectly passive role, in the second case one had to demonstrate one's reliability from the very outset, through betrayal. Only then was it possible to advance to a higher rank. Ultimately, then, the revolutionary was caught in a situation which was the very reverse of his original intentions: the police concealed their secrets from him, but squeezed out of him the revolutionaries' secrets.[6] Furthermore, this option had a highly negative effect on the revolutionaries' morale. Such were the confusion and bewilderment among the organization's members when they discovered that one of their number was serving as a secret agent, that there was no choice but to divulge his true role; and once it became necessary to inform everyone, clearly the secret could not be kept from the Okhrana for long. Thus when all aspects of this option were weighed in the balance, the conclusion was that the sole beneficiaries were the police, and not the revolutionaries. Since 'the advantages and disadvantages [of this course] are distributed very differently than in the first case',[7] its use was entirely ruled out. Despite the differences between the three cases, and at times despite their different results, their common starting point was their good intention, and this sometimes blurred the differences and the dividing lines between them.

Two representatives of the Executive Committee of the *Narodnaia Volia*, Zlatopol'skii and Grachevskii, had the Kletochnikov model in mind when each in his turn effectively assented to the Degaev brothers' ties with Sudeikin. The same was true of the periodical *Byloe* ('The Past') which served its editor, Burtsev, in his unrelenting war against provocation. In 1907–8 Burtsev published Kletochnikov's lists and lauded his 'tremendous contribution' to the revolutionary movement: 'Kletochnikov has given us an excellent example of collecting information about the enemies of the liberation movement,' the preface to the first list stated. Readers were invited to fill out the lists by supplying the names of persons who had had ties with the institutions of political investigation, not only in the past 'but at any time, any place and in any manner . . . with the Third Section, the Okhrana, the Police Department or other agencies of detection'.[8]

Undoubtedly this call posits counter-espionage as beneficial to the revolutionary movement and as an exemplary model worthy of emulation. Indeed, the very fact that there were a number of cases in which ties with the Okhrana were accounted for, after their exposure, by citing revolutionary intentions, demonstrates – irrespective of the veracity of these contentions – that this is how the message was understood, albeit without sorting out the methods or the means.

It was this phenomenon which forced the SR party's Organization Bureau to issue a statement warning that any party organization that consented to any of its members joining the Okhrana would be disbanded by the Central Committee.[9] About comrades who assumed such a role wholly on their own initiative, there was no question: ever since the 1870s the accepted rule was that they would be expelled from the party immediately, and the party's Fourth Council had given this tradition the force of law.[10]

We may assume that a veteran party member with a wealth of revolutionary experience such as Petrov, was aware of the party's stand regarding connections with the Okhrana, but only on his release did he grasp the full gravity of what he had done. His description of his devastated feeling when his initial plan failed is surely identical to what must have gone through his mind when he arrived in Paris to meet his veteran comrades: a feeling that he had committed an irrevocable crime, that he was caught up in a situation from which the only way out was to put an end to his life in a spectacular act of terrorism which would expiate his sin and purify his name in the eyes of his revolutionary comrades. Confessing fully to the Central Committee, he asked for its help.

The party's representatives related that Petrov's story had left them with a difficult choice: on the one hand Petrov had committed a serious crime that violated the revolutionary tradition and was harming the revolutionary cause, necessitating his immediate expulsion from the party and the publicizing of his name and his actions. On the other hand, they knew him well, his past activity was unblemished, and they believed him. To refuse to accede to his request, they felt, would be to deprive him of any possibility of penitence – a punishment they did not think he merited. It was decided to allow him to return to St Petersburg in order to assassinate Gerasimov, 'one of the heads of detection in Russia'. One consideration may well have been that Gerasimov's liquidation would go some way towards enhancing the tainted standing of the party and its central institutions. This at least is the impression created by the detailed description of the affair and the Central Committee's part in it that appeared afterward in the party's organ.[11] At all events, Petrov was assured of all the technical assistance he might require.

Clearly, Petrov could not return to Russia at once, both because of his shaky mental health, and so as not to arouse the suspicions of the police who expected him to provide information about the Paris SRs. Petrov was therefore exempted from all party activity, to avoid the possibility of exposure in case the police were trailing him. A representative of the Central Committee stayed in constant touch with him, helping him to draft his letters to his case officer in St Petersburg and to the contact who was supposed to follow him to Paris. In these letters Petrov claimed to have information about 'extremely urgent matters', and described the progress he was making in becoming acquainted with members of the party's central organs. Everything was designed to convince his dispatchers that his penetration of the centre was proceeding apace.[12]

At the suggestion of the Cental Committee representative, Petrov wrote to Gerasimov that he possessed certain information about Savinkov's plans and actions in which Gerasimov was particularly interested and about which the police were so apprehensive, adding that he would soon be leaving for Russia in connection with this information. But the preparations for Petrov's return to Russia dragged on. His contact, Dolgov, failed to turn up, leading Petrov to complain to Gerasimov. By now the Central Committee was also losing its patience. The committee seems to have feared that the entire affair would be discovered, generating a new provocation scandal even before the storm of the Azef affair had abated. On 23 November the committee informed Petrov that if he did not execute the plan by 1 January 1910 it would have no choice but to make the entire matter public. Finally, a few days after the Central Committee's warning, Petrov set out for St Petersburg to meet with Gerasimov. Petrov, who was carrying dynamite which he had received from Savinkov, was accompanied by two party members, Bartold and Lukanov, and was trailed by agents of the Okhrana's Foreign Agency.[13] In the meantime, Gerasimov was replaced as Okhrana Commander in St Petersburg by Sergei Karpov, to whom Petrov was now to report.

Petrov's relations with Karpov proved no less felicitous than those he had maintained with his predecessor. Indeed, Karpov, who was positive that with Petrov's help he was on the verge of exposing a major terrorist conspiracy, trusted him implicitly. Violating every accepted rule of prudence, he rented a flat with him, which was to serve as a safe apartment for the two of them. Only in this way, he claimed, could he maintain contact with Petrov without arousing the suspicions of the revolutionaries. He left it to Petrov to find and furnish the apartment. The latter rented a three-room flat and purchased an old sofa and a round table with one wide, hollow leg. He also installed a system of electric bells, hooked up to the front door and to the front gate. The entry bell could be disconnected by a special switch. Petrov planted a large explosive device in the table's hollow leg, attached it to the doorbell and disconnected the bell from the gate. He then sat down to await his victim.[14] According to Martynov, Petrov was expecting higher-ranking personages than Karpov. Gerasimov maintains that these personages were himself, the Director of the Police Department, Kurlov, and his deputy, Vissarionov. His transfer to another post, he adds, prevented Petrov from carrying out his plan. For this reason Petrov told Karpov that he had all along been in secret contact with Gerasimov, who had given him money to kill Kurlov whose position as Police Department Director Gerasimov wanted. Karpov lost no time in conveying this information to the Director and his deputy. Believing Petrov's story, they agreed to his suggestion that he invite Gerasimov to a secret meeting at his apartment while they eavesdropped from behind a closed door. But the entire scheme collapsed, according to this account, because of Karpov's surprise appearance to celebrate the house-warming, bearing wine and delicacies. Since the bell at the gate was cut off, he called to Petrov from outside and the latter went down to let him in. Petrov had no choice but to eat and drink with his guest at the booby-trapped table. Suddenly Karpov decided that the tablecloth was not clean enough and began to remove it. Petrov froze. The wires connecting the device to the door-bell were visible beneath the tablecloth. 'Never mind, never mind,' he said, 'I'll take care of everything.' Rushing out, ostensibly to bring a new tablecloth, he activated the switch connecting the entry gate with the system of bells, then ran downstairs and pressed the doorbell. The device went off, killing Karpov instantly.[15] Petrov was seized by the landlord and handed over to the police. He was tried and hanged.

Gerasimov did not believe the account published in the party's organ. He thought that Petrov had lost his confidence because of Dolgov's tardiness in arriving in Paris. Under the watchful gaze of Burtsev's agents, in constant fear of exposure, and lacking any support from the Police Department, he finally decided to confess all to the revolutionaries but to present the story as though his ties with the police had been a deliberate pretence. Gerasimov was certain that this version of events was totally unfounded. Had Petrov wished to kill him, he argued, he had a perfect, risk-free opportunity at their second meeting in St Petersburg. They always met alone, in an empty secret apartment. Indeed, Gerasimov, claimed that at their last meeting he himself had given Petrov a loaded pistol. Petrov could have done the deed and reached Finland safely using the passport and the money Gerasimov had given him. That he did not take advantage of this opportunity was proof for Gerasimov that Petrov had some quite different purpose in coming to the meeting.[16] But Gerasimov's account does not refute that of the SR party's Central Committee. All the correspondence in the archives shows that Petrov confessed to the Central Committee long before he could have lost his nerve for the reasons adduced by Gerasimov. It does, however, lend credence to the above mentioned hypothesis[17] that the Okhrana's pressure on political prisoners was so intense that even revolutionaries like Petrov buckled under it, believing that if they only agreed to the proposal they would later be able to elude the grasp of the police. The police, however, were certain that anyone who fell into their hands would not get away so quickly. Very few were capable of retracting, like Petrov, and then choosing the only course of action left.

The rumours rampant in party circles concerning the Petrov affair even before the story was published in the party organ, and then its actual publication, generated a furore within the SR party about the Central Committee's role in the affair. The impression in St Petersburg was that the assassination had been recognized as an operation executed in the name of and on behalf of the party, and had been approved by the Central Committee. The St Petersburg organization thus held the committee responsible for new and deplorable tactics in the struggle against provocation. The organization protested vehemently, demanding that the Karpov murder should not be considered a party operation. Arguing that the party could not accept responsibility for the behaviour of the Central Committee, the organization called for the Committee's resignation, urged that its members be placed on trial, and requested the convening of an all-party congress to elect a new Central Committee. This resolution was adopted also by the SR workers committee in St Petersburg and discussed in the worker's clubs in the capital.[18]

Abroad, the Regional Committee was the first to react. On 4 January it adopted a sharply worded protest resolution against the participation of party members in the Karpov assassination. It went on to level harsh criticism at the Central Committee for having seen fit

> to maintain contacts with a person who had approached , albeit for special purposes, the heads of provocation and detection, allowed him to carry out an operation, received financial reports from him, gave him technical assistance, and in dictating for him a letter about 'important information for the Okhrana' entered into indirect contact with the secret police.

The Regional Committee did not evaluate Petrov's personality or consider whether he deserved the trust placed in him by the Central Committee, but concentrated exclusively on its course of action. That course, the resolution asserted, was 'intolerable and debased the party's moral prestige'.[19]

The debate that followed this proclamation caused a storm in SR circles abroad that was not easily abated. Five months later the matter was still on the agenda of the Paris Group for the SR party. Everyone concurred in denouncing Petrov's ties with the Okhrana. Opinion was divided, however, with respect to two other questions: had the Central Committee acted properly in helping Petrov to assassinate Karpov? And did the Regional Committee abroad have the right to express a protest against the Central Committee in general and in the name of the SR groups abroad in particular? A protest against the Central Committee did not necessarily entail support for the reaction of the Regional Committee. In fact, most of the groups abroad passed resolutions condemning the behaviour of the Central Committee because they had a matter-of-fact approach to the question of relations with the Okhrana – however also condemning the position taken by the Foreign Committee which was supposed to represent them. We find, then, that intra-party political considerations also played a role in the debate, since the Foreign Committee had long since become a centre of opposition to the veteran leadership, and its organ a forum for ideological dissent. The debate therefore focused more on the stand of the Central Committee than on Petrov's act, as emerges from the divergent stands of the Lausane and London groups.

The former supported the decision of the Central Committee, viewing its behaviour as proper, indeed as the only possible course in this instance:

> The Central Committee faced a dilemma: to cast a decent, dedicated revolutionary to his fate and refrain from providing him with

> moral or material support; or to help him extricate himself honourably from the situation he has fallen into and to repay the government in kind for its provocationist bacchanalia.[20]

In contrast, the London group resolved that:

> from the viewpoint of revolutionary ethics, under no circumstances must a party member be allowed to enter the Okhrana Section, with or without the knowledge of the central institutions, not even to sow demoralization among that filthy criminal gang which trades in humanity's conscience.[21]

The upshot was that if until then the official position regarding contacts with the Okhrana had been determined on utilitarian grounds following an examination of whether or not these were advantageous, a new, emotional dimension was now added to the debate. The emotional posture was manifested not only by the intensity of the debate but by the acerbity of its style. Expressions like 'provocationist bacchanalia' and 'that filthy criminal gang which trades in humanity's conscience' do not emanate from cold, utilitarian thought but from the realm of the emotions and primal drives. Henceforth the police represented not just a political enemy, but a wicked, degenerate force which would corrupt anyone who got close enough – so that one seeking to preserve his soul or maintain his standing had better keep his distance.

If the Central Committee actually thought that the assassination of a key police official would enhance its reputation and help towards clearing the foul atmosphere that had settled over the party, it could not have been more mistaken. The very fact that the Committee was at the centre of a party storm – irrespective of the degree of support for it – further undercut its already shaky standing. The furore also demonstrated that provocation – any provocation, not necessarily one as far-reaching as the Azef affair – was, besides a police means of struggle, of political import in the party's inner life. This fact had not escaped the notice of the leadership, which acknowledged that mistakes were made in the Petrov affair. The ferocity of the reactions against it was attributed to timing, to the fact that the mistakes followed so closely on the heels of the Azef case and before the deep wounds it had caused party members had healed. 'Perhaps in a different, better period for the party, [these mistakes would] not have assumed such major significance and would not have sparked off such a row in the party's rank.'[22] Indeed, it was a very bad time for the party – not just because of the Azef affair but because of the whole series of additional exposures that followed it.

In 1909–10 a large number of secret agents was uncovered in all the revolutionary parties. This followed the defection to the revolutionary camp of Leonid Men'shchikov, a retired senior police officer. He arrived in Paris at the beginning of 1909 bearing a large number of secret documents which he claimed to have collected during his twenty years of service in the Police Department.

In his youth, in the early 1880s, Men'shchikov was a member of a revolutionary students' circle at Moscow University. A fellow student, Zubatov, was already then a secret agent, who informed on the group to the police. Arrested, Men'shchikov believed himself to have been victimized by a police provocation. He decided, he states, to take his revenge on the Tsarist police using the same base and brutal measures as those employed by the police in their suppression of the revolutionary ardour and the innocence of Russian youth. He began by making a full confession of his revolutionary activity, thereby gaining the trust of his interrogators. In 1888 he himself joined the police, launching a career that was to take him from the post of a simple detective in the Moscow Okhrana to that of assistant to Zubatov, by then Head of the Special Section: the assistant, that is, of the person who had brought about his original arrest. Throughout the entire period, Men'shchikov later claimed, his sympathies remained with the revolutionaries, and he unflaggingly collected documents which he intended one day to hand over to the revolutionaries. Once he even attempted to make contact with them. It was he who sent the anonymous letter in 1905 warning the SR leaders against Tatarov and Azef. In 1908 Burtsev made efforts to get in touch with him. Ever since Bakai's defection from the police, Burtsev had several times attempted to lure away other police officials as well. He had noticed Men'shchikov two years earlier because of the stories that were circulating about him: that he was a bibliophile and a bibliographer who owned a large collection of revolutionary literature and was well-versed in the history of the revolutionary movement. As the editor of *Byloe*, a historical periodical whose subject was the annals of the revolutionary movement, and as a relentless opponent of provocation, Burtsev felt that Men'shchikov might prove of some use, either specifically to the paper or to his own struggle against police agents. He wrote to Men'shchikov, suggesting a meeting abroad. They met in Belgium shortly after Men'shchikov's retirement. Burtsev said the meetings convinced him of Men'shchikov's sincerity, and the way was paved for the latter's return to the revolutionary fold.[23]

There is another version of the motives that led Men'shchikov to co-operate with Burtsev. It seems to have originated in police circles, and was published about a year after his defection, when his identity, which until then had been guarded zealously, was finally revealed. In this version, Men'shchikov's defection was in revenge for his expulsion from the Police Department and his demand for an enlarged pension. His decline began with the assassination of Plehve, which put an end to Zubatov's influence in the Police Department. Although Men'shchikov remained in the Department, he was transferred to Warsaw, and upon his recall to St Petersburg 18 months later, was told that his services were no longer required. Hurt, he tendered his resignation and demanded a pension of 700 roubles per month. This was rejected. Suddenly he disappeared from St Petersburg without a trace. Only in the autumn of 1910 did it emerge that he was behind the letters to the editor signed 'Ivanov', which contained details about secret police agents and were published in the press.[24]

For a time Burtsev and Men'shchikov worked together. However, Burtsev soon began to cool towards him, accusing him, *inter alia*, of seeking publicity and of attempting to have the best of both worlds: to be a hero in the eyes of the revolutionaries on the one hand, but to keep his true identity secret so as not to lose his police pension on the other hand. Be that as it may, his defection led to the exposure of a good many police agents who were operating in the ranks of the revolutionaries. Between August 1909 and January 1910 Men'shchikov provided lists of 200 agents classified according to parties: 90 among the Social Democrats, 21 in the Bund, 28 among the SRs and 75 in the Polish organizations. Zinaida Zhuchenko was conspicuous among the agents in the SR party.[25]

For the definitive identification of secret agents, the information provided by Men'shchikov, based on his documents, was insufficient. As will be recalled, agents in police documents appear under codenames, and in some cases their identities were only hinted at. This made further investigation mandatory. Thus, for example, Men'shchikov told Burtsev that among the SRs was an extremely important female agent, and that it was she who had informed the police of the plot to assassinate the Tsar in Moscow. Nothing further was known about her. Nevertheless, this information led Burtsev to recall another affair, also set in Moscow, involving some of the persons who had been connected with the plot against the Tsar; among them was a woman named Gerngross. About a month later the SRs' Central Committee informed him that in Moscow suspicions had been raised against Zinaida Zhuchenko.[26]

The first to suspect Zhuchenko was her comrade in the Moscow organization, Anna Pribyleva. It was not the fact that Zhuchenko always managed to survive all the calamities that came and went around her that alerted Pribyleva, but a seemingly minor detail: Zhuchenko's repeated deferrals of her trip abroad to visit her son, even though her comrades urged her to go. Every time she was to have gone, she reappeared without offering a satisfactory explanation. Pribyleva had the impression that Zhuchenko was determined to conclude some urgent business which she was concealing from her comrades. It subsequently emerged that she was on the verge of turning in the organization members to the police. Finally on the eve of her journey, as she was taking her leave of Pribyleva over the phone and wishing her well, Zhuchenko suddenly laughed bizarrely and incongrously, a kind of guffaw of *Schadenfreude* which Pribyleva could on no account reconcile with the laugh of a person departing from a friend and sincerely wishing her well. Shortly afterwards, when she was arrested along with her comrades in the organization, she no longer had any doubt as to Zhuchenko's true role.[27] Although these suspicions were as yet unverified, an investigation was nevertheless launced. As was customary, comrades who had operated with Zhuchenko in various periods were asked to tell what they knew and to indicate any signs that seemed even the least suspicious. It turned out that Zhuchenko's previous name was Gerngross.[28] Thus the circle closed around her. The Central Committee thought it best not to issue an immediate communiqué about the betrayal. Instead, they suggested to Burtsev that as the editor of *Byloe* he try to extract a detailed confession from Zhuchenko, covering everything she knew about 'the world of provocation'. Burtsev made contact with her and they arranged to meet in Berlin. Zhuchenko admitted to having served in the Police Department all along, though in their ensuing correspondence she maintained repeatedly that her motivation was purely ideological.[29]

Zhuchenko's exposure caused wide reverberations in circles where she had been known as a key activist on the Moscow Regional Committee. Once again there were some who refused to believe the charges, while others were quick to draw parallels with the Azef affair and accused the Central Committee of having opposed Burtsev's inquiry against her. So intense did the rumours become that Burtsev was forced to issue a denial in the SR party organ, in which he explained what had happened and assured his readers that ever since the Azef affair he and the Central Committee had been working in close conjunction.[30]

The Central Committee had altered its attitude toward provocation in the wake of the Azef affair. All the organizations were instructed to examine meticulously their membership lists; those of unassailable reliability were to single out comrades who, for one reason or another, had aroused their suspicions. In every such case the local organizations were advised to establish a special commission of inquiry to clarify the matter.[31] In the meantime, new exposures were reported, rumours were rife about Men'shchikov, and there was tense expectation of imminent and spectacular new revelations. This atmosphere is reflected in the files of the Okhrana's Foreign Agency in reports such as: 'Lists of names and copies of documents of secret agents are about to be published. There is talk of mass exposures, particularly of persons connected with the Okhrana in Moscow.'[32] 'Attached is a copy of issue no. 24 of *Parizhskii Listok* ('The Parisian Leaflet') which contains a letter to the editor signed by "Ivanov". . . . According to information supplied by the Agency, this "Ivanov" has already exposed some 40 agents, and the list of their names which was conveyed to the parties will shortly be published. . . . To date it has proved impossible to discover the identity of "Ivanov".'[33]

The call for alertness, combined with the constant anticipation of exposures and revelations, led to an obsessive preoccupation with the provocation issue. Suddenly the SR party's Foreign Delegation was flooded with reports, suspicions, mutual recriminations and gossip from all sides, to the point where it could no longer handle it all. Until then the Delegation had received this kind of information and had then passed it on for handling to the Central Committee. If it proved substantive, an *ad hoc* commission of inquiry was appointed, as in the case of Tatarov; that is, a commission of inquiry to examine the one specific case. But beginning in 1911 the Delegation was forced to convey all this incoming information to the Conspiracy Committee, which was in touch with comrades in Russia. Through them the preliminary clarifications were made, and only if anything of substance turned up was the matter referred to the commission of inquiry.[34]

Unlike the past, the commission of inquiry was now a permanent, active institution. Appointed by the Central Committee, it was generally composed of two members. Even though it was an appointed body, it could not be dissolved, and it even enjoyed the power of veto *vis-à-vis* comrades who were co-opted to it for certain cases. Its work was conducted on two levels: investigation of certain persons who were accused of provocation, and clarification of the reasons for the downfall of organizations or of various revolutionary enterprises.[35] Thus the element of provocation became institutionalized within the party: no longer was it dealt with according to a specific ephemeral set of circumstances, nor was it handled by the Delegation or the Central Committee within the framework of their responsibilities. Instead, it was entrusted to a special institution vested with defined powers and functioning in line with fixed procedures. The commission might undertake an investigation on its own initiative, or on the basis of complaints it received. Following the inquiry, it had to conclude whether the defendant's guilt had been proved, basing itself solely on documentary evidence and objective data – that is, without resort to interpretations or circumstantial evidence.[36] As a result, its conclusions were, effectively, oriented in one direction only: if definitive evidence was found, the commission could determine the suspect's guilt with certainty, but without such evidence all it could do was to note that fact, without being able to determine the suspect's innocence unequivocally – for there were no documents or objective data that could demonstrate beyond doubt that someone was not in contact with the Okhrana.

The case of Vasilii Leonovich was unique in that it seemed possible, on the face of it, to determine his innocence on the basis of a written document. But since this was the exception that proves the rule, and since it also serves to illustrate the commission of inquiry's method of operation, as well as other points mentioned in the study, it deserves our attention.

Leonovich was a member of the Northern Regional committee and served as its liaison with Karl's Flying Detachment. The detachment had been created parallel to the establishment of Zil'berberg's Central Organization, following the temporary dispersal of the Battle Organization. After Zil'berberg's arrest and the liquidation of his Organization, the detachment was placed under the direct authority of the Central Committee. However, if until then the detachment had chalked up successful operations such as the assassinations of Generals Min and Pavlov, once it established ties with the Central Committee it sustained one failure after another (some, though not all, of which were explained by the Azef exposure). Between the beginning of November 1907 and February 1908 all its members were arrested and most of them executed. The downfall of the Flying Detachment unleashed a major row in the party. At that time Burtsev was already in the midst of his struggle against Azef; the party's Conspiracy Committee (one of whose leading members was Iudelevskii, of the Paris opposition) asserted unequivocally that provocation existed at the party centre and the Paris opposition itself was accusing Azef openly and explicitly.

It will be recalled that Bakai, a Warsaw Okhrana official who defected from the police, played a major part in exposing Azef. Within the framework of his efforts to get other Okhrana officials to defect as well, Burtsev instructed Bakai to write to his former police colleagues in Russia, proposing that they follow his course and defect abroad, or at least supply information to Burtsev. Although both Burtsev and Bakai were convinced that most of the recipients of these letters would bring them to their superiors' attention, they nevertheless hoped that at least a few might produce an impact. One addressee who did reply and even struck up a correspondence with Bakai was Gerasimov's assistant, Dobroskok, who had himself launched his police career as a secret agent among the Social Democrats. Although it was perfectly clear to Burtsev that Dobroskok's letters were being dictated in full by Gerasimov, he maintained the correspondence with great interest, seeking to elicit the message that Gerasimov wanted to convey to him, so that he could draw the appropriate conclusions. For his part, Gerasimov was convinced that he had led Burtsev to believe that Dobroskok's letters were genuine and were thereby leading him astray.[37] While Gerasimov hoped to thwart suspicions of Azef, Burtsev hoped the letters would reveal clear proof of Azef's guilt. In one letter, Bakai, at Burtsev's instructions, asked Dobroskok what he knew about four persons he mentioned. The first name was fabricated, the second was someone whose reliability was in question, the third was Azef and the fourth was also made up. In their reply Dobroskok and Gerasimov wrote that the first was undoubtedly a *provocateur*, the second was a victim of false accusations, the third – Azef – was not known, while there were doubts about the fourth. Burtsev was well aware that Azef's name must be known to Gerasimov and Dobroskok, either as a revolutionary or as a *provocateur*. Thus their claim never to have heard of him could have only one meaning: they were trying to protect him and to divert suspicions elsewhere. Indeed, they had even enclosed a fake document, ostensibly showing that Leonovich, a veteran, high-ranking Socialist Revolutionary, was a paid secret agent.[38] Burtsev claimed to have grasped immediately that the document was false – since it sought to cast aspersions on a blameless revolutionary – and had therefore disregarded it.[39] However, the document's existence became known, and since the collapse of the Northern Organization had raised such strong feelings, and the exposure of Azef had been so traumatic, rumours about Leonovich's supposed treachery also began to circulate early in 1909. On 31 January Leonovich wrote to the Central Committee:

> Rumours have recently reached me which are tarnishing my personal honour and my revolutionary repute. Since I do not know the source of these rumours and have no way of freeing myself of the burden of this base suspicion – even though I have done absolutely nothing to merit it – I demand to be tried by the party at once, so that all aspects of my twenty-year party activity can be investigated . . . .[40]

A special commission of inquiry was appointed to look into the Leonovich affair and began its work at the end of February. Unlike the Tatarov case, for example, the inquiry was not almost exclusively based on the testimony of the suspect himself, but evidence was given by many comrades who had known him during his lengthy period in the revolutionary movement. The witnesses were requested to point to any detail that might have aroused their suspicion. The Leonovich case produced two written testimonies, while 11 persons testified orally before the commission. Testimonies of this kind were normally taken from comrades abroad as well as in Russia, and included a good many details about the life of the person under investigation. The commission was also given the fake document and Dobroskok's six letters to Bakai which reiterated the charge contained in the document. In addition, the commission examined copies of the indictments handed down in the trials of several members of the Flying Detachment, including that of 'Karl'. Leonovich himself was questioned during six sittings, four of them consecutive. It was no simple matter to withstand such an interrogation. It meant being ready to reveal and explain every detail of one's personal life without contradicting not only one's own previous statements made during a protracted inquiry, but also the evidence given (in this case) by 13 other persons whose testimonies remained secret and whose reliability, unlike one's own, was not in question. In fact, no sphere was deemed irrelevant in these inquiries, and there was no question that the suspect was permitted to evade. The inquiry was designed to determine whether there was anything suspicious about the suspect's life, to examine his financial resources, and to clarify as far as possible whether details, whose discovery by the police had led to the failure of party actions or projects, might have been available to the suspect. Normally the person under investigation was suspended from all party activity for the duration of the inquiry. He was kept at arm's length from his organization, indeed he was effectively removed from the party, entailing his social isolation, in some cases, for months on end. Leonovich decreed such isolation for himself when he approached the Central Committee; however, if the suspect was connected with party activity in Russia, the delegation imposed the isolation.[41]

Besides the fake document and Dobroskok's letters to Bakai, incriminating evidence against Leonovich came from Eduard Trauberg, the brother of 'Karl'. He related that the series of failures sustained by the Flying Detachment had led 'Karl' to suspect the handiwork of a *provocateur*, and he had therefore decided to conduct an experiment to ascertain whether the source of the provocation lay with the detachment itself or at the centre, meaning the Regional Committee. To that end he had met the Committee's representative, Leonovich, at Viborg to discuss an assassination plan. On the day agreed for the attack he stationed unarmed persons who were not members of the Detachment at prearranged locations. One of them, a woman who was to appear with a pram as the signal for the operation to commence, was arrested even before she reached the designated site. The others, who were waiting in a restaurant, noticed an unusually large number of policemen and managed to escape. 'Karl' was convinced that the traitor was Leonovich. Although, according to Eduard, 'Karl' did not inform the Detachment members about his experiment in the course of a consultation with them, the Detachment's conditions of secrecy were improved and contacts with the Regional Committee were severed. 'Karl' refused even to speak to Leonovich.

The commission of inquiry perused this testimony thoroughly, seeking by various means to clarify which details of the assassination scheme Leonovich might have known. Finally, after two months of inquiry, the commission published its conclusions: Leonovich, it was noted, had pledged to reveal everything he knew and to conceal nothing – and had kept his word. His replies to the commission's queries about insufficiently clear points were perfectly credible and satisfactory. No contradictions emerged in his re-examination. The commission itself found fault with the police document, and the explanations of Burtsev, who was one of the witnesses, proved its suspicions about it to have been well-founded. A precise examination of Eduard Trauberg's incriminating evidence led the commission to conclude that Leonovich could not have had the slightest idea about the assassination plan; nor, indeed, had there been any meeting with 'Karl' at Viborg. Thus, the entire experiment proved nothing against Leonovich. Nor did the commission discover anything amiss in the defendant's style of life or with his financial resources. In view of these findings, the commission ruled that Leonovich was not guilty of the charges against him and that he was cleared of any suspicion of contact with the police. Moreover, the commission noted that in the course of the lengthy investigation it had considered all possible information, adding that it was inconceivable that new evidence on the subject would come to light. Since the affair had been thoroughly exhausted, the commission recommended to the Central Committee that the case be considered closed.[42]

Although the commission of inquiry's *modus operandi* was evidently more thorough and more reliable than other investigative possibilities, it nevertheless fanned the flames of suspicion and mistrust that were rampant in the party following Azef's exposure and the others in his wake. That many acquaintances of a suspect were asked to testify about his activity could not long remain a secret, and this also fanned rumours already rife. The same applied to the custom of isolating comrades for the duration of an inquiry against them. Undoubtedly this was an important precautionary measure, taken due to the lessons gleaned from the experience with Azef, who throughout the inquiry against him had remained at his post, where he had access to the most closely guarded party secrets. However, the isolation process also necessitated letting many persons in on the fact that an inquiry was underway, causing the wave of whisperings and suspicions to mount, which in its turn brought about numerous charges and applications to the commission. Thus, paradoxically, the party's heightened caution following its blatant failure in handling the Azef affair, only brought it new troubles – to the point where an inquiry's effectiveness was sometimes harmed if the general good required that secrecy be maintained.[43]

The commission's recommendation in the Leonovich case – to regard it as closed – was exceptional among the rulings of similar commissions. Since the chief source of the suspicions against him was the police document whose forgery and malicious purpose had been established, the commission was able to rule that no new information was likely to be forthcoming and to hand down a definitive, final judgment. This contrasted with many other cases as mentioned above, in which not only were no objective proofs or documents available which could actually demonstrate that no contacts with the police had taken place, but further information could always be expected from sources to which there was no access. Some inquiries lasted for years, reappearing on the agenda of the commission each time new facts surfaced: for example, the case of Iashchurzhinskaia-Postnikova, which dragged on for over five years.[44] These limitations, primarily the result of the need to conduct an inquiry in underground conditions, were not the lot of the SRs alone. Yet it was precisely among the Socialist Revolutionaries that these circumstances produced grave and at times tragic results, due to their obsessive preoccupation with provocation in an agitated, tension-ridden atmosphere. The victims of the inquiries were sometimes honest and untainted revolutionaries, such as Tatiana Lapina, who, unable to muster the strength to cope with this tortuous justice, took her own life.

The suspicions that eventuated in her death first surfaced during a friendly dinner of several SRs from circles close to the party centre. At the table a conversation was mentioned which, it was rumoured, had taken place among several Russian Senate members. They had ostensibly referred to

> a woman, not so young, who is very close to terrorist circles and who has been gaoled more than once and borne the prisoner's share of suffering, a revolutionary in every fibre of her body, and yet for all that – in the service of the police.[45]

It was said to have been Prince Urusov, who sympathized with the revolutionaries and may have maintained secret contacts with them, who mentioned the rumour.[46] Although the identity of the Socialist Revolutionary in question was not revealed at that dinner, those present could not but brood lingeringly on who she might be. Suspicion fell on Tatiana Lapina, known in the party by her code-name 'Bela'. Everything seemed to fit. She had been a member of the Battle Organization since 1905, had worked hand in hand with Azef, had held important posts in the party. Now in her thirties, she had already been serving the cause of the revolution for close to 20 years. She had been arrested several times and exiled to Iakutsk, but had escaped and made her way to Paris in 1908. The phrase 'a revolutionary in every fibre of her body' fitted her perfectly. She was known for her absolute dedication to work, disdaining any talk of rest. 'She had no life except the [revolutionary] struggle, and she knew no other way of struggle but terrorism.'[47] The comrades exchanged glances. Without a word being said, it was clear they all suspected the same woman.[48] They urgently demanded that the Central Committee should check the information and as an interim measure asked the Committee to caution all her close friends. This the Committee refused, although it did decide to take all the necessary measures to expedite the inquiry into the *provocateur's* identity. However, after a lengthy investigation failed to turn up any results, the committee yielded to the comrades' vigorous remonstrations and warned persons close to Lapina about the suspicions against her. Rumours now spread rapidly, evidently from an additional source. Lapina sensed the change in attitude towards her. One of her friends disregarded the Central Committee's admonition and told her that she was under suspicion. When the committee replied to her query by informing her that no investigation was underway, she demanded an immediate inquiry to clear her name.[49] She was ready to tell the commission members whatever they wanted to know. However, to determine her innocence unequivocally, the commission required factual material which was not in her possession.[50] Lapina then decided to leave the party. In a letter to the Central Committee she declared that her continued work under such conditions was impossible, adding that 'the atmosphere that has been created is destroying all faith in the sanctity of party activity'. She also resolved to leave Russia, turn herself in to the police, and to renounce her membership of the Battle Organization. She sought to save her revolutionary honour by going to the gallows. After she made her decision known to the movement's Fifth Council, which was then in session, two comrades were sent to dissuade her from this course of action – but to no avail. Broken in spirit, she shot herself. In her suicide note she wrote, 'I am forgoing my plan only because my physical strength has given out. I have only one request: be careful how you treat others. In this atmosphere I am incapable either of working or of living.'[51] A few days later it emerged that the secret agent referred to by the rumour was Zinaida Zhuchenko.

The demands for documentary or objective proofs in order to determine a suspect's guilt or innocence could lead to tragic results in the case of a loyal and dedicated revolutionary such as Tatiana

Lapina. On the other hand, this method was precisely the hope of secret agents who came under suspicion. They evinced great self-confidence, dismissed the accusations contemptuously – and ran to their case officers in order to seal gaps in their defence. It will be recalled, for example, that Alexander Mass told his comrades in Paris that he had inherited a large sum of money, no less than $125 000. When Mass learned that Burtsev had told the members of the delegation that he had information concerning Mass's connections with the Okhrana, he remained calm and said offhandedly that even though such declarations had of late become rather routine, he was still surprised and hurt. . . . Nevertheless, he could not but smile, and he certainly would not remain silent. He also demanded to see the evidence of his supposed guilt. Mass, who was personally close to Sletov, a member of the commission of inquiry, and enjoyed the confidence of the leadership, felt quite sure of himself. He himself suggested that the commission look into the matter. Naturally the question of the inheritance came up at once. Mass claimed that the money had been deposited in the National Bank in Paris and that each month a notary received part of the interest from the bank, 1000 francs (the amount of Mass's salary from the Okhrana), and then transferred the funds to him. The fortune had been left him by relatives, he explained, but it would be a few years before it actually came into his possession – after it was absolutely clear that he had severed his ties with the revolutionaries, had found gainful employment and had achieved a certain social standing. By the terms of the will, Mass claimed, his sister, who lived in the United States, could halt the interest payments and deprive him of the inheritance should it emerge that he had not broken his relations with the party. The notary handling the matter had informed him of this, Mass explained. Although nothing could have been simpler than to ascertain the veracity of the story from the bank, the commission of inquiry opted to allow Mass to produce confirmation in the form of a letter from the notary. Promising to produce the document, Mass immediately asked the Foreign Agency to find someone who would confirm the tale. The Head of the Agency made great efforts in this direction, he fired off an urgent request to the Director of the Police Department to allow him to give the notary a sum of money. However, the immense amount cited by Mass, together with the detailed fabrications he had conjured up to lend the story credibility, now backfired. Obviously the Police Department could not come up with such a vast sum of money, nor could a notary be found who would agree to sign a false confirmation. The result was that after repeated delays, which Mass accounted for by citing all manner of technical problems stemming from the terms of the will or the notary's absence from Paris, he was unable to explain his financial sources and therefore was declared an *agent provocateur*.[52]

Another agent, also in the Paris Group for the SR Party, made a more modest request. To account for his economic resources, he asked that a sum of money equal to three months' salary be deposited in a bank in his name. The benefit this agent had brought the Police Department led the Okhrana's Paris office to recommend that the request be fulfilled; the 3600 francs were subsequently deducted from the agent's salary at a rate of 200 francs per month.[53] This agent, Andrei Demetrashvili, managed to ward off the suspicions raised against him and was only finally exposed after the Revolution of 1917.

The cases of both Mass who was exposed and Demetrashvili who overcame the charges against him, contributed, each in its own way, to the foul, embittered atmosphere that now pervaded the party: the former due to the surprise and gloom generated by his treachery; the latter because of the anger at what seemed to be unjust and at times fatal blows to innocent victims. Most of the wrath was directed at Burtsev who, as the moving force behind the relentless series of revelations, was also held responsible for the social climate they had produced.

The SRs' relations with Burtsev were complex and complicated. Memories of the bitter struggle Burtsev had waged against them in the period preceding the Azef exposure were just one reason for the grudge they held against him. An equally important element in the relations that were created between him and the party because of the role he undertook – as the hunter of traitors in the ranks of the revolution – involved his political motives.[54] The fact that in the Azef affair Burtsev had been right while the others had been forced to pay the heavy price of his triumph certainly did not increase their sympathy for him, though it did force them to be ultra-cautious in order to avoid further scandals or accusations. This ambivalent attitude found expression in, for example, the remarks of Sletov, a member of the commission of inquiry and a personal friend of Mass, who prior to the final proof of the latter's guilt held a friendly conversation with him, and while expressing a warm attitude of trust and comradeship, evinced 'surprising hatred' for Burtsev. He said he was certain Burtsev was wrong and that another agent was actually hiding behind

Mass. He accused Burtsev of 'having already gone beyond the bounds of simple ethics', adding that he, Sletov, would be happy to put an end to the demoralization that Burtsev had injected into the party, and stating his hope that he could effect this by proving Mass's innocence.[55] In contrast, in another case that was referred to the Delegation, a veteran party member whom Burtsev suspected of maintaining ties with the Okhrana requested to be allowed to carry on with his non-party post as an organizer of tours for teachers from Russia. However, even though Burtsev's investigation turned up nothing, even though the absence of any factual basis for the suspicion meant that the matter was not even referred to the commission of inquiry, and even though the Delegation formed a favourable impression of the man, some comrades, including Natanson, nevertheless argued that the party could not risk giving such permission in case it should ultimately turn out that Burtsev was right. One comrade even suggested that the Delegation and Burtsev grant the permission jointly so that responsibility would not devolve exclusively on the Delegation.[56]

Burtsev's activity may be compared with that of the commission of inquiry in terms of its heightening of the atmosphere of agitation and tension in the SR party. His connections with the party's central institutions had no formal basis. Customarily, he would send official letters to the Delegation, or inform Natanson personally about his suspicions, since the latter was a member of the party's Conspiracy Committee. Only if the suspicions were sufficiently grounded to enable their publication would Natanson bring them on to the knowledge of the Delegation, which then passed them on to the commission of inquiry. Natanson justified this procedure by citing the need to keep insufficiently grounded suspicions a secret until the time when enough evidence was accumulated for the matter to be referred to the commission. The result was that many items of information that Burtsev gave Natanson were never handled by the commission of inquiry, nor indeed were they ever brought to the official knowledge of the Delegation. This procedure, combined with the commission of inquiry's insistence on the rule that a person could be convicted only on the basis of objective or documentary data, was another reason for that constant tension between Burtsev and the SR leadership. If Burtsev thought that his information was not getting the attention it deserved or that an inquiry was not being conducted vigorously enough, he would present his case to various comrades and thereby help to spread the rumours.[57] This activity may have exerted pressure on the party's investigative institutions, but it definitely intensified opposition to Burtsev and to his methods. Many comrades were fed up with the mood that had enveloped the party and held Burtsev largely responsible for that frame of mind. Nor did this help dissipate the tension or to divert the obsession with provocation to a less emotional, more rational path. On the contrary, it only added one more emotional element to an already turbulent state of affairs.

One such emotional storm flared up following the suicide of Ivan Tsytsin. Burtsev suspected him of being in contact with the Okhrana, but since he himself was not completely certain of the reliability of his source and lacked the required factual proof, he acceeded to Natanson's request to keep the matter a secret. Burtsev's suspicion was aroused by a conversation whose content was made known to him. In that conversation Dobroskok spoke of the random circumstances to which a secret agent was liable to fall victim. As an example, he cited the case of a postcard inviting Tsytsin to a meeting at the Eiffel Tower, and which had been found by Tsytsin's lodging companion – fortunately without arousing his suspicion. However, since in itself this story was not an adequate basis for an inquiry to be launched, Burtsev approached the suspect and several of his friends. They retorted fiercely, charging that Burtsev was simply a maniac being fed false reports by Okhrana personnel whose aim was to destroy loyal and dedicated revolutionaries. None the less, following pressure from Burtsev, Natanson agreed to summon Tsytsin for an inquiry to explain the meaning of the postcard. On the morning of the date set for the inquiry, Tsytsin shot himself in the railway station at Versailles. He left a note stating that he had been compelled to take his own life because of the severe and suffocating conditions in the party. That same day Natanson appeared at Burtsev's flat; furious, and deeply upset, he told him about the suicide and requested that the scheduled inquiry remain a secret.[58]

The Tsytsin affair emphasized Natanson's ambivalent attitude towards Burtsev. On the one hand he feared that he would be accused of inaction if Tsytsin's guilt were eventually established, and so he consented to the inquiry even though Burtsev's evidence was extremely meagre. On the other hand, when Tsytsin took his own life – which was considered proof of his innocence – Natanson feared the ensuing scandal if the Delegation were held responsible for causing the death of a blameless revolutionary.

It should be noted that this was the third suicide since the Azef affair against a background of suspected provocation. Thus the SRs, convinced of their comrade's revolutionary integrity, followed his coffin carrying red banners and wreaths in the name of the party. One of the eulogists at the funeral maintained that Tsytsin had fallen victim to party rivalries and to a new tendency towards mutual suspicion. Burtsev declared that he was assuming moral responsibility for the affair.[59] It was only afterwards, when Tsytsin's papers were being sorted, that his correspondence with his Okhrana case officer was found, including the postcard in Dobroskok's handwriting. An official party communiqué definitively declared Tsytsin's guilt.[60] Nevertheless, even if the episode was a triumph for Burtsev, and despite its unexpected *dénouement*, it did far more to whip up agitation than it did for the overall good of the cause as Burtsev understood it.

The most lethal consequences of provocation were not in the area of the human relations within the party. The mutual suspicion and mistrust generated by the manifestations of provocation seemingly affected the SRs at a far deeper level of revolutionary identification: their sense of moral quality. Paradoxically, this moral crisis stemmed precisely from the perception of the Tsarist police as the forefathers of the abomination, and treachery and provocation as its offspring. If these constituted utterly loathsome crime, baseness and sin, then anyone who suspected the innocent drove them to suicide. No moral, decent person could allow himself to be the subject of such an accusation.[61]

Tatiana Lapina's suicide proves at least the first part of the assessment, namely, that in her view the accusation of provocation was a moral accusation of the worst possible kind, while Natanson's behaviour in the Tsytsin affair indicates that for many SRs its second part was also correct. His demand that Burtsev should keep the scheduled investigation secret, shows that he could not bear the moral responsibility for Tsytsin's death. The evidence cited shows that so routine had accusations and suspicions become that the Delegation came to view the defence of innocent revolutionaries as one of its major tasks, and more important than the exposure of the *provocateurs* themselves.[62]

The party's smooth absorption of *provocateurs*, who were considered of inferior human quality, also raised doubts about the party's entire social fabric. Was the party comparable to a pus-infested body? Was it possible that in the last analysis the human quality of the party members and the leaders was not as fine as was initially believed, so that the *provocateurs* had not appeared to deviate from the norm?[63]

Inevitably, besides the comrades' sense of moral quality, the situation also adversely affected the party's unswerving confidence in the justice of its way and its members' sense of solidarity and revolutionary partnership. Only those qualities could be a driving force behind the dedication and self-sacrifice which were a prerequisite for genuine revolutionary activity. A sense of moral quality, unassailable confidence in the rightness of the struggle, revolutionary solidarity: these were the functional constituents of the revolutionary and any vitiation of that ethos must lead to questions and doubts centring on ethical issues. It is precisely such problems that are raised in the letter of the Munich Group for the SR Party to the Foreign Delegation:

> Due to a whole chain of circumstances, a tendency is discernible among the *émigrés* in our party to legalize party activity by voluntarily returning to the place of deportation (*ssylka)*, by providing guarantees to the State authorities, or even, simply, by submitting a request to the Tsar and Stolypin to regard their time abroad as part of the deportation period. This tendency has led some of us to seek to examine these and similar concessions from the point of view of revolutionary ethics.[64]

There is no similarity between this stand and the behaviour of Lev Tikhomirov or the Executive Committee of the *Narodnaia Volia* who forsook his revolutionary life, asked permission to return to Russia, and became a declared supporter of the Tsarist régime. The members of the Munich group had no intention of foregoing their party allegiance; in effect, they were willing to forsake their revolutionary essence but not their right to be called revolutionaries – hence their soul-searching over questions of ethics. In their letter they call into question the party's traditional ethical posture in whose name generations of revolutionaries had refused to co-operate with the Tsarist courts or to recognize their right to judge, not to mention any thought of compromising with the authorities.

For the Munich group its proposal was a compromise, not unlike residence abroad remote from the revolutionary struggle – yet no one was questioning the oddness of remaining abroad while Russia bled. Moreover, there was no difference between those who requested that the Tsar or Stolypin regard their period of residence abroad as part of their term of deportation, and those who asked to be sent abroad instead of being deported. Any distinction between those two courses of action was not qualitative but merely quantitative, the group maintained. Having made these two points, the group requested the party's institutions to place a list of questions it submitted on the agenda, the intention being to show that essentially these questions did not differ from the party's stand on the issue of the return to Russia on the terms it proposed; yet this was considered acceptable among revolutionary circles, and at any rate led neither to condemnation nor expulsion. Was it permissible to negotiate with the authorities about reducing a prison sentence, through relatives, personally, orally or in writing? Did a comrade have the right to consider himself a party member after pledging to the authorities that he would not engage in revolutionary activity in order to get his sentence reduced? Under what circumstances and to what degree could the bribing of government officials be condoned from the point of view of revolutionary ethics? Could one in the name of those same ethics, violate one's word of honour to the authorities? In terms of revolutionary ethics, were there any qualitative differences between political *émigrés* and 'returnees', between someone who wrote a 'declaration' to a governor in order to have his sentence reduced and made use of guarantees provided by his relatives or his lawyer, and a person who submitted a request to the Tsar, even if only formally? Was the Central Committee aware of cases of party members who had made compromises of this kind, and if so, could its silence about them be explained? Was such behaviour condoned in principle, or was it something shameful which was to be tacitly disregarded? If the latter, would the Central Committee suggest to such a person that he should leave the party or not? Had efforts been made to prevent such behaviour? From the point of view of revolutionary ethics, was a member of the SR party permitted to surrender to the government without a struggle, to turn himself in to the court and to go to prison of his own volition, to recognize the court, and to yield to the prison or the deportation authorities who humiliate the revolutionary honour? And could a party member who had been deported or gone abroad adopt a line of minimal resistance in his private life? In other words, was the private life of a party member his own personal matter or was it open to a general critique?[65]

The existence of an ethos is not necessarily contingent on a strict adherence to its tenets by each and every individual. An ethos also can exist as an attitude or an ideal. Yet the moment violations of its tenets are sanctioned or given official recognition, the ethos ceases to exist. What is the import of the refusal to recognize the Tsarist courts and their power to pass judgment if not an unequivocal declaration that the revolutionary identity is nobler and morally higher and the utter rejection of the Tsarist régime and all its institutions?

Only the revolutionaries' sense of justice and morality, as against their perception of the autocracy as the domain of evil justified their uncompromising terrorist struggle in their own eyes. Readiness to return to Russia by the grace of that régime and on its terms was tantamount to forsaking a moral identity as a supreme existential value, one which could not come to terms with the rule of evil and certainly could not co-exist with it. That readiness in itself voided the revolutionary essence of all content. The demand to place the question of such readiness on the agenda for discussion in order to gain assent and recognition shows that at least for those who wished to discuss this element of the revolutionary ethos, it no longer existed.

Among all the events that afflicted the party after the Azef affair, it is a reasonable assumption that in this crisis over its ethos, the issue of provocation played a considerable role.

(ii) PROVOCATION AND INTERNAL STRIFE

The potentially explosive nature of all evidence or suspicion of provocation was now clear to all. The Azef affair, followed by many other episodes, demonstrated that the exposure of treachery or a suspicion of its existence never ended with the indictment of the traitor or the clearing of a suspect. Everyone unfortunate enough to be involved was swept up by the cyclone: those who should have suspected but did not, those who were subsequently blamed for harbouring false suspicions, comrades who fervently and in good faith defended a colleague whose treachery was later proved, or those who had unknowingly nurtured a *provocateur* whose exposure cast a heavy shadow over them and their activity. It is obvious why provocation was apprehended as a contagious disease which was to be avoided at all costs. Just as the shock waves of the Azef affair made it a convenient tag on which to hang all manner of controversial opinions, so too did provocation as a whole become an effective instrument for deliberate use in political power struggles within the party. This may well be a further reflection of the ethical crisis that developed in the party's ranks. Irrespective of the substantive content of the debates or disputes, the very use made of the provocation issue indicates its transformation into a destructive political weapon employed, most ironically, by the revolutionaries against one another. As we have seen, the reason for this lay in the emotional charge that suddenly burst into the open after years of repression, against the background of the shock caused by the Azef affair, combined with the sense of failure and the questions the affair posed for the party's past and its achievements. The methods and the mode of this deliberate usage will be examined in three cases which were far from accidental in the annals of the party: that of the Paris opposition, the Veber-Argunov affair, and the Postnikova (*née* Iashchurzhinskaia) case.

The first conscious and deliberate usage of the provocation issue occurred in the struggle of the Paris opposition against the veteran SR leadership, which had begun even before the eruption of the Azef affair. Originally, the opposition had organized on ideological grounds, over a reassessment of the defeat of 1905. However, there seem to be good reasons for the police appraisal [66] that personal ambitions also played a key role in the course of events that eventually led to the Paris opposition's total withdrawal from the party framework abroad (and effectively from the entire official party framework) and to the publication of a separate opposition organ called *Revoliutsionnaia Mysl'* ('Revolutionary Thought').[67] In it the opposition gave expression to the Socialist Revolutionary aim of the 'Initiating Minority' (*initsiativnoe men'shinstvo*) with which the group regarded itself as being affiliated although it understood its application differently. It was for this reason that it chose the term as its name.

The idea of the Initiating Minority actually harked back to the tactics of the Narodnaia Volia, criticizing the SR leadership which, because of its pointless expectation of a mass uprising, had missed the great opportunity of 1905. That expectation, the opposition surmised, was based on a dual idealization whose damage was also two-pronged: on the one hand full confidence in the inevitable historical process leading to a mass uprising; on the other, complete faith that the oppressed strata of the people were ready and willing to take up arms and join the struggle. This idealization had, in the opposition's view simultaneously generated harmful optimism and crippling pessimism, since the expectations were not realized. History knew many instances of the suppression and enslavement of a majority by a minority which had endured for generations. Why then should the Russian revolutionaries view a mass revolution as axiomatic? And if it were in fact not feasible due to certain historical constraints, this outlook decreed that the revolutionaries should sit with folded hands or confine themselves to cultural activity. Thus the party would lose its role as in independent entity, while its role as an Initiating Minority would become inconsequential. 'Only the narrow-minded and the disbelievers regard the principle of the operation of the Initiating Minority as a foolish idea.' To this criticism the opposition added that the leadership was disregarding the prodigious role such a minority had played in the history of science and technology, and in human culture generally. True, the opposition acknowledged, in the political sphere the struggle for liberation depended on the reciprocal relations between the various social forces, but those relations were not quantitative. Just as a majority could be exploited by a minority, so could the majority be liberated by an initiating minority whose strength lay in its moral supremacy, its manner of organization and its methods of struggle.

A political revolution, the opposition argued, could be fomented only by a revolutionary minority, and this held true also *vis-à-vis* absolutism in Russia. Pointing an accusing finger, the opposition contended that instead of extensive mass activity the party leadership should have organized an intensive struggle against the régime, with the mass support the party enjoyed among all strata of the population throughout the country serving only in an auxiliary role. What Russia needed was an intensive struggle, not an extensive one, which led nowhere. 'Now or never', the opposition summed up its case.

> The Russian revolution will triumph only through the tactics of the initiating minority. It has no need for hollow revolutionary rhetoric or for mere cultural activity. What it requires is combat activity. No longer a miserable life of stagnation in a harsh atmosphere employing well-worn patterns of action, but a courageous initiative and a creative struggle.[68]

The idea of the 'Initiating Minority' was an old one which had been bandied about in various forms throughout the party's history. Its resurfacing now meant a return not only to the tactics of the Narodnaia Volia, but also to debates which had preceded the party's first congress. The idea of the autonomous battle units, mentioned above in connection with the debate that followed the Azef affair, was a byproduct of the concept of the Initiating Minority. For those who advocated this idea or this organizational solution, as the opposition understood it, the autonomous battle squads were the instrument that was to realize it. Since they were subsequently posited as the only way to prevent the centre from being harmed by provocation, we find here yet another example of the political use of the provocation issue and its transformation into a driving force of ideas within the party.

However, this ideological argument served only as a framework for a bitter personal campaign between the opposition members who headed the Paris SR group at that time, and the party's veteran leadership, and it was only at a relatively late stage in the struggle that it made its appearance in this form. Its origins evidently lay in personal tensions between key party figures such as Argunov, Avksentiev, Fundaminsky, Nikolaev, Bilit, Seliuk and others, all of whom had held or were holding central party posts. Against them were aligned comrades of the second rank such as Agafonov and his wife and Iudelevskii – 'persons of the periphery' (a term drawn from Chernov's letter describing his ouster from the hierarchy at one point). They began to voice complaints against members of the Foreign Committee. This criticism seems to have been taken particularly seriously because it smacked of the Maximalist secession, which was still a sore spot for the party. The activism manifested by the group's members as reflected in the ideas of the Initiating Minority was also suspected, and not without reason, of being close to Maximalism. At all events, the opposition members maintained that according to the constitution which was accepted in most of the foreign groups, a comrade who wished to return to Russia for operational activity was to be referred by his group to the Foreign Committee in order to obtain recommendations, addresses, passports and financial means. However, the Paris group committee – which was made up mainly of opposition members – alleged that any comrade it referred to the Foreign Committee suddenly faced an interrogation as to his party orthodoxy, his support of the party platform and similar queries, and was invariably informed that the committee lacked the required means to send him to Russia on its behalf. Yet the Paris group claimed, there was no such lack of resources when it came to the dispatch of comrades whose views were consistent with those of the Foreign Committee. This seems to have been the background to the bitterness felt towards the Committee members, leading to calls for the severance of all contact with it.

Some of those who were turned down chose to go to Russia in Maximalist groups. This and other developments led to heightened accusations that the Paris group tended towards Maximalism.

Compounding everything were personal tensions between persons such as Iudelevskii and Rubanovich of the Bureau of Socialist International. There were also allegations that the party was being run 'in a police atmosphere.[69] Finally, after protracted squabbles, charges and counter-charges, Minor and Sletov disbanded the Paris group by virtue of their membership of the Foreign Committee. Claiming that this violated the accepted rules of the constitution, the opposition group refused to recognize the validity of the act, insisting that it was they who continued to constitute the Paris Group of the Socialist Revolutionaries. For their part, Minor and Sletov organized their supporters into a new group called the Paris Group for the SR Party. Thus two rival groups co-existed, both within the framework of the party's institutions; the orthodox 'rightist' group with 176 members, and the opposition 'leftist' group with 56 members.[70]

Prior to the dissolution of the Paris Group by the Foreign Committee, the Group's members seemed unwilling to exacerbate the dispute with the Committee or, alternatively, with the party hierarchy. Instead they sought to convene a conciliation commission to clarify the differences between them and the Committee, tried to reach understanding with Rubanovich via mediation, and agreed to retract certain offensive statements.[71] But from the moment of the dissolution, relations began to deteriorate to the point where the SR opposition group could not allow itself, as a group, to accept the 25 francs sent to needy members by the rival group.[72]

When the Group associated itself with Burtsev's charge that the downfall of Karl's Flying Detachment and the hanging of seven of its members was the result of a provocation at the party centre, an irrevocable rift occurred. It is likely that the Group's accusation did not stem from cold political calculations. In all probability its hostile stand towards the party leadership led it to believe from the outset in the possibility of treachery at the centre, and to accuse the Central Committee which was ignoring it. Yet the manner the Group chose to express its stand demonstrates that a deliberate attempt was made to exploit the pain and shock generated by this downfall in order to besmirch and undermine the moral credibility of the party leadership – in this case, members of the Foreign Committee.

As part of the leadership, the Foreign Committee rejected the accusations against Azef and the attempt to link them to the downfall of the Northern Organization. Its organ published a report stating that rumours concerning a massive provocation to which the Northern Organization had fallen prey were exaggerated. There were reasons for believing that the entire squad had been apprehended in the wake of police surveillance which had come across the trail of one of its members, Lebedintsev-Kalvino, who attracted the attention of the police in Rome, and was followed wherever he went. The report also directed the readers' attention to a Geneva periodical which had ostensibly published articles confirming this surmise.[73] On the other hand, the SR's Paris Group believed – and informed everyone – that all the facts pointed to systematic provocation that had long been brewing at the party centre.[74] However, instead of sparking a debate in which the facts would either be verified or refuted, the affair became a touchstone for 'morality' and for 'an atmosphere of comradeship'. In this raucous dispute, during which the Paris Group circulated its own resolutions accompanied by appendices on the resolutions of the other side, people were not right or wrong but moral or immoral. Not even at the height of the fiercest struggle between Burtsev and the SR party had the debate revolved around questions of morality but had been centred on facts alone. The question of Burtsev's motives or his integrity simply had not been an issue for the great majority of his opponents.

In a resolution it passed on 16 May 1908, the Group shifted the issue from the level of a substantive argument to that of a vituperative moral clash. The Group expressed deep mourning for the downfall of the Northern Organization – 'an unprecedented catastrophe' which had cost the lives of many dear comrades. Averring that the combination of circumstances indicated a systematic provocation at the party centre, the Group called on all members of the party, its activists and its institutions to do everything in their power to investigate the causes of the downfall while being aware of 'the full extent of the atrocity that has afflicted the party and every atrocity that still awaits it as long as the source of the affair is not clarified, as long as the network of the provocation is not torn apart or the evil uprooted'. At the same time, the Group accused the Foreign Committee of publishing a report of doubtful veracity designed to cast responsibility for the disaster on 'comrades who sacrificed their lives for the enterprise and who consequently are no longer able to defend their good name'.[75]

The Foreign Committee did not take this lying down. In reaction to the resolution of the Paris Group of Socialist Revolutionaries it declared that the item it had published in its organ was no more than the transmission of simple information and did not constitute a definitive allegation. Consequently, the Committee held the resolution of the Paris Group to be groundless and a manifestation 'completely out of place within a collegial framework'. As for the view that the Committee had twisted the true import of things in order to take advantage of a fallen comrade's inability to react, this was 'so stupid and unfair that its very assertion is an absurdity that hardly befits a revolutionary. As for the Paris Group's contention that all the facts pointed to a systematic provocation, if the group actually possessed such facts, its clear duty was to convey them to the party's institutions; since this had not been done, the Committee viewed its resolution as unfounded. Indeed, the Committee seemed bent on stifling the debate, and therefore explicitly rejected the demand of the Paris Group to publish its resolutions, while also refraining from publishing its own reaction.[76]

The Paris Group decided to put a stop to the public debate, but not before maintaining, in addition to its rejection of the committee's explanations and accusations, that its members' behaviour cast doubts on their morality.[77]

The first public testing ground which could indicate the degree of support for the opposition, was the party's Fourth Council, which convened in London from 21 July to 3 August 1908. It proved to be the largest party forum for many years to come. Seventy-four delegates, including 48 from Russia, took part in the 11 days of deliberations; in addition to the members of the Central Committee there were 11 guests, including former members of the Narodnaia Volia, who had been inmates at Shlissel'burg prison: German Lopatin, Vera Finger and Mikhail Frolenko. The Council session was opened by the eldest party member, Felix Volkhovskii, who spoke elegaically of the members who had recently died and had left a vacuum at the heart of the party. Among them were Karl Trauberg and Lebedintsev-Kalvino, of Karl's Flying Detachment, whose deaths were 'a gash in the living flesh of the party, a wound that will never heal'.[78] But when Iudelevskii advanced his explanations for their fall and the outlook of his group, he was rejected by a majority vote of the Council.[79] Moreover, the Council explicitly voted in favour of concentrating its best forces on centralist terrorism,[80] a resolution that contradicted both the ideas of the Initiating Minority and the opposition's allegations concerning provocation at the party centre.

The failure at the Council did not act as a deterrent. Immediately following the deliberations, Iudelevskii and other opposition members went to Italy, and apparently to Russia as well, in order to drum up support for their stands,[81] raising the banner of provocation in order to assail and embarrass the party centre. One typical incident occurred when Chernov briefed the two SR groups in Paris about the London Congress. His optimistic speech about heightened party activity was disrupted by two members of the Agafonov group who asked him what the Central Committee thought about the fact that news of its resolutions reached the police even before they were implemented. Chernov's terse reply that the matter was being looked into put an end to the discussion.[82]

Police agents in Paris assessed that Iudelevskii and Agafonov were bent on obtaining places in the Central Committee. What is clear is that the Paris group did not call itself a 'Group *for* the SR Party', but the 'Paris Group *of* the Socialist Revolutionaries'. More than a semantic difference was involved here. By its very definition as an SR group it asserted its affiliation to the party, unlike the other foreign groups. While the latter were only groups for the party, they provided outside aid and support. This definition was chosen deliberately in order to open the party's doors to sympathizers who did not regard themselves as clear-cut party members. The differences were reflected, *inter alia*, in representation at congresses and in the right to membership in party institutions by virtue of membership in the group. Although this did not rule out the possibility that a Central Committee member might also be a member of the Group for the SRs, the group as such did not have the right to send representatives to party institutions. For this reason the opposition's name – the 'Paris Group of the Socialist Revolutionaries' – was in effect a declaration of the right to hear and be heard as a fully fledged party group, and certainly also of its members' right to be elected to any party institution whatsoever. The different definition of identity, then, indicates the intention of the opposition leaders, to become a bridgehead for a new party force.

Against this background, the opposition heard the news of Azef's exposure almost joyfully. As described above, the Paris opposition outdid other groups in its reaction. Unlike most of the others, who expressed their shock at the revelation and their apprehension about the impact the betrayal would have on the party – though without blaming anyone – the opposition openly accused the Central Committee, and unlike some *émigrés* who also tended to accuse the Central Committee, the opposition rattled off its charges one by one in a manner which implicitly cast suspicion on the entire leadership.

First, like everyone else, they called for the establishment of a commission of inquiry to investigate the matter exhaustively, and also put forward a series of questions that required elucidation:

> Under what conditions and circumstances was Azef able to flourish and act in the party? What damage did he and can he cause the party? What traces did his party activity leave behind? Who might he have infiltrated into the party as his aides and successors? For it is obvious that the police could not rest satisfied with Azef's activity alone, and certainly must have instructed him to infiltrate other *provocateurs* into the party who would continue his path should he be caught.[83]

By stressing earlier in the resolution the years of close activity between the leadership and Azef; also by mentioning the leadership's stubborn and consistent defence of Azef despite various indications and evidence; and by maintaining that it was not the fact that Azef never erred that enabled him to persist with his treacherous activities – indeed, by the mere fact of putting forward the possibility that Azef had planted other *provocateurs* in the party, the opposition was implicitly casting suspicion on the entire leadership without taking the risk of saying so outright.

The Azef exposure fired the opposition with considerable self-confidence; its members believed that everyone would now acknowledge that they had been right all along and that, as the former leaders' prestige waned, their's would rise. This certainty would seem to account for the aggressive tone of all its resolutions which were circulated among the foreign groups. Their failure at the Fourth Council of the SR party was now reduced to insignificance. Although that Council had convened in the shadow of the Azef affair, Azef himself had not yet been exposed. However, the Third Congress of Foreign Groups met after the exposure, when it seemed to the opposition that

> despite the immensity of the blow . . . everyone was in the thrall of an atmosphere of change and betterment, with voices from all sides calling for a severe inquiry, a thoroughgoing purge and unsparing scrutiny . . .[84]

Thus the opposition regarded the Congress as a platform for an attack on the Central Committee.

Nevertheless, when the Congress opened, the opposition encountered a hostile atmosphere which remained unaffected by the nature of their allegations or their possible justification. The dispute broke out at once over the issue of the essence of the discussion of the Azef affair. The majority of the delegates, it turned out, did not support the opposition's viewpoint, being satisfied to hear supplementary facts about the case without addressing themselves to what the opposition termed 'its fateful consequences'. At the same time, the opposition found itself the victim of a concerted attack because of the communiqué it issued immediately following the discovery of the betrayal, entitled 'Statement about the *Provocateur* Azef'.

Although the opposition representation expressed its regret over part of the phraseology of the statement, which was 'judicially incautious', it stood by the communiqué's content and facts. The opposition delegation contended that the Congress had no right to pass a resolution concerning its statement, since the Congress represented persons and institutions who were themselves being accused of having supported Azef; thus certain participants in the Congress actually constituted an interested party which was seeking to transform itself from accused to accuser. However, this argument was not fully accepted and the delegates decided to take the minimal step of condemning the opposition's statement, though without reference to its content and essence.

Countering this, the opposition delegation charged that to examine the form of the statement without appraising its content was illogical, adding that it would refuse to be present when such a resolution was passed. It proposed the immediate appointment of an objective commission of inquiry into the entire affair which would summon witnesses, examine documents and then determine its position *vis-à-vis* the document as a whole. This suggestion, too, was rejected by majority vote. The opposition then submitted a written protest and stalked out of the meeting – a move which did not prevent passage of the resolution of condemnation:

> The Congress of the Federation of Foreign Groups heard the statement of the Paris Group of Socialist Revolutionaries which expresses regret at its methods of discussion, and for its part protests vigorously against the introduction of such methods into the party and declares its firm resolve not to permit them among members of the Foreign Federation.

In the eyes of the Paris opposition the discussion of its Azef affair statement was designed to divert attention from the affair itself, thus rendering the congress hostile not only to ideas but also to individuals and groups.[85]

After the delegation's withdrawal from the Congress, it reported to the group which reiterated its support for both the form and the content of statement.[86] This statement was also circulated among all the foreign groups, and once again generated an adverse reaction. The Brussels group, for example, responded to the Paris opposition's resolution by stating that 'its insistence on the rightness of the form and content of the "Statement about the *Provocateur* Azef" violates all concepts of party and human ethics.'[87] This resolution once more indicates a perception of the situation in terms of a crisis of ethics.

The Paris opposition hoped to benefit from the Azef affair; to present itself as the blameless group in place of the leaders who had gone astray and fallen out of favour. It admitted this in stating that 'all hope has been lost for the party's regeneration within the framework of the current official structure'. Therefore it had decided to withdraw from the Federation of Foreign Groups (which was tantamount to leaving the party) and to examine all the means for forging ties and conducting joint activity with groups and comrades in Russia that sympathized with it ideologically and organizationally.[88]

There is no evidence that they were successful in this aim, perhaps because of their ideological stance, which deprived them of all declarations of support abroad, even from comrades whose views about the Azef affair and about the lessons to be learned from it were similar to their own, such as the 'Group of Fourteen'.[89] Perhaps the organizational situation within Russia itself ruled out such a possibility, but it is also a fact that the personal dispute with the veteran leadership played a considerable role in the affair. In 1908–9 the opposition still faced a united leadership whose organizational influence enabled it to repel any assault. In this connection, it is of interest to note that the only persons known to have joined the Paris opposition were former members of the Moscow opposition which had been dissolved in 1906 by the Central Committee.[90] Some of its members who reached Paris joined the opposition and adopted its stands on issues which had not previously preoccupied them.[91] As in the protracted struggle which preceded the Azef exposure, the arguments of the Paris opposition and its acerbic style were said to reflect an anti-collegial and unethical attitude, which permitted their rejection without the necessity of any substantive discussion.

The following years saw a radical change in the atmosphere. If

Iudelevskii and Agafonov had raised the question of ideological conflict and a personal dispute and, by utilizing the Azef affair, sought to translate them into the organizational and personal conclusions which they had believed the affair called for, the opposition that surfaced in 1914 no longer needed an ideological excuse when it launched a frontal assault on the veteran leadership in an effort to seize control of the party. Far from acting in the name of ideas and their interpretation, or seeking refuge behind a respectable mantle of ideological debate the opposition sought control, and provocation provided the means. The ground for this had been prepared by years of incessant preoccupation with suspicions, investigations and exposures, as well as by the publication of 'The Conclusions of the Commission of Inquiry for the Liquidation of the Consequences of the Azef Provocation' – all of which seemed to make the party leadership more vulnerable to the use of this political instrument.[92]

The opposition intended to wage the struggle in two phases, its first target being the committee of the Paris Group for the SR Party, and its second objective the party centre. The committee of the Paris Group was also under the direct influence of the party leadership, either through its members or their confidants, such as Shura Kartielova, wife of Nikolaev who for many years had headed the committee of Foreign Groups; Maria Seliuk, one of the founders of the SR party; Nastasia Minor, wife of Osip Minor, who was from the generation of the party's founders and was a veteran of the Narodnaia Volia; Vasilii Leonovich, who was close to the Foreign Delegation; as well as persons close to the party veterans such as Natan Bogoraz, Boris Bartold and others. They confronted a group of some 20 persons of a lower rank, headed by Veber.

The presentation of candidacies for the new group committee was designated for 13–26 November. A few days earlier the opposition held a secret meeting in a Paris café, with the participation of 18 persons. The issue being deliberated was phrased as follows: 'How to react to the inaction of the committee of the Group for the SR Party and of persons who are close to the committee.' For some time, it was noted at the meeting, a large group of Socialist Revolutionaries had existed which was not satisfied with the activity or the behaviour of those heading the party. This was expressed in the fact that only people amenable to the veteran leaders were co-opted to the committees in their various forms. Moreover, these 'usurpers' and their friends were supercilious, overbearing, and at times even contemptuous of others. At group meetings the opposition members utilized every pretext to level criticism against the group committee. Systematically they prepared to oust the old committee and its cronies, feeling that such a move would be within their power. This is also attested to by the fact that a key police agent in the Paris Group for the SR Party now joined the ranks of the opposition. Had failure been anticipated, he certainly would not have risked losing his position in the group.

Confidently, they planned their moves with a view to the next meeting of the Paris Group for the SR Party. It was decided that Veber, the leader of the opposition, would deliver a withering criticism of the old Committee's activity, to which end the members of the opposition would give him information about the failures or blunders of the outgoing Committee, including even the most minute details. The other opposition members would express support for Veber's critique. Demetrashvili, a police agent, was made secretary. Topel'berg was to ensure that the meeting began and ended on time, and that none of the opposition members left before its conclusion. In the previous elections, the committee had been elected and important decisions made by those who had stayed until the end of the meeting – namely, those who had a personal interest in the proceedings. To ensure that a similar bloc of self-interested supporters of the veteran leadership would not emerge at the forthcoming meeting, one of the comrades was given the task of forcing all the opposition members to remain until the conclusion of the assembly, and by the same token to see to it that the meeting ended at the scheduled time. The opposition also decided to vote for the candidates of their group. But to propose the candidacies of two members of the other camp, in order to avoid the impression that the opposition faction had taken any prior decision – and because it was known that the two persons in question would refuse to accept the posts. This was only an interim stage. In the second phase, the opposition members intended to launch a struggle against the party centre itself, and particularly against Argunov and Leonovich.[93]

The meeting to choose a new committee took place on 8 December. The opposition's prior organization did not remain a secret, and the anticipated clash brought out a large number of comrades who did not generally turn up for meetings of the group. A tense, agitated atmosphere prevailed. A lengthy debate ensued over whether voting was to be open or secret; there were no fewer than 39 candidates. Finally a secret vote was held, resulting in the election of four opposition candidates to the six-member committee.

In the meantime consultations had already begun between the elected members of the opposition and their comrades regarding the Committee's future activity, and chiefly about how to overcome the central party members and their 'governmental' (*pravitel'stvennye*) supporters who, the opposition was certain, would be loath to turn over the party's organizational and financial affairs to the elected opposition members.[94] The struggle with the party leadership was launched immediately after the victorious takeover of the group's committee.

At the beginning of 1913 the Okhrana agent Movsha Glikman – who had infiltrated the SRs in 1910 – was exposed. Just before the exposure Argunov recommended him for membership of the Labour Committee, to conduct propaganda among workers arriving from Russia. Veber knew that Burtsev was already suspicious of Glikman when his candidacy was proposed, although there was no reason to believe that Argunov was aware of this. Nevertheless, at the assembly of the Paris Group held on 20 November 1913, Veber attacked Argunov directly during a speech against the veteran leadership, accusing him of having known that Glikman was an *agent provocateur* when he recommended him for the Labour Committee. In the ensuing furore Argunov branded Veber a liar and added that everything he had said was fabrication and deceit.[95]

According to Demetrashvili's report, the attack launched by Veber and the opposition on the members of the outgoing committee was unexpected and had a considerable impact. The victims of the onslaught, he claimed, were particularly embarrassed because the criticism was well founded to a large extent. The opposition's sense of triumph made them confident that they would be able to form the majority of the new Central Committee. According to Demetrashvili the incident with Argunov had not been concluded, and everyone was waiting impatiently for further developments.[96] This evidence, combined with the actual continuation of the affair, shows that Veber's charges were not the result of impulsive anger but were debating tactics in expectation of the reaction of comrades who responded with extreme emotion to any charge of provocation or anything smacking of it. Nor, indeed, did Argunov let the matter pass: he appointed Sletov and Nikolaev to represent him in a party trial of Veber for slander.[97]

For his part, Veber appointed Pavlov and Fedorov from his own group.[98] The trial commenced on 16 December 1913, with the court deciding to rule on whether Veber's declaration against Argunov at the Paris Group meeting was correct. If it was found to be correct then the court would be entitled to declare its opinion of Argunov's behaviour; whereas if it were demonstrated that Veber's allegation was false, the court would address itself to that question. For six sittings the court heard the arguments of the two sides and their witnesses. Argunov's representatives sought to restrict the inquiry to the narrow question of whether Argunov had known about the suspicions against Glikman when he proposed his candidacy for the Labour Committee. Veber's representatives worked to expand the deliberations and transform the court into a platform for the accusation of the entire delegation and its confidants.

Burtsev was, in fact, the chief witness. His testimony reveals that, as was his custom, he had made his suspicions known, informally and without definitive proof, first to Bilit, then to Natanson and finally to Veber. Only at a later stage did he begin to deal with the matter more vigorously, demanding an inquiry. In this connection Veber's representatives also raised the question of Tsytsin, whom Burtsev claimed was a *provocateur*[99] as well as Burtsev's complaint that Natanson had not seen fit to convey his (Burtsev's) information to other delegation members. They also contended that inquiries were not always energetic enough, meaning that this dissatisfaction was not confined exclusively to the Glikman affair, which in his view was not dealt with soon enough, but was more general.

Argunov's representatives, as already mentioned, wished to restrict the deliberations to proof that Argunov had not been aware of the suspicions against Glikman when he proposed his membership of the Labour Committee, and that his lack of knowledge was due to the party's customary way of dealing with the entire provocation issue. The court, however, decided to expand the deliberations, to ward off any possible allegations of 'silencing of opinion', or charges that witnesses could not be interrogated properly. But when Veber's representatives tried to raise the case of the secret agent 'Mikhnevich', Gersh Iakobson, the court ruled that this was irrelevant to the present discussion and that it was inadmissible on formal grounds.[100] This ban and the argument that followed it provided a pretext to accuse the judge of bias and for Veber's second representative to declare that he was withdrawing from the proceedings, the other representative having withdrawn earlier. In his report the judge wrote:

> I must point out that the attitude of the sides towards the trial was as follows: despite the displeasure of Argunov's representatives at the broadening of the trial's framework and their protests against

this, they nevertheless obeyed the court and did all they could to bring the matter to a close. The representatives of comrade Veber, who previously had not complained even once, unexpectedly announced their withdrawal . . . and did not allow the work to be completed. Under these circumstances it does not seem to me to be possible to resolve the conflict in the accepted manner of comrades' trials . . .[101]

The withdrawal of Veber's representative may have been precipitated by the judge's comment that the judicial inquiry was almost concluded, and that the testimonies of the witnesses had proved beyond any doubt that Argunov had not known that Glikman was a *provocateur* when recommending him for the Labour Committee.[102]

It is apparent from the proceedings that the provocation issue did not serve as grounds solely for the Veber-Argunov trial. The opposition did not rest content with trying to prove Argunov's guilt – which it probably did not believe itself – but tried to place the entire delegation in the dock, while dredging up affairs such as those of Tsytsin and Iakobson, and accusing the delegation of indifference to and negligence in dealing with provocation. In this effort it found support in Burtsev's stand.

At the trial itself Burtsev in effect testified in favour of the delegation, maintaining that he had not notified Argunov of his suspicion of Glikman and that Natanson often kept such reports to himself. Indeed, he explained, in the case of Glikman this was justified due to the absence of incontrovertible evidence, although it was clear that he had subsequently informed Veber, an opposition figure.[103] Burtsev played a dubious role in the Veber-Argunov clash. Violating his custom of informing only Natanson, he had conveyed his apprehensions to many others, and in this case to the opposition member, Veber. Well aware that provocation had become a political instrument within the SR party, Burtsev did not hesitate to use it for his own purposes.[104]

The Veber-Argunov trial preoccupied the Paris Group for the SR Party for over six months. Throughout the trial the subject remained high on its agenda, reaching a peak only in June 1914, when the Group was disbanded. According to police reports its members were divided in their opinions and so rancorous was the dispute between the two sides that there was no possibility of reconciliation. Nor could a continuation of joint work be considered under these conditions. The only way out seemed to be the expulsion of the opposition, or at least its leading activists, from the Group.[105]

Representatives of the two sides had their say at a meeting held on

11 June (new style). The first speaker, Glotov, gave an extensive, detailed history of the 'so-called opposition' group, going on to demonstrate that this opposition had not been formed in order to present a critique of the Group or of the party's central institutions, but to besmirch and undermine it in every way possible. Since it was out of the question to allow such activity, the Group must be disbanded to ensure its continued normal operation in the future.

Countering this argument, the opposition spokesman, Polushkin, asserted that the opposition had been formed in order to ensure the party's 'good work'. The total inaction of the party's institutions and its central personages had left all the activity in the hands of foreign groups. This was a serious and ruinous situation, particularly when a new revolutionary wave was beginning in Russia. Moreover, Polushkin said, this inaction had produced other undesirable results as well: a decline in the comrades' moral level, and heightened provocation within the party's ranks while the responsible party officials were doing nothing to counter the phenomenon, not even when those accused of such grave crimes were known to them.[106]

Once again, this argument demonstrates that the Veber–Argunov affair was no more than a political gambit and that in the arguments presented both in the trial and in the discussion, the opposition as a group tried to make political gains out of the tense social climate in the party.

As had been the case with the first Paris opposition group, the provocation issue was once more demonstrated to be a two-edged sword. It undercut the prestige of the leadership and preoccupied the Paris Group with a scandal that took up most of its time for months on end. Yet the accusation itself seems to have been grasped in moral terms, like the accusations of Iudelevskii and Agafonov; as an act that was designed to serve personal ends and was therefore anti-social. This is attested to by the very fact that the slander trial took place, and by the framework of the proceedings established by the court. True, the trial did not conclude in the usual manner due to the withdrawal of Veber's representatives. But according to Shabel'skii, the chairman of the court, Veber's charge was refuted beyond any doubt. Under these conditions the group's continued existence seemed impossible; the opposition's ouster, it was argued, would benefit the entire party by ridding it of people who only interfered with party activity, and would thereby aid the revolutionary cause.[107]

As always in such cases, the prerogative of dissolution and reconstitution lay with the committee which ranked above the Group, in this case the Foreign Committee. The group was in fact disbanded and it was decided that members would be accepted to the new group only on the basis of stringent recommendations – and that no opposition members would be admitted. Thirteen persons were expelled.[108] Demetrashvili, however, was not among them; he continued to report faithfully to the Okhrana about the new group, and through it about other significant aspects of party activity.

The two attempts to oust the SR party's historic leadership by a direct assault and use of the provocation issue failed, and on the face of it the party hierarchy defended its acts and its standing with one voice. In fact, however, it was not immune from this political weapon once its internal cohesion had been undercut by the publication of the Azef inquiry commission's conclusions.[109]

The case of Postnikova[110] demonstrates that the impact of provocation was not confined to personal relations between frustrated *émigrés* – former revolutionaries seeking something of interest when all the genuine channels of revolutionary activity were closed to them. It permeated the party, including the uppermost level. Indeed, it is precisely there that it may well have had the deepest and most lasting impact. The Postnikova affair thus encapsulates the height of the consequences of the phenomenon in the SR party. Its characteristic features once more demonstrate its destructive power, the intensity of the emotional storm it could unleash, the permanent stigma caused by the lingering questions about a comrade's integrity even if he was exonerated by the commission of inquiry, the social agonies he experienced due to the methods of inquiry. No less important was the far-reaching effect of the suspicion, which went far beyond the suspect himself, in this case Chernov. On the surface, Chernov, who barely knew Postnikova, seemed to have nothing to do with the case. Nonetheless, Postnikova's indirect association with his literary activity and his poor relations with the members of the Foreign Delegation were his links with the affair. These two factors combined to convince Chernov that the entire matter was serving as a weapon in the hands of the delegation against him and his project. His furious reactions and fierce charges, countered by the responses of the delegation, are evidence that the provocation phenomenon had long since gone beyond the narrow sphere of defendants and accusers. Beyond the personal tragedy of Postnikova the case assumed both a political dimension that had nothing to do with her and which must be viewed against the background of Chernov's standing in the party at that time, and against the intra-party ideological struggle, which was also wholly unrelated to Postnikova. Chernov's wrath had nothing to do with Postnikova's fate, but stemmed from the anxiety about his own fate and that of his project, which in turn derived from his absolute certainty that the entire matter was but an instrument wielded against him by his adversaries.

Postnikova was active in the SR organization in Baku until it was broken up by the police in 1907. She had taken part in organizing a shipment of literature and arms to Moscow which was seized by the Okhrana. Among the activists who were arrested at the time of the Baku downfall was a certain Ratner, who was apprehended in the summer of 1907 at Kerch. Ratner had long born a grudge against Postnikova. Although the reasons for this are not clear, his enmity sufficed to convince him that she was responsible for his arrest. The subject became an obsession. In 1909 he approached the commission of inquiry, but no proof of his allegations was forthcoming. Nevertheless, he never missed an opportunity to declare that Postnikova was a secret agent.

In 1911, having lost her patience, she herself asked the commission of inquiry to place her on trial in order to refute the allegations. The commission examined all the written material, and interrogated Ratner's witnesses as well as party members who had encountered Postnikova during their party activity and might be able to shed light on certain aspects of her revolutionary past. The commission also heard all of Ratner's story. Its conclusion was that the accusations were groundless. Ratner had direct and personal knowledge of only two instances; all the others he cited originated with various sources, since he himself was not directly acquainted with Postnikova's activity, and moreover, several of his witnesses denied that they even knew her. Others pointed to a totally arbitrary interpretation that Ratner had attached to the information they had given him; and as for the two downfalls of which Ratner had personal knowledge, they were amenable to different explanations.

Ratner's allegations were declared baseless; their continued dissemination would be viewed as slanderous. Yet not even this ruling put a brake on his charges. He continued to make them at every opportunity and flooded the commission of inquiry with letters claiming that he had new proof. He also sent threatening letters to Postnikova, writing, 'To the Okhrana agent Elizaveta Viktorovna Iashchurzhinskaia . . . '. He even sent letters to her mother. Finally, after the commission of inquiry refused to heed his protestations, he threatened to publish an open letter abroad, as he had previously done at Baku.[111]

It is noteworthy that despite his persecution of Postnikova – disregarding two judgments in her case – no measures were taken against him. On the contrary, Bilit, a member of the commission of inquiry, actually replied to him at intervals, explaining that he did so only in extreme instances in order to pacify him and deter him from generating new scandals.[112] However, the very connection that the commission of inquiry maintained with him, irrespective of its motives, lent a kind of official stamp to his continued activity.

Early in 1914 Burtsev told the SRs' Foreign Delegation that rumours had reached him concerning the presence of a secret agent in the circles close to the journal *Zavety* ('The Legacy') published legally in Russia. He could add nothing more. Bilit immediately made the connection: Postnikova worked in the magazine's St Petersburg office.[113] Once more we find that even the investigators who had cleared a suspect were never totally free of a latent suspicion. Two unusual circumstances led Bilit to suspect Postnikova: the fact that she had never been arrested despite her years-long party activity, and that she was able to live openly in the capital.[114]

The moment suspicion fell on her, Bilit saw fit to warn the periodical's editor, Chernov, while in his pacifying letters to Ratner he noted that if Postnikova were actually guilty, this would soon come to light. However, he maintained, he did not mention Burtsev's remarks. The commission of inquiry, it will be recalled, dealt with two spheres: the investigation of persons suspected of being *provocateurs*, and clarification of the circumstances of downfalls. Burtsev's comment concerning provocation in circles close to *Zavety* spurred the commission of inquiry to investigate the downfalls at Baku and the seizure of the shipment to Moscow. The investigation encompassed a good many persons besides Postnikova. Although Bilit evidently did not convey to Ratner what Burtsev had told him, Ratner heard it from Burtsev himself. So Ratner was now certain that he was right, with a letter in his pocket from the commission of inquiry assuring him that the truth would soon come to light, or as Ratner himself put it, 'The rope around Postnikova's neck is getting tighter and tighter'. Meeting Chernov on a train in Germany, he told him the story, explaining that he had heard all the details from Bilit.

Naturally these rumours did not long remain secret, and soon reached the Postnikovs in St. Petersburg. They rushed to Paris to discover the meaning of the new accusations and the truth of the reports about the renewal of the inquiry. For the purposes of the inquiry, Postnikova agreed to remain in Paris for its duration, to refrain from all party or political activity, and to place herself within reach of the commission on the conclusion of the inquiry, whatever its findings.

With the hasty arrival of the Postnikovs in Paris, a special commission to examine their case was again established, which received and showed them all the material of the 1911 inquiry. The couple was not informed about the investigation of the downfalls in which Postnikova had been involved. The inquiry thus proceeded on two levels, one secret – an ostensibly non-personal investigation of downfalls – and the other open. Upon its conclusion Postnikova and her husband were handed a document reviewing the final stage of the affair, which declared explicitly that since no new facts had been made known to the delegation following its decision of 1911, no grounds existed for reopening the case.[115]

The Postnikovs, who knew only half the truth, returned to St Petersburg greatly relieved that no one suspected them or had any complaints against them. Since the rumours were circulating around *Zavety*, a special meeting of the editorial staff was convened in St Petersburg at which it was averred that once again Ratner was the source of the rumours about the periodical, combined with 'intrigues within the editorial staff of *Zavety*'.[116]

At this point we must turn our attention to Chernov, who, it will be recalled, left the party leadership in a fury following the publication of the judicial commission of inquiry's conclusions, since he, like others among his colleagues, considered them tantamount to a personal accusation against himself. His anger at the leadership only increased upon the arrival in 1912 of Azef's letter, sent from his place of hiding, in which he declared his readiness to stand party trial provided he sustained no harm during the proceedings. Chernov and others like him who had been close to Azef and to the party's terrorist activity, and who had been tainted by the commission's conclusions, were extremely anxious for such a trial to be held, since 'it alone will clarify everything that has remained dense and unclear in this case'.[117] However, they ran up against the unbending objections of the delegation members, who refused to reopen the painful affair. Complaining bitterly that as 'a person from the periphery' who lacked any formal rights but possessed 'an unassailable moral right', and seized with a sense of outrage, Chernov launched a fierce attack on 'our wise men', the members of the delegation.[118] Clearly his new literary venture in legally publishing the periodical *Zavety* did nothing to better his relations with the party leadership. Chernov regarded the very establishment of the periodical as making him the centre of ideological renewal in the party.[119] Moreover, the lawful publication of the periodical in Russia dovetailed with the 'liquidationist' tendency which had been gaining strength in the party for some years. The advocates of this tendency, members of the *Pochin* group, sought expressly to shift party activity from its underground terrorist course to a lawful track, while taking advantage of the possibilities for legal activity that existed in Russia – such as the Duma, professional organizations, co-operatives, and the Zemstvo bodies – and thereby to disseminate the ideas of SRs. Chernov himself was not among the advocates of this approach, nor was he in the *Pochin* group, but the very fact that *Zavety* was legally published in Russia reinforced a tendency that conflicted with the orthodox stance of some influential members of the Foreign Delegation.

To Chernov, the re-eruption of the Postnikova affair and the accusations voiced by *Zavety's* editorial staff concerning intrigues being woven within circles close to the periodical, seemed to be part of a deliberate attempt by delegation members to harm him. As he saw it, it was delegation members who had reopened the inquiry into the Postnikova case; who had been in correspondence with Ratner and had informed him about the renewal of the inquiry, assuring him that Postnikova's end was near; and who had misled the Postnikovs by concealing the truth from them, thus generating the backbiting that had led to accusation of intrigues. Against this background, vituperative and mutually insulting, a correspondence began between Chernov and the Foreign Delegation through Boris Moiseenko, with Chernov charging the party hierarchy of manifesting 'cool relations' towards him,[120] while they countered by alleging that he was demonstrating mistrust and contempt towards them.[121] In the meantime the Alexander Mass affair[122] was also dragged into the debate, when Chernov accused the Delegation of having lied in its contention that Mass had not left for Russia on its behalf. 'Since when has it become the custom among us not to tell the truth?' he asked, implying that he doubted the Delegation's integrity altogether. The Delegation also minced no words. Chernov's accusations were like salt on open wounds. The Delegation again denied that Mass left for Russia with an authorization from it, adding, 'We would have thought that after all we experienced together in the Azef affair, you would have learned to distinguish between rumour and truth' – a remark containing more than a hint of an admonition that he who lives in a glass house should not throw stones.

Whether, as the delegation maintained, Chernov's ire actually stemmed from a series of misunderstandings and a desire to ascribe malicious intentions to the leaders, or whether, as he believed, it was an attempt to strike at him through the mishandling of the Postnikova affair by leaking the story to Ratner, it is evident that the provocation issue now assumed unprecedented dimensions and importance within the party. Although rivalries and tensions were hardly confined to the SR party alone, the fact that charges of provocation began to appear in their wake meant that these relations were tinged with an unremitting sense of bitterness. This in turn undermined inter-personal trust not only among rank-and-file members, who felt themselves hurt, but worse, it produced the same effect within the leadership itself. Instead of maintaining a sense of trust and partnership, or a perception of the party as a single cohesive and integral entity, the leadership also began to be afflicted by incipient indications of internal disintegration and by rifts between factions, which were not wholly devoid of personal interests. Thus the circle was completed. The process had begun with the virtual disregard of the provocation issue, gained intensity after the shock generated by the Azef affair, and climaxed in an obsessive preoccupation with accusations and mutual suspicions to the point where they were utilized as a deliberate political instrument. This cycle is reflected in Savinkov's second book, *To chego ne bylo* ('What Never Happened').

Savinkov himself was an unusual figure in the SR hierarchy. Chernov depicts him as lacking any solid ideological position, and in fact he was more of a fellow traveller than a committed party comrade. At one point he declared himself a *Narodovolets*, although following a visit to Kropotkin in London he pronouned himself an anarchist, and for a time he leaned towards spiritual-religious revolutionism. He injected a new note into the terrorist ranks, one which Chernov maintains could never have been voiced in the more democratic period of Gershuni. It was a unique stance, based on the psychology of a fighting terrorist faction which took a supercilious view of other forms of party activity and regarded them as less heroic.[123] These later comments of Chernov, which are strongly reminiscent of certain conclusions of the judicial commission of inquiry into the Azef affair, actually constitute an attempt to adopt those parts of the conclusions which shift responsibility from the party leadership to the Battle Organization. Savinkov was stunned and pained by the treachery of his close friend Azef. Yet it was he who adamantly demanded his execution. Unlike Chernov, Savinkov rejected the allegations directed at the terrorists themselves. Terrorism, he wrote in the party organ, remains as pure as ever. Indeed, as will be recalled, to demonstrate its purity he headed a group that intended to go to Russia to perpetrate a spectacular terrorist act. When this plan fell through he returned to his foreign base and decided to settle accounts with those who seemed to him to be the truly guilty, not just in the Azef affair but in all the provocation cases which had brought about the party's disintegration. This he did in his second book.

Andrei Bolotov and his colleagues in the Central Committee constitute one side of the story. On the other side – separated from the first by an unfathomable abyss – are the members of the battle squads. Andrei Bolotov and his friends felt inwardly that they were the exlusive masters of a vast estate: the huge party, spread across the entire length and breadth of Russia. This party, with its dynamite laboratories, secret printing presses, battle squads, regional and provincial committees, its fraternities of peasants and workers' groups, its student circles and associations of officers and soldiers, all its successes and its failures, strikes and demonstrations, conspiracies and arrests – all this they saw as their own complex domain over which they were to keep a watchful eye at all times. In the meantime, while they were wasting their time with empty verbiage that was totally unrelated to the great deeds being done in the field, the members of the battle squads were waging a heroic struggle on the barricades during the days of the Moscow revolt, and perpetrating daring acts of terrorism on missions from the Central Committee. One day Andrei Bolotov, ignoring the protests of his comrades, decided to join these fighters who were doing the work and paying with their lives, when it emerged that a secret agent, Dr Berg, had for years been operating in the Central Committee. Like Azef's colleagues in the leadership of the SR party, the Central Committee members in Savinkov's book also refused to believe the reports about the treachery of their comrade. Like their real-life counterparts they protected him and regarded the accusations against him as lies fabricated by enemies of the party who were seeking to besmirch a dedicated and blameless revolutionary. 'But even though they thought they were protecting Dr Berg's honour and stature, they were actually protecting themselves against agonizing thoughts and severe pangs of conscience.'[124]

When the absolutely irrefutable proof turns up, Savinkov also describes a revolutionary who is on the verge of taking his own life out of despair:

> yet even though the comrades saw that the provocation had slashed through the party like a sickle through grass, and even though inwardly everyone recognized the shame of the deceit and the downfall, not one of them recognized his own guilt. Dr Berg's betrayal seemed to them an act of nature. They did not consider themselves to blame that a base murderer had craftily wormed his way into the committee, and since there were many persons in the party, most of whom liked Dr Berg and had 'worked with him', obviously no one was to blame. . . . Not one of them [the Central Committee members] was capable of understanding that the provocation was not accidental or that responsibility devolved wholly upon them.[125]

According to the author, their guilt and responsibility lay in the fact that they had for years been shielded from the consequences of terrorism, and on top of that were insensitive to the many losses; the result was that they had not bothered to examine and probe the situation until the moment came when the facts could no longer be denied. Manifestly, then, it was the SR party's leadership, the members of the Central Committee, who were to blame for the disaster which had struck the party, while Savinkov and his ilk were on the other side which was paying the price of their guilt.

Yet in Savinkov's view this was not the full extent of their guilt. Later on in the story, about a month after Dr Berg's exposure and murder, nearly the entire Central Committee was arrested and the party was left leaderless. Terrorist affairs were entrusted to the insecure Alexander Bolotov, brother of Andrei. Alexander, a young naval officer who had defected to the revolutionaries, is portrayed as the polar opposite of the members of the old Central Committee. Vigorous and energetic, he is ready to carry out the revolution on his own. Even in his small group suspicions were voiced about the presence of a *provocateur*, but by the power of his personality Alexander discovered the traitor immediately and, in marked contrast to the Central Committee members in the Berg affair, assumed responsibility for meting out the punishment. Yet it was too late; the disease had penetrated too deep for the party to be saved.

> If the party were more pure, if it contained no 'generals', no pettiness, irresponsibility, acts of robbery, if everyone honourably and wholeheartedly served the revolution, then there would have been no Dr Berg. . . . He could not have existed. . . . He would

have been exposed within five minutes. . . . But now it is too late.[126]

Whereas in Savinkov's first book provocation is not even mentioned, in his second book it becomes the axis around which the entire story revolves; nor is it depicted only as an instrument in the hands of the police, but as the mirror which reflects the moral quality of the party leadership. Savinkov's story leads to the conclusion that it was the leaders' moral degeneration that paved the way for provocation, and will, in the end, cause its final downfall. The source of the evil was not terrorism, as some had held as early as 1909 immediately after Azef's exposure, a claim which was also voiced by the *Pochin* group; rather it lay in *general'stvo*, the 'landlord' type of leadership which, itself remote from events, dispatched persons to kill and be killed without having the slightest conception of what it all signified, and without the respect due to human life. In the absence of a fitting leadership, terrorism also degenerated into mere robbery, and as the human and moral level declined, even veteran revolutionaries were liable to become police agents out of greed.

Such, then, was Savinkov's opinion about the state of the party and such was his settling of accounts with the leaders. It is hardly surprising that his books elicited a furious reaction, to the point where there were calls for his expulsion from the party. Essentially, the manner he chose to get back at the party leaders was not very different from that of Agafonov and Iudelevskii, or Veber and his colleagues. This was because the moment provocation became an ongoing party issue, no more effective political instrument seemed to be available.

4 Exposures as a Political Tactic

Many of the SRs were fully aware of the damage wrought by the Party's preoccupation with the provocation issue. According to this view, the detrimental effect of the exposures and the inquiries was far greater than any benefits they could possibly bring. The police too were kept fully abreast about the party's internal disintegration and about the part played in this process of social and ideological degeneration by the exposure of secret agents. In its detailed reports the Foreign Agency described the depressed atmosphere, the poisonous relations among party members, and the near total paralysis of the Paris group's activity.[1] Wide coverage was given to the growing voices that linked the party's gloomy state to its obsession with the provocation issue on the one hand, and to the terrorist tactics that made it a principal police target on the other hand. Indeed, according to these reports, some party members blamed terrorism not only for the disaster that had struck the party, but for the reactionary régime in Russia.[2] The reports singled out ranking figures such as Fundaminskii and Avksentiev as decrying the use of terrorism. The history of the Battle Organization also features prominently in the abundant reports, which held that its activity had now ceased almost completely due to internal squabbling, and most strikingly because of suspicions of provocation which had led to the suicide of two agents.[3]

Against the backdrop of these ongoing reports, and of the general awareness of the party's situation, particular importance attaches to the stand of the Police Department and Burtsev alike. As the representatives of the opposite extremes in the duel between the régime and the revolutionaries which was based on the secret agent, the two played key roles in developments within the SR party: the police in their use of the Internal Agency with the aim of liquidating the forces of the revolution and uprooting terrorism, and Burtsev by systematically engaging in the exposure of police agents, thus making himself 'a one-man espionage agency'.[4] On the face of it, internal developments within the SR party favoured the deep and long-term interest of the police, while harming those revolutionaries whose activity Burtsev sought to protect from the searching gaze of the authorities. It seems that from every point of view the police should have been satisfied with the course of events in the SR party after the exposure of their most important agent, Azef. Their great bane, terrorism, was reduced to an empty threat. Not only did the party lack the forces to carry out terrorism, but there were growing calls among the SRs to abandon it altogether. Nevertheless, in the absence of eye-catching revelations about terrorist plots conceived secretly that the police had managed to abort, the régime's dependence on the police actually seemed to decline, and with it the Department's prestige. On the other hand, the police could point proudly to the diversion of most of the SRs' revolutionary forces and energy from subversive activity to self-destruction, and rub its hands in glee at every new exposure which generated yet another internal crisis in the party. At the same time, Burtsev, as the moving force behind so many revelations and inquiries, could only wonder how far his unflagging activity was actually serving the revolutionary movement of which he considered himself a part. However, just as there is nothing to indicate that the police viewed the situation it had brought about within the SR party as a desirable trend – certainly it did nothing to further that situation – so, too, we find no let up in Burtsev's exposure activities nor any sign that might attest to doubts he harboured about the actual benefit of his activity for the revolutionary movement.

The letters of the Foreign Agency to the Police Department are permeated with a sense of despair and impotence due to the demoralization that had seized its agents since the defection of the two policemen, Bakai and Mensh'chikov. Instead of voicing satisfaction at the bewilderment sown among the most dangerous revolutionaries, the letters sound an apologetic note because the Foreign Agency was not meeting the request for the required information, whereas Burtsev was constantly bemoaning the fact that the revolutionaries were not assisting him in his vital campaign.[5]

Parallel to its 'extraordinary' efforts to forestall the resignation of frightened agents, the Foreign Agency made Burtsev a paramount object of surveillance and detection in an attempt to discover his sources of information which, it was believed, lay within the Police Department itself. The agency sent special agents to Burtsev, who posed as police defectors and declared that they were ready to reveal all its secrets to him. The reports of two of them, External Agency member François Jollivet and his son, served as the basis of a letter from the head of the Foreign Agency to the Director of the Police Department:

> Following the reports I conveyed to your excellency. . . . I have the honour to inform you of new information I have received from the agent Jollivet, which casts a unique light on the sources from which Burtsev obtains facts about the affairs of the Foreign Agency and which are, perhaps, capable of directing special attention to anything that might help expose the person or persons from whom Burtsev obtains his information. In my absence, Jollivet and his son continued to maintain contact with Burtsev and carried out various missions which they had been assigned. On 11/24 December (1913) Jollivet and his son went to a party, and on their return they saw Burtsev, who left them with the impression that he lacked his sources of information.

A few days later Jollivet himself wrote: 'Burtsev now seems less conversant with the affairs and work of the Russian police. He no longer declares as frequently as he did in the past that he is waiting for information from St Petersburg.' On the basis of another source St Petersburg was told that

> from conversations with Burtsev we must infer that while he does have sources within the Police Department, it is not possible to clarify whether he personally is in contact with someone from the Department or whether his contacts are maintained through another party. This is because of late Burtsev has become particularly gloomy, and seems to be deliberately refraining from talking about his exposure activities. Previously, Burtsev spoke quite willingly about the inquiry into provocation, and it is noteworthy that those conversations always touched on his contacts in St Petersburg, for whose maintenance he lacks sufficient means. It is probably that in his remarks Burtsev indicated the source from which he obtained his various items of information. This is partially confirmed by external signs: unrest, outbursts of anger, and Burtsev's expectations of reports from Russia about matters related to provocation.[6]

This extract is but a small portion of a far lengthier report which shows also how the police were groping in the dark where Burtsev's sources were concerned, as well as their desperate desire to seize on anything that might lead to those sources, not excepting even such nebulous hints as someone's impression of his state of mind. Aware of the situation, Burtsev was able to utilize it for his own ends. His actual source of information from 1912 to 1914 was Petrishchev, of the Okhrana administration in Paris. As camouflage, he sought to create the impression that the source was actually in St Petersburg, by delivering via Petrishchev a fake letter ostensibly addressed to Burtsev. The letter mentioned that a woman whom Burtsev would identify by her diamond earrings would come to him in Paris from St Petersburg bearing a verbal message which he would be likely to find of interest.

In 1918 Burtsev and Beletskii, a former Director of the Police Department, were imprisoned in the same Bolshevik cell, where they spent much time talking about the period in which they had been antagonists; for both of them it was now past history. Beletskii told Burtsev how he had agonized over the fake letter, which had disrupted the entire functioning of the Police Department. Because of it the organization of the sections had been revamped completely, twice investigation procedures had been altered, and personnel dismissed. Everyone's attention was riveted on the woman with the diamond earrings who was supposed to travel to Paris. Beletskii said the police had begun to interrogate all its personnel whose wives owned diamond earrings and who went to France at about that time. Finally suspicion fell on Gerasimov's wife and she was placed under surveillance.[7]

This point redirects our attention to the aims behind the utilization of the Police Department and the problem of their adaptation to the changing conditions within the revolutionary movement as a whole and in the SR party in particular. The explanation for the incongruity between the intensity of revolutionary activity and the rate of infiltration of secret agents into the revolutionary movement is confirmed also by the Police Department's agitated reaction to the stepped up exposure of its agents. Since it perceived liquidation as its very *raison d'être* it gave pride of place to an uninterrupted flow of information of the kind which would enable it to carry out liquidations. Because the police perceived the revolutionary threat, and more specifically the danger posed by the SR party, on a one-dimensional level – in terms, that is, of terrorist acts which it must be ready to prevent at any cost – they failed to react to the deep and destructive inner meaning of the exposure process and of the party's preoccupation with it: what the Police Department feared was the loss of sources of information. This one-dimensional attitude, which overlooked the totality which forms and facilitates revolutionary activity, brought about a situation in which the police, paradoxically, undermined their own interests. Evidently the exposure of Mass or Glikman or dozens of other agents served the police far better than any information these agents might convey about plans which the police knew lacked the necessary basis. Yet the Foreign Agency did all it could to save them. One can easily imagine what the exposure of Patrik or Demetrashvili – two prominent members of the Paris Group for the SR Party – would have caused the party had the Foreign Agency not moved to save them.

Nor is the hand of the police noticeable in the debate that split the party between the *Pochin* group and the orthodox wing. The identification of the agent Mass with the latter, and the 'legacy' money he was supposed to provide in order to establish a printing press and consolidate his standing in orthodox circles, did not seem to be part of an effort to strengthen the conservative section of the party against the opponents of terrorism, out of an institutional interest, but rather an attempt to consolidate a strong agency among those whom the police never ceased to regard as their prime objective. Although, as we have seen, the initiative failed when Mass was exposed, this does not offset the shortsightedness of the police who, out of fear of the orthodox terrorist wing of the party, was on the brink of actually strengthening it.

Provocation caused the SR party incalculable harm, but the police were unable to exploit its full latent potential and deliberately to destroy its narrow organizational base among the *émigrés*, which the police themselves viewed as a prime danger for the future.

The contradiction between Burtsev's exposure activity and its ruinous consequences for the SR party was incidentally referred to by Natanson. According to Natanson, Burtsev believed that no revolutionary struggle could be launched until provocation was extirpated from the revolutionary camp. Natanson argued that a revolutionary struggle must be waged, part of which, in limited spheres, would be directed against provocation. To that end special arrangements for communication were instituted between Burtsev and Natanson by virtue of the latter's membership on the Conspiracy Committee and the Foreign Delegation. However Burtsev did not always follow the procedures, thereby incurring the wrath of the SR leaders. Indeed, he was also the target of the fury of the SR opposition and was criticized by other revolutionaries as well. Natanson's account cannot explain Burtsev's adamant stand in the face of the price his activity exacted. To understand his position, we must comprehend the roots of his political outlook. Although Burtsev's anti-police activity was concentrated in the period from 1908 to 1914, the political viewpoint that underlay it evidently crystallized as early as the 1880s. In his memoirs, Burtsev attests that he continued to adhere to this viewpoint throughout the entire period of his activity and that it guided him from the moment he first joined the emigration in July 1888, after having escaped from his place of exile in Siberia.[8] From the outset, Burtsev defined himself as a *Narodovolets* – the same name he gave the periodical he published in London at the end of the 1890s;[9] this despite the fact that he himself was never a member of *Narodnaia Volia* and that, as he said, he formed his political outlook precisely under the influence of those elements that were critical of Russian populism. These included, according to Burtsev, the journals *Golos* ('The Voice'), *Vestnik Evropy* ('The European Courier') and others. Burtsev says he was struck by the criticism they levelled against inciting one part of the people against another in the name of the popular revolution. As an example, he cites the pogroms against Russian Jews in the Early 1880s, viewed by many populists as essentially a positive revolutionary manifestation which in the future they would succeed in channelling towards the appropriate objectives. In contrast, Burtsev saw the pogroms as merely a manifestation of the ugliest instincts of the masses against the Jews; and he viewed the position of the populists who supported the pogroms as a manifestation of the sacrifice of the interests of certain elements among the people in the name of narrow class interests. In this connection Burtsev quotes A. D. Gradovsky who warned in *Golos*: 'Don't release the beast!' The 'beast', in Burtsev's view, consisted of the dark and dangerous instincts of the masses, 'an irrational and merciless Russian *bunt*', and 'spontaneous (*stikhiinye*) popular movements'. Among these he included 'the sick hopes' that populist revolutionaries pinned on a popular revolutionary movement.[10] It was this same criticism which later underlay his attacks on the SRs, to whose revolutionary propaganda he attributed the 'terrible consequences' of 1917. Under the influence of this criticism, Burtsev writes in his memoirs, he formulated, at the very outset of his public career, his stand of opposition both to Lavrov and the members of his group, and to Social Democrats like Plekhanov.[11]

If Burtsev actually was a *Narodovolets*, he adhered to no more than the minimum programme of the *Narodnaia Volia* – a struggle of political terrorism until the attainment of complete civil liberties – or, as he put it:

> I gave prime place to the constitutional struggle in the name of the all-national tasks, and I attached great importance to the intelligentsia

and to the revolutionary organizations and their struggle. It was just for that reason that I insisted then on adopting the most acute revolutionary means in the struggle against the government.[12]

This combination of constitutionalism and terrorism led to Burtsev's being derided as a 'liberal terrorist'. Yet the inherent irony of the description notwithstanding, it does in fact convey well the operative political conclusions that Burtsev drew at the time. Believing that the revolutionary struggle alone would not save Russia, and attaching considerable importance also to lawful struggle, he began to form ties among both the revolutionaries and the liberals in order to publish, together with 'moderate oppositionary forces', a periodical which would wage a struggle against the Russian autocracy to guarantee civil rights in the country, and to that end would also support terrorism. In 1889 he managed to set up a short-lived partnership with Mikhail Dragomanov and Vladimir Debagory-Mokrievich: together they published the periodical *Svobodnaia Rossiia* ('Free Russia').[13] Only three issues appeared before the partnership collapsed due to the constant tension between its two components: the liberal and the terrorist. Burtsev sought to repeat this enterprise in 1908 when he again joined the emigration after three years of lawful activity in St Petersburg. Convinced that the failure of the revolution and the intensification of government repression necessitated the united mobilization of all the elements struggling against the régime in an uncompromising war against reaction, he began once more to seek ways and means to found a 'free' periodical to be based on a platform which was 'not Lenin, not Chernov and not reaction'.[14] Once more he failed and when he found himself unable to establish a periodical along the lines of *Svobodnaia Rossiia*, he began to publish his own *Obshchee delo*[15] ('Common Cause') which soon folded, and thereafter *Budushchee*[16] ('The Future'). The latter became not only a platform for his ideas but also an instrument in his struggle. Through it he sought to convince, to precipitate the struggle, to accuse, and finally also to operate on his own in a manner he regarded as serving the goals he preached.

'Never in the past 50 years,' he wrote, 'has the effort of the forces of reaction reached a level such as this. Never has the influence of the forces of darkness been greater than in the years after the revolution. Clearly, the struggle for the freedom of Russia must begin afresh.'[17] In this struggle, all citizens and all opposition forces must co-operate with one another, because a regime of political freedom is as necessary to them as the air they breathe.[18] On that basis, he asserted, all parties could co-operate despite their deep differences.[19] To reinforce his argument, he cited the example of *Narodnaia Volia*, whose well-known letter to Alexander III had put forward demands for constitutional guarantees and for the establishment of a constituent assembly, even though these issues were not contained in its platform. By doing so, according to Burtsev, it posited political freedom as a precondition for its existence as a party, since it sought a formula for action which would be acceptable to the entire nation and not just to a narrow circle of like-minded persons.

> *Narodnaia Volia* began to speak in all-national terms . . . and to that end did not flinch even from the price of undertaking to forgo the tactic which had typified it until then [i.e. terrorism]. It adopted this behaviour because it understood well what was called for at that time and [realized] that on its own it lacked the strength to meet those needs.[20]

Similarly, Burtsev argued, the struggle for the freedom of Russia was still beyond the strength of individual groups or parties. In his view, the experience of 1904–06 had demostrated that the government's resistance could be broken only with the aid of united forces – requiring a common goal and conception[21] – even if this meant temporarily forgoing long-term goals. This common goal and conception he found in the issue of the Duma, for a number of reasons: first and foremost, because the sovereignty of a legislative assembly is the crowning glory of civil liberties in general; and also because the Duma, its severe limitations notwithstanding, remained the only platform in Russia from which it was possible to exercise freedom of speech – hence its great importance as a means of propaganda.[22] Very probably Burtsev also took into account the fact that the Duma was the only arena in which most of the forces struggling against the régime participated, and he saw it as a means which would facilitate further co-operation among them. In any event, in his articles he stressed the first two reasons cited above as binding on representatives of the opposition parties in the Duma, writing:

> Nowhere more than in Russia does society have the right to demand of its representatives the courage to protect its interests so fiercely. Nowhere should the position of the delegates be a sinecure or a means to a personal career, and especially not in Russia. In all countries the possibility exists of taking part also in

extra-parliamentary activity. Only in the Russia of our day are the avenues closed to any serious political activity save for that in the Duma.[23]

At this point Burtsev offers explicit and trenchant criticism of the part played by the opposition parties in the Duma, while expressing disappointment at his own failure to create a common front for action among them. He accuses them of having failed, in their discussions of the most burning issues facing Russia to take a clear and unequivocal stand, of having demonstrated neither courage nor vigour, and of having adopted no political tactic. Moreover, 'when they occupied their seats in the Taurida Palace they seemed to be engaged in forced labour'. They allowed the government to intimidate them and refrained from appealing to the public on a series of vital questions when discussion of them was still within the realm of possibility.[24]

None the less, Burtsev argues, whatever the opposition may do in the Duma, forces of struggle against reaction also exist outside that body; and just as successful activity within the Duma contributed significantly to agitation in Russia, so too agitation and struggle outside the Taurida Palace were a crucial condition for bringing activity in the Duma to the requisite level.[25] With these explicit words, then, Burtsev took on the task of exerting external pressure on the opposition parties in order to force them to co-operate even against their will. However, since he regarded himself as a person whose 'political life took place not in public assemblies, not in the street and not in party meetings or international talks . . . [but as] a *littérateur* and a journalist',[26] Burtsev transformed his paper *Budushchee* into the main platform for his political struggle, while also making use of his other writing activities, including his historical periodical *Byloe*.

His intentions were clear and he made no secret of them, asserting overtly that his goal was to bring about the organization of a broad all-national movement for the establishment of a sovereign Duma and universal franchise; and that this, the paramount task in the life of Russia, required the participation of all citizens, though chiefly of the opposition parties. Burtsev declared forcefully that he did not intend to create a new party but to work for the advancement of the paramount task in order to make the opposition (i.e. revolutionary) parties aware that they must give that task priority in their 'realistic programmes'.[27] Thus, he declared in advance that he would not relent on the subject of the Duma and would follow its activity closely. He asked 'his correspondents in Russia' to help him keep meticulous track of everything that happened in and around the Duma. Behind all this lay the desire to undermine the Tsarist autocracy internally and externally by 'exposing its corrupt nature'.[28]

On the surface, the struggle against the Okhrana and against provocation – the Police Department's main instrument in its war against the revolutionary movement – suited Burtsev's purposes perfectly. From his point of view, the Okhrana was one of the bases on which the Tsarist régime rested, and to attack it was to attack the entire régime. The struggle necessarily involved all the elements in the opposition camp, since, as we have seen, there was not a single movement or party in Russia into whose ranks secret agents had not infiltrated. The exposure of secret police agents usually generated a political storm and was charged with powerful emotions. No one could remain indifferent. To raise the issue of the Duma within the framework of the question of the legality of the police *modus operandi* would perforce cause a raucous scandal in which all the opposition parties – the protestations of the revolutionaries among them notwithstanding – would be swept up in the imbroglio of the struggle against the government and its supporters. Thus, in the very nature of things, Burtsev's one-man struggle against provocation would bring into his political struggle those elements in whose participation he was interested, though to date they had remained largely aloof. Finally, the entire subject aroused curiosity and reverberations among the general public both in Russia and abroad. The struggle, then, was not intended to protect the revolutionary camp by exposing the secret agents in its ranks; it was not, as some contend, aimed primarily at uprooting this affliction because of the immense damage it was causing to the revolutionary movement. Burtsev himself attested to this when he wrote: 'We have launched a struggle against provocation, not because it is one of the major obstacles to the revolutionary struggle but because it constitutes – so we are convinced – the basis for all current Russian politics. We wanted to direct attention to it – *not of other revolutionaries but of the entire Russian public*.'[29]

The conflict between the political interests of Burtsev and of the SRs was first revealed immediately after the exposure and flight of Azef. Burtsev's actions as the affair developed showed that the issue of Azef's guilt or innocence constituted only one aspect of the dispute between him and the SR leadership, and in the last analysis perhaps not the most important one. While the SRs did all they could to sever any possible connection between the successes of terrorism and the heads of the Police Department, it was precisely with the aid of that connection that Burtsev could transform the affair into a political instrument, a lever for his purposes. Only that connection could impart significance to Burtsev's battle against the Okhrana. His principled advocacy of terrorism prevented him from supporting the conclusion drawn by the detractors of terrorism – in large measure thanks to Burtsev himself – that the naïve members of the Battle Organization were not, as they believed, sacrificing their lives for the good of the people, but were in fact puppets whose strings were pulled, through Azef, by rival police factions.[30] Burtsev argued that even if the police had not actively supported the terrorist actions, and even if it had been unaware of Azef's role in them, several of its heads realized that Azef was not getting his information about the SRs thanks solely to his connections with several of the party's leaders, but because he was the person closest to Gershuni and Savinkov, and as such perforce took part in a number of terrorist acts. However, the police chose to ignore this because of the benefit they derived from it; or, as Burtsev put it in 1917: 'The govenment, knowing that it was Azef who headed the party, tolerated the fact that he perpetrated these acts, as though to say: "He is useful to us and we will exploit him – and if someone is killed, what can we do? It is of no importance".'[31]

On the basis of these accusations, Burtsev demanded that Gerasimov, as Azef's case officer and commander of St Petersburg Okhrana Section from 1905 to 1909, be placed on trial. Repeating his accusations in 1911, he insisted in a letter to the Minister of Justice, Ivan Shcheglovitov, that Trusevich (1906–9 Director of the Police Department), Kurlov (1909 Deputy Minister of the Interior) and Leonid Rataev (1902–6 head of the Foreign Agency) also be tried in connection with additional affairs of provocation.[32] We need not assume that Burtsev expected his demands to be acceded to, though through his letters he did obtain part of what he sought: the affairs were once again raised in the Duma. First was the Azef affair, which generated a turbulent debate; against the defensive Stolypin were aligned representatives of the Cadets and the Social Democrats.

Burtsev did not rest content with exerting journalistic pressure on the parties or with making the issue of provocation a subject of general discussion. Simultaneously, he set up his own machinery of information and detection in order to expose police agents in the ranks of the revolutionaries. He used his own private resources in this work and ran publicity campaigns to drum up additional funds. With the money he obtained he would bribe Okhrana agents in Paris, inducing them to defect to him and reveal police secrets. Meticulously he gathered one bit of information after another about persons who for some reason – a hint from a certain source, or his own intuition – had aroused his suspicion. He employed detectives to trail the objects of his investigations and exerted heavy pressure on the parties to conduct their own inquiries to prove suspects' guilt. He thus became a standing threat to the Foreign Agency and his activity generated strong pressure on the parties' centres there. The Bolsheviks established a commission of inquiry, of which Burtsev was a permanent member, on issues relating to provocation.[33] As we have seen, Burtsev stayed in formal contact with the SRs through Natanson. Whatever one may have thought about Burtsev personally, neither he nor the information he possessed could be disregarded. As was described above, in the SR party his activity fanned the atmosphere of suspicion and mistrust which had so devastated it since the Azef affair. But the party leadership was caught between the devil and the deep blue sea: between the fear of falling prey to a new Azef affair, and its efforts to calm down its members. Burtsev's aim of placing the issue of provocation at the head of the revolutionary agenda and of making it a banner in the anti-Tsarist struggle could no longer be consistent with the party's interests. However, the SRs' distress tempered neither Burtsev's fervour nor his adamance that the issue of provocation be dealt with as he saw fit.

Burtsev was utterly insensitive to the SRs' attitude towards Azef. About three years after the shock the party had experienced, in 1911, Azef made his well-known appeal to the SRs, requesting that he be tried before his comrades and given the opportunity to explain his deeds. A fierce debate erupted afresh in party circles. There were some who had never ceased searching for Azef with the intention of taking revenge on him,[34] while others maintained that under the revolutionary code of justice a judgment handed down *in absentia* was invalid from the moment the accused could be heard.[35] A third opinion held that by the very act of fleeing, Azef had relinquished his right to be heard.[36] Those who advocated the latter view effectively supported the position of the party's official representatives, led by Natanson, who rejected totally the idea of a formal party trial for Azef, but who tended not to oppose such a trial if it came at the initiative of interested comrades and under their full personal responsibility.[37] What was abundantly clear was that all these approaches had their origins in the powerful emotional storm whipped up by the affair and which had not yet abated. The entire matter focussed on settling past accounts, whether by liquidating Azef in revenge for what he had wrought, or by bringing him to trial in the hope that this would purge the guilt that had rubbed off on others. (As Chernov expressed it: 'In my opinion, only those who support terrorism can be members of the court, and not those who oppose it'; or: 'I believe that a trial of Azef would necessarily clarify the entire Rutenberg affair which he [Rutenberg] maliciously exploited against us in order to justify his cowardly behaviour.')[38] The absolute refusal to speak with him and reopen the painful affair, with all its destructive ramifications, also originated in this attitude towards the past.

Burtsev joined the debate in the pages of his own paper:

> We think that a different attitude must be adopted towards Azef's declaration. In our view, we must do in this case what *Narodnaia Volia* did at the time in the Degaev affair. Azef must be interrogated if he ever decides to appear for trial. . . . Azef has something to tell about the Stolypins, the Gerasimovs, the Truseviches, and right now he has no need to cover for them. He has no interest at all now in preserving their secrets. In our view, like any paid agent, deep down he is always contemptuous of those he served, particularly the Okhrana and the government representatives. Yes, indeed, otherwise he would be wholly incapable of thinking about them. And the various Plehves he killed 'with a revolutionary's happiness of heart', as he put it. At the same time he is utterly devoid of any moral scruples. He was always just as easily ready to inflict disaster on Kaliaev as to throw a bomb at Plehve. Now, when the Okhrana no longer has any need for Azef, after all the revelations, and he is out of the Police Department, there is nothing more natural for him than to expose the Gerasimovs whom he has always despised. . . . At all events, whether Azef will face a revolutionary trial, whether he will explain himself or not – none of it makes any difference. The Azef period, the Azef affair are gone for good. Now begins the exposure of the Azefs, and in this period Azef's revelations themselves could play an important role.[39]

In the midst of the debate, Burtsev made a secret trip to meet Azef, after having assured him, naturally, that he would not reveal his hiding place. He had one purpose in mind: to obtain from Azef additional ammunition for the political war he was then waging against the Tsarist government.

It is not difficult to understand the unbridled fury of the SRs when they learned of the secret meeting, after their efforts to find Azef at an address given to them by Burtsev proved unavailing, which led them to conclude that Burtsev had kept from them his information about Azef's hiding place.[40] Moreover, they could not help thinking he had conspired with Azef against them. 'When they hear Burtsev's name,' Evgenii Kolosov wrote in a letter to his wife, 'they tremble with rage. They threaten – God knows what. They accuse him of having deliberately given them an incorrect address so they would not kill him [Azef]: "He led us astray", "We will never forgive him", "A shameless fraud", etc.'[41]

Whether this was a genuine misunderstanding due to which Azef's pursuers were unable to track him down and were therefore frustrated in their plan to murder him, or whether Burtsev deliberately misled them because he opposed their plot, the affair reveals the basic conflict of interest between Burtsev and the SRs. Their attention was focused entirely on the problem of their past. Burtsev's struggle was perceived as striking at the party's very essence, and therefore as being inadmissible and unethical.

Thus, despite the fact that Burtsev never ceased to explain his political goals and their significance, his methods were not discussed in that context but were explained solely in terms of personal motives: publicity seeking, attention getting, headline making. Burtsev himself rejected all this criticism. He replied in his own paper *Budushchee*:

> We are sometimes accused of giving too much space in our paper to the issue of provocation. A strange rebuke! We do not know whether the legal press in Russia will, under special circumstances, be given the opportunity to deal with issues like these. In the meantime it must remain silent [with respect to them] or make use of quotations from foreign papers. Russian readers are now getting reports about how Eremin in 1906 organized Ryss's escape in Kiev; how Gerasimov fabricated, through Brodsky and others, the charges against the members of the Second Duma; how Azef actively participated in the assassination of Plehve, the Grand Duke Sergei, and others. All these matters were covered long ago in our paper. We believe wholeheartedly that ultimately the Russian public will recognize our charges against the government regarding how provocation was organized, nor will the government be able to deny them. We have spoken and we are continuing to speak so much about the Okhrana for two reasons: first and

foremost, because the Okhrana is the pillar of Russian reaction . . . and secondly, because until a very short time ago it was impossible to speak about it. Whereas now it is being talked about incessantly, albeit within the framework of the censorship. As to the current place of provocation in Russian political life, that is indicated by the fact that the session of the Duma has been reopened with two entire meetings devoted to that subject – and the entire Russian reading public is following with baited breath its discussions on provocation. No, we cannot be accused of talking over-much about the Truseviches, the Gerasimovs, the Eremins and the Azefs – but of talking too little about them. However, to that rebuke we reply that we are doing all we can, and if anyone can do better – let him![42]

Externally, then, Burtsev was satisfied with the results of his activity. But since in implanting the issue of provocation in the public consciousness he was in fact seeking to serve a more important purpose, it is difficult not to conclude that, his own remarks notwithstanding, his success was at best partial.

It is clear, then, that for Burtsev the social and moral effects of his actions were negligible in comparison to the political aim he sought to further. Likewise, the SRs could not accept Burtsev's wider purpose, for which his exposure of provocations was merely tactical. These conflicting approaches are reflected fully in Vera Figner's reply to Burtsev's complaint that he was being left without support, isolated in his struggle against provocation:

> What a dark figure you represent, Vladimir Lvovich! You stride about like the angel of death bearing the scythe, even worse than the angel of death . . . like a black phantom with long, twisted fingers . . . and your dark shadow falls everywhere that you turn. From your black bag you pull out broadsheets on informers, on betrayal, on the selling of one's soul, on crimes against comradeship, against friendship, against everything that man holds precious and sacred. You sow suspicion, you sow loathing and contempt for people, for mankind in general. . . . You are a terrible person, you are dark-souled. . . . You call for a struggle against provocation – with what means? Is there any other way to root out wild weeds than by revolutionary and cultural activity inside Russia, among the people, in the cities, the villages, the factories and the fields – everywhere, amongst all classes? . . . That leprosy [provocation] will be transformed into a minor rash when freedom prevails in

Russia. We must call for its achievement, for activity aimed at obtaining it. But you issue no such call. . . . You want the institution of espionage itself. You want endless exposures, condemnations, proofs, judgments. Is that creative work? Is it for that that we must call on those who still remain in the ranks? To waste the few pennies yet remaining in one's empty pocket? No, it is better that you remain alone. Go by yourself and complain about the cool indifference [accompanying you] in this murderous campaign.[43]

Vera Figner's letter sums up the essence of the phenomenon of provocation which rendered it such a powerful factor in revolutionary life. It also clearly elucidates two of its major constituent elements which were discussed in this book: the terror of death that provocation evoked, and its perception as the embodiment of all that was evil, corrupt and inhuman. These characteristics enabled the SRs to transform it into a political weapon in their internal struggles, while allowing Burtsev to hope that he could utilize it for a comprehensive political strategy. But precisely the immense emotional weight of provocation turned out to be a double-edged sword. These SR opposition members who dared seize it unthinkingly paid for their attempt by being ousted from the party, while Burtsev himself ran up against a wall of criticism and hostility throughout most of his years of activity. If he could actually console himself by drawing on his powerful faith in the rightness of his way, it was difficult for the SR party to find consolation in the failure of those who challenged the party leadership. Their failure was only technical; ultimately, it was the entire party that paid the true price.

Conclusion

Due to a combination of several basic factors the police agents in the SR party profoundly influenced its development and this significant element must be taken into account when studying the party's history. These factors were interconnected. Some of them derived from the police perception of the possible uses of the secret agents, and the manner in which they attempted to put it in practice, while others stem from features that were unique to the party itself.

The conception that took root in the Police Department was based on the exploitation of the secret agents in order to collect information which should be then used in the cause of liquidating revolutionary organizations. Since the secret agent was perceived as the optimal instrument for thwarting revolutionary activity, every new situation appraisal by the police following an escalation in the revolutionary struggle brought in its wake an upgrading of the secret agent's role, to the point where the agent became the linchpin of political police work. Ideas mooted by senior police officers concerning a subtler use of secret agents – to undermine morale among the revolutionaries, or to wield internal political influence within their organizations – failed to receive serious consideration due to the structure of the Police Department, its institutional interests, and its attitude towards terrorism. Because of the division of the political police between the Gendarmerie administration and the Okhrana sections – which had been established in various periods in response to changing needs, but which continued to fulfil parallel functions – a structure evolved which was bound to generate competition between the two bodies and prevent the kind of co-operation which is essential for such clandestine activity. Moreover, the Police Department encouraged its investigative bodies to aspire to immediate and blatant achievement – in the form of liquidations – rather than to work with a view to the long term results. The rationale was that liquidation underscored the revolutionary threat and the government's consequent dependence on the police, whereas the results of internal activity are inherently of a less immediate and less impressive nature. The stress on the immediate also imbued the Okhrana and Gendarmerie Commanders with this spirit of competition. Its ultimate effect was to lead the Police Department to reach a distorted assessment of the revolutionary danger. Compounding the matter was the Police Department's perception of terrorism in general and central terrorism in particular as constituting the major threat to the régime and to its own position, leading it to concentrate its attention on the perpetrators of terrorism. As a centralist terrorist organization the SR party became a prime target of police activity, a major objective for the growing penetration of secret agents, virtually irrespective of the actual spurts and declines in party activity.

However, even if the police did not deliberately set out to exert an internal political-social influence on the SR party, it was precisely on this level that its impact was most pronounced. This was the result of certain traits of the party which from the outset was marked by deep ideological divisions. Its adherence to centralist rules of organization enabled the police to place obstacles in its course and prevent it from realizing these principles which were fundamental to the party's constitution. The upshot was that the party was controlled by a more or less cohesive group of veterans of the founding generation and their followers.

As long as revolutionary activity was on the upswing – until 1907 – the ideological differences remained for the most part unarticulated; no overt opposition arose to the veteran leadership and no awareness existed of the high price being exacted by the presence of the secret agents in the party. The latent suppression of the threat facilitated revolutionary activity which otherwise would have been unfeasible, since by its nature such activity must be based on close relations of trust. But the clampdown which followed the revolution of 1905 and the shock generated by the Azef exposure, continued to bring to the surface the ideological disagreements, the opposition of certain groups to the traditional leadership and an awareness of the presence of secret agents within party ranks and its price. The issue of provocation which gradually assumed a central place in party consciousness was emotionally charged both because of the accusations and suspicions which reached the party's centre from every direction, and because of the ways prescribed for dealing with them, given their multiplicity and the leadership's earlier failure in the Azef affair. From 1909 to 1914 the party engaged relentlessly in investigating suspicions in an agitated and highly tense atmosphere, with each such inquiry inevitably dragging in persons guilty of baseless suspicion, others who should have been more suspect and those whose proximity to an exposed traitor cast a dark shadow over them as well. The potentially explosive effect inherent in every hint or revelation of provocation was apparent to all and seized on as an effective and deliberately employed instrument in intra-party political power struggles.

The absence of an appropriate forum rendered difficult any campaign launched from the periphery against a veteran, united leadership, and resting on ideological arguments alone. However the prospects for the success of such a campaign were strikingly enhanced by the atmosphere prevailing in the party, when ideological issues were linked to the question of provocation. The upshot was that this loaded and highly resonant issue became a convenient means for the advancement of internal political goals, whether ideological or personal. That this was the case is manifest from the discussion of the Fifth SR Party Council, the affair of the Paris opposition group, and other major events that preoccupied the party between 1909 and 1914. What all these had in common was the interlacing of the provocation issue with internal disputes, initially in order to justify a certain political line, subsequently in leadership struggles and finally to settle personal accounts within the leadership itself. Thus, in flagrant contrast to the suppression of the consciousness of the danger posed by the presence of secret agents, which characterized the SR party until 1909, the following period was marked by an obsessive preoccupation with the provocation issue, whose clear political nature was highly charged with moral significance which was not lost upon many party members.

Yet a quantitative analysis reveals that, despite the impression formed by the contemporary actors concerning the scope of the phenomenon, the actual number of secret agents operating within the revolutionary camp was smaller than they believed. Their impression, then, derived from the qualitative impact the agents exerted on the party's political and social life. Similarly, the notion that the SR party was permeated with secret agents, far in excess of any other revolutionary party, is also inaccurate. Proportionately, the number of secret agents among the anarchists was far greater.

The activity of Burtsev was a factor in the prevailing impression of the extensive nature of provocation within the revolutionary camp. Until now the explanation adduced for his unceasing struggle against the police and their agents was Burtsev's desire to protect the revolutionary movement from their ill effects. However, it emerges that he, too, made use of the issue to promote his own ideas. Through it he sought to impose a common political strategy on the entire opposition – liberal and revolutionary – within the framework of the Duma. We find, then, a certain analogy between the role provocation played in his hands, and the selfish uses made of it within the SR party.

Burtsev's activity demonstrates cardinally that provocation as a permanent political factor in the revolutionary camp was not confined to the SRs alone. On the other hand, given the fact that the nature of its influence stemmed from the reciprocal effect of police activity and the distinct characteristics of each of the separate police fields of action, the results would presumably differ from party to party. Nevertheless the special role played by provocation among the SRs hastened the party's organizational and ethical breakdown, deepened the rifts within a leadership which had begun as a cohesive group with strong internal ties, and brought to the surface the opposition to the traditional leaders and their associates which undermined their authority. These results were to leave their mark on the party's history until its liquidation by the Bolsheviks, and even later, on the relations between its *émigré* leaders. Even if provocation itself was not the sole cause of the state of the party its significance cannot be underestimated. This definitely had a bearing on the party's disappointment with the results of the revolutionary awakening following the Lena events. The disillusionment found expression in the party's organ which complained of its remoteness from the people and the dispersion and shattering of its forces, which prevented the party from exercising influence on the masses. This already serious state of affairs was further aggravated as a result of the relations which developed between the SR leaders at the outbreak of the First World War, which produced a total break between them. The personal enmity which had been evident beforehand now overcame the party interest and the good of the cause, even though an attempt was made to conceal the situation. Similarly, with respect to the SR party's stand *vis-à-vis* the Bolsheviks after October 1917, the rift within the party leadership was deeper and more bitter than their disagreements with their rivals.

The explanations offered for the SR party's failure in 1917 are of two kinds: the ideological stands taken by its leaders on the fateful issues that emerged between 1914 and 1917, namely between the First World War and the seizure of power by the Bolsheviks; and sociological, demographic and ideological factors that influenced the party's organizational makeup from the very outset. However, additional dynamic elements affecting existing structures and their development must be taken into consideration for their bearing on the historical import of these factors at a given moment. The presence of provocation within any social movement is one such element; without taking it into account, no analysis of the significant data discussed in previous studies is complete.

Notes

NOTES TO THE PREFACE

1. For a detailed account of this famous affair see B. Nikolaevsky, *Azeff the Spy: Russian Terrorist and Police Stool* (New York, 1934).
2. M. Hildermeier, *Die sozialrevolutionäre Partei Russlands* (Cologne, 1978) pp. 206–14.
3. R. C. Elwood, *Roman Malinovsky: A Life without a Cause* (Newtonville, Mass., 1977).
4. B. D. Wolfe, *Three Who Made a Revolution* (New York, 1964) Ch. XXXI, pp. 535–90.

NOTES TO THE INTRODUCTION

1. R. Pipes, 'Narodnichestvo: A Semantic Inquiry', *Slavic Review*, XXII (1964).
2. I. Kol'tsov [L. Tikhomirov], 'Shatanie politicheskoi mysli', *Delo*, III (1883) 5, cited in Pipes, 'Narodnichestvo', p. 445.
3. Hildermeier, *Die sozialrevolutionäre Partei*, p. 146.
4. A. Lopukhin, *Nastoiashchee i budushchee russkoi politsii* (Moscow, 1907) pp. 8–9.
5. S. Monas, 'The Political Police: The Dream of a Beautiful Autocracy', in C. E. Black (ed.), *The Transformation of Russian Society* (Cambridge, Mass., 1970) pp. 164–90.
6. Lopukhin, *Nastoiashchee i budushchee*, p. 30.

NOTES TO CHAPTER 1: THE CHALLENGE TO THE POLICE

1. L. Andreiux, *Souvenirs d'un préfet de police*, vol. I (Paris, 1885) pp. 35–9, 158–63.
2. Monas, 'The Political Police', in Black (ed.), *Transformation*, pp. 164–81. According to Monas throughout the period of Alexander III's reign the total number of secret agents did not exceed 100.
3. Ibid., p. 166.
4. A. P. Martynov, *Moia sluzhba v otdel'nom korpuse zhandarmov* (Stanford, Calif., 1972) pp. 5–6.
5. Lopukhin, *Nastoiashchee i budushchee*, p. 25.
6. The description of the Degaev affair is based on A. Pribyleva-Korba,

'Sergei Petrovich Degaev', *Byloe*, no. 4 (April 1906) and 'Degaevshchina: materialy i dokumenty', ibid.

7. W. Laqueur, *Terrorism* (London, 1977) p. 102.
8. L. P. Men'shchikov, *Okhrana i revoliutsia*, vol. I (Moscow, 1925).
9. A. Gerassimoff, *Der Kampf gegen die erste russische Revolution* (Leipzig, 1934) p. 33.
10. A. I. Spiridovich, *Partiia Sotsialistov-Revoliutsionerov i eia predshestvenniki 1881–1916* (Petrograd, 1918) p. 126.
11. A secret circular from the Special Section to the chiefs of the investigative institutions, 4/17 August 1905, no. 10950, Okhrana Archives, XIII d(1), fol. 9.
12. P. P. Zavarzin, *Rabota tainoi politsii* (Paris, 1924) p. 9.
13. 'General-Gubernatoram, Gubernatoram i Gradonachal'nikam' [?] 1906, Nicolaevsky Collection, no. 37, fol. 2.
14. V. K. Agafonov, *Zagranichnaia okhranka* (Petrograd, 1918) p. 132.
15. J. Kucharzewski, *Od białego caratu do czerwonego* (Warsaw, 1931) vol. IV, p. 15, cited in Z. Ivianski, *Individual Terror: Theory and Deed* [Hebrew] (Tel Aviv, 1977) p. 243.
16. Spiridovich, *Partiia Sotsialistov-Revoliutsionerov*, pp. 128–9.
17. Martynov, *Moia sluzhba*, p. 56.
18. Secret personal circular from the Police Department to the chiefs of the investigative institutions, 16/29 September 1914, no. 190791, Okhrana Archives, XIII d(1), fol. 11.
19. P. M. Shchegolev (ed.), *Padenie tsarskago rezhima, po materialam Chrezvychainoi komissii Vremennago Pravitel'stva, stenograficheskie otchety doprosov i pokazanii dannykh v 1917 g. v Chrezvychainoi Sledstvennoi Komissii Vremennago Pravitel'stva* [hereafter *Padenie*] (Leningrad, 1925) vol. III, p. 286.
20. Elwood, *Roman Malinovsky*, p. 34.
21. Police Department to Foreign Agency, 11/24 March 1914, no. 168123, Okhrana Archives, XVI n, fol. 7.
22. Foreign Agency to Police Department, 2/15 March 1904, no. 48, Okhrana Archives XVI, b(3), fol. 4.
23. Martynov, *Moia sluzhba*, p. 100.
24. Ibid., p. 116; Zavarzin, *Rabota tainoi politsii*, p. 21.
25. Zavarzin, *Rabota tainoi politsii*, p. 21.
26. 'Ubiistvo Karpova', *Za kulisami okhrannago otdelenia* (Berlin, 1910) p. 274.
27. Martynov, *Moia sluzhba*, p. 169.
28. B. Savinkov, *Memoirs of a Terrorist* (New York, 1931) p. 325.
29. 'Soobshchenie sotrudnika "Vinograd"', letter no. 2, Nicolaevsky Collection, no. 32, box 3.
30. Foreign Agency to Police Department, 20 November/3 December 1913, no. 1837, Okhrana Archives, XXIV c, fol. 2.
31. Martynov, *Moia sluzhba*, p. 51.
32. Foreign Agency to Police Department, 29 November/12 December 1911, no. 1588, Okhrana Archives, VI e, fol. 1.
33. Martynov, *Moia sluzhba*, p. 139.

34. The secret agent M. Gurovich initiated and published the first legal Marxist organ *Nachalo* (Beginning) with police funds. A similar attempt was made by N. Tatarov in 1905, but this plan was frustrated by his exposure. Another example of a police attempt to advance its agent in a party hierarchy is that of I. Kokochinskii. It was suggested that he should be provided with the means for organizing a PPS congress (see Foreign Agency to Police Department, 29 November/12 December 1911, no. 1588, Okhrana Archives, VI e, fol. 1.
35. Elwood, *Roman Malinovsky*, p. 35.
36. Shchegolev (ed.), *Padenie*, vol. III, p. 275.
37. Ibid., p. 278.
38. Ibid., p. 279; Agafonov, *Zagranichnaia okhranka*, pp. 198–9.
39. A. T. Vassilyev, *The Ochrana: The Russian Secret Police* (London, 1918) p. 63.
40. Ibid., p. 89.
41. Ibid., pp. 198–200.
42. Shchegolev (ed.), *Padenie*, vol. I, p. 298; for details of Zhuchenko's career see below pp. 70–3, 136–7.
43. Gerassimoff, *Der Kampf*, p. 222; Shchegolev (ed.), *Padenie*, vol. III, p. 258.
44. Ibid., vol. I, p. 298.
45. Martynov, *Moia sluzhba*, p. 154; Shchegolev (ed.), *Padenie*, vol. III, p. 272.
46. Vassilyev, *The Ochrana*, pp. 75–6.
47. Ibid., p. 53.
48. Shchegolev (ed.), *Padenie*, vol. III, pp. 268–9.
49. It is, however, noteworthy that some senior officers started climbing up in the police hierarchy while they were secret agents. Most famous among them was S. Zubatov. Their attitude was presumably different (see Vassilyev, *The Ochrana*, p. 76).
50. Okhrana Archives, XII d(2), XII d(3), fols 3, 4, 5.
51. Shchegolev (ed.), *Padenie*, vol. III, p. 272.
52. Ibid., vol. I, p. 197.
53. See Tables 7 and 8.
54. Shchegolev (ed.), *Padenie*, vol. I, p. 298.
55. Agafonov, *Zagranichnaia okhranka*, p. 235.
56. Police Department to Foreign Agency, 28 December 1909/10 January 1910, no. 1958, Okhrana Archives, XI b, fol. 1/A.
57. *Byloe*, n.s., no. 2 (August 1917) p. 233.
58. Agafonov, *Zagranichnaia okhranka*, p. 122.
59. V. B. Zhilinskii, 'Organizatsiia i zhizn' okhrannago otdeleniia vo vremena tsarskoi vlasti', *Golos minuvshago*, no. 9/10 (September/October 1917) p. 252.
60. 'Instruktsiia no. 98 po organizatsii naruzhnago nabliudeniia', p. 2, Okhrana Archives, VI f, fol. 1/A.
61. Zhilinskii, 'Organizatsiia i zhizn', p. 254.
62. Martynov, *Moia sluzhba*, p. 252.
63. Zavarzin, *Rabota tainoi politsii*, p. 17.

64. 'Pokazaniia Doktora Arseniia Bel'skago', Arkhiv Sledstvennoi kommissii, zasedanie XII, Nicolaevsky Collection, no. 224, box 1.
65. 'Zapiski ispovedi provokatora 1909–11 Mikh. G. Rips', Nicolaevsky Collection, no. 95, box 3, fol. 14.
66. Martynov, *Moia sluzhba*, p. 99.
67. Gerassimoff, *Der Kampf*, p. 39.
68. Shchegolev (ed.), *Padenie*, vol. III, p. 272.
69. A. V. Pribylev, *Zinaida Zhuchenko: Iz vospominanii* ([Paris], Izdatel'stvo Byloe, n.d.) p. 31.
70. Gerassimoff, *Der Kampf*, p. 131.
71. Shchegolev (ed.), *Padenie*, vol. III, p. 271.
72. Agafonov, *Zagranichnaia okhranka*, p. 196.
73. [List of agents], *Ultra Rossii*, 6 May 1917.
74. Police Department to Foreign Agency, 6/19 January 1903, no. 76, Okhrana Archives, VI a, fol. 2.
75. Shchegolev (ed.), *Padenie*, vol. III, p. 271.
76. See below, pp. 119ff.
77. 'Zapiski ispovedi provokatora 1909–1911 Mikh. G. Rips'.
78. Foreign Agency to Police Department, 4/17 August 1910, no. 763, Okhrana Archives, XII d, fol. 5.
79. Vassilyev, *The Ochrana*, p. 76.
80. Martynov, *Moia sluzhba*, pp. 172–3, 206–7.
81. 'Zapiski ispovedi provokatora 1909–1911 Mikh. G. Rips'.
82. Ibid.
83. 'K ubiistvu polkovnika Karpova', *Znamia Truda*, no. 25 (January 1910) p. 9.
84. See p. 125.
85. 'Izveshchenie TsK PS-R', *Znamia Truda*, no. 25 (January 1910) p. 9.
86. Foreign Agency to Police Department, 15/28 October 1912, no. 1303, Okhrana Archives, XVI c, fol. 2; 19 November/2 December 1912, no. 1530, ibid., XVI b(3), fol. 8.
87. N. Metal'nikov to the Central Committee, PS-R Archives, no. 714.
88. Shchegolev (ed.), *Padenie*, vol. III, p. 268.
89. Ibid.
90. Vassilyev, *The Ochrana*, p. 59.
91. Martynov, *Moia sluzhba*, pp. 170–1.
92. 'Expropriation' – a term used to describe robbery for revolutionary needs. Occasionally referred to in short as 'Eks'. Foreign Agency to Police Department, (no day) 1910, no. 1056, Okhrana Archives, III f, fol. 9.
93. Foreign Agency to Police Department, 22 March/4 April 1910, no. 260, Okhrana Archives, XVII, n, fol. 5/B.
94. Foreign Agency to Police Department, 2/15 March 1914, no. 46, Okhrana Archives, XVI b(3), fol. 4.
95. Foreign Agency to Police Department, 6/19 March 1912, no. 327, Okhrana Archives, VI h, fol. 5; 12/25 March 1912, no. 361, ibid., XII, fol. 1; 14/27 March 1912, no. 372, ibid.
96. Secret circular from the Police Department to the chiefs of the investigative institutions, 15/28 June 1912, Okhrana Archives, III f, fol. 10.

97. Zavarzin, *Rabota tainoi politsii*, pp. 8–9; Martynov, *Moia sluzhba*, p. 25. According to Martynov each case officer was in charge of 8–10 secret agents.
98. A. Volkov, *Petrogradskoe okhrannoe otdelenie* (Petrograd, 1917) pp. 4–6, 8–10.
99. Gerassimoff, *Der Kampf*, p. 187.
100. Martynov, *Moia sluzhba*, p. 239. Some doubt the number specified by Martynov and argue that according to other credible sources the number of detectives in the Moscow Okhrana was seven times as high (ibid.). However, Martynov's figure is more or less consistent with that cited by Volkov, if we deduct from the number of agency personnel in St Petersburg those who had assignments unique to the capital. Zhilinskii also contends that there were 700 men in the External Agency, but he adds to Martynov's 100 the precinct detectives in every police station as well as various volunteers.
101. Ibid., p. 254.
102. Ibid., p. 107.
103. M. LaPorte, *Histoire de l'okhrana, la police secrète des tsars, 1880–1917* (Paris, 1935) pp. 61–2.
104. Vassilyev, *The Ochrana*, p. 38.
105. Ibid.
106. Zavarzin, *Rabota tainoi politsii*, p. 20.
107. Police Department to Foreign Agency, 9/22 February 1912, no. 112154, Okhrana Archives, II d, fol. 14.
108. Police Department to the Ministry of the Interior, 9/22 December 1909, cited in Agafonov, *Zagranichnaia okhranka*, p. 45; Foreign Agency to the chief of agency in Berlin, 4/17 May 1903, [no no.] Okhrana Archives, II b, fol. I.
109. Foreign Agency to Police Department, 19 September/2 October 1911, no. 1213, Okhrana Archives, II d, fol. 9.
110. Foreign Agency to Police Department, 28 August/10 September 1907, no. 376, Okhrana Archives, X c, fol. 5/C.
111. Foreign Agency to Police Department, 4/17 August 1906, no. 260, Okhrana Archives, VI f, fol. 2.
112. R. J. Johnson, 'The Okhrana Abroad, 1885–1917: A Study of International Police Cooperation' (PhD Thesis, Columbia University, 1970) pp. 74–94.
113. Foreign Agency to Police Department, 24 August/6 September 1913, no. 1631, Okhrana Archives, II d, fol. 5.
114. Foreign Agency to Police Department, 9/22 November 1913, no. 1757, Okhrana Archives, II d, fol. 2.
115. Martynov, *Moia sluzhba*, pp. 80–1.
116. Ibid.
117. Zavarzin, *Rabota tainoi politsii*, p. 47.
118. Degaev and Petrov murdered Sudeikin and Karpov respectively during meetings which were held in apartments that did not meet the required standards of secrecy.
119. S. B. Chlenov, *Moskovskaia okhranka i ee sekretnye sotrudniki* (Moscow, 1918) p. 24.

120. M. E. Bakai, 'Iz vospominanii M. E. Bakaia: provokatory i provokatsia', *Byloe*, no. 11/12 (July–August 1909) p. 162.
121. Martynov, *Moia sluzhba*, pp. 189–90.
122. Shchegolev (ed.), *Padenie*, vol. III, p. 286.
123. Police Department to Foreign Agency, 2/15 November 1914, no. 177312, Okhrana Archives, IV c, fol. 2.
124. Shchegolev (ed.), *Padenie*, vol. I, p. 85.
125. Police Department to Foreign Agency, 27 April/10 May 1910, no. 604, Okhrana Archives, IV e, fol. 2.
126. Police Department cable to Foreign Agency, 12/25 June 1907, no. 1294, Okhrana Archives, XIV d, fol. 1/A.
127. M. Perrie, 'The Social Composition and Structure of the Socialist-Revolutionary Party before 1917', *Soviet Studies*, XXIV (October 1972) p. 226.
128. Martynov, *Moia sluzhba*, p. 279.
129. Ibid., p. 23.
130. Foreign Agency to Police Department, 26 March/8 April 1909, no. 191, Okhrana Archives, X e, fol. 55/F; 14/27 May 1909, no. 282, ibid. XVI b(4), fol. 1; 29 May/11 June 1909, no. 317, ibid.
131. Foreign Agency to Police Department, 20 February/5 March 1910, no. 159, Okhrana Archives, XVI b(3), fol. 4.
132. Foreign Agency to Police Department, 26 January/8 February 1911, no. 122, Okhrana Archives, XVI b(3), fol. 9; 30 October/12 November 1911, no. 1414, ibid.; 12/25 November 1911, no. 1473, ibid., XVI b(3), fol. 4; 22 November/5 December 1911, no. 1544, ibid., XVII g, fol. 2.
133. Foreign Agency to Police Department, 13/26 July 1911, no. 916, Okhrana Archives, X e, fol. 57/C.
134. Gerassimoff, *Der Kampf*, p. 210; Martynov, *Moia sluzhba*, p. 260.
135. The Foreign Agency files are full of requests from the Police Department to check information on various SR terrorist plans, such as rumoured bombing attacks from aircrafts. Police Department to Foreign Agency, 27 August/9 September 1913, no. 103448, Okhrana Archives, VI h, fol. 1; Foreign Agency to Police Department, 12/25 November 1913, no. 1780, ibid.
136. The reference is to Beletskii's policy aimed at intensifying the dissension between the Bolsheviks and the Mensheviks; see Shchegolev (ed.), *Padenie*, vol. III, p. 286.
137. Foreign Agency to Police Department, 29 January/11 February 1905, no. 25, Okhrana Archives, XXIV i, fol. 2/A.
138. Spiridovich, *Partiia Sotsialistov-Revoliutsionerov*, pp. 311–13; Gerassimoff, *Der Kampf*, pp. 130–2.
139. Gerassimoff, *Der Kampf*, pp. 130–2.
140. Even then it would be impossible to say that the attack could have been prevented. The reference is solely to the fact that all supervision was withdrawn and that one central agent only was relied on. This, according to Gerasimov, was not done even at the height of Azef's activity in the Battle Organization.
141. Shchegolev (ed.), *Padenie*, vol. III, p. 76.

142. D. Lane, *The Roots of Russian Communism* (Assen, 1969) p. 13.
143. M. Ivich, 'Statistika terroristicheskikh aktov', *Pamiatnaia knizhka Sotsialista-Revoliutsionera* (Paris, 1914) pp. 5–23.
144. Gerassimoff, *Der Kampf*, p. 89.
145. Ibid., p. 15.
146. Police Department circular, 19 May/1 June 1912, no. 112555, cited in Agafonov, *Zagranichnaia okhranka*, pp. 207–9.
147. Martynov, *Moia sluzhba*, pp. 225–6, 229.
148. Foreign Agency to Police Department, 19 April/2 May 1914, no. 781, Okhrana Archives, VI h, fol. 5.
149. Police Department Circular no. 112555.
150. Handwritten list, Okhrana Archives, III f, fol. 6. It is possible that one of the three anarchist agents did operate in Paris.
151. *Bericht der russischen Sozial-Revolutionären Partei an der Sozialistenkongress zu Stuttgart, August 1907* (n.p., 1907) p. 105.
152. Police Department circular, 19 May 1910, no. 110825, Okhrana Archives, XII d, fol. 10.
153. N. Krupskaya, *Memories of Lenin* (London, 1970) p. 83.
154. Foreign Agency to Police Department, 19 January/1 February 1907, no. 42, Okhrana Archives, XI c(4), fol. 1; 13/26 February 1907, no. 56, ibid.; 21 February/6 March 1907, no. 70, ibid.
155. A. Kubov [A. Argunov], 'Pora gotovit'sia', *Znamia Truda*, no. 50 (April 1913) p. 10.
156. Gerassimoff, *Der Kampf*, p. 240.
157. 'Piaty sovet partii', *Znamia Truda*, no. 19 (July 1909) p. 1.
158. Hildermeier, *Die sozialrevolutionäre Partei*, p. 202.
159. Agafonov, *Zagranichnaia okhranka*, p. 343. Different types of motivation were referred to in this research. It should be noted that Zhuchenko's motivation is not cited here as a typical example.
160. Unless otherwise indicated this description is based mainly on Pribylev, *Zinaida Zhuchenko*.

NOTES TO CHAPTER 2: THE REVOLUTIONARY RESPONSE

1. At a meeting of the Foreign Committee on 5 January 1905, G. A. Bokhanovskii complained that the exposure of Iakov Mash had not been made public. Following his complaint the Committee adopted a resolution to publish a statement in the next issue of *Revoliutsionnaia Rossiia*, the party's organ. PS-R Archives, no. 18.
2. 'Kak otvechat' na pravitel'stvennyia zverstva', *Revoliutsionnaia Rossiia*, no. 12.
3. 'Belyi terror pravitel'stva i fon-Pleve', ibid., no. 32.
4. 'Chernosotennaia vakkhanaliia', ibid., no. 76.
5. Zavarzin, *Rabota tainoi politsii*, p. 51–5.
6. Lane, *The Roots of Russian Communism*, pp. 211–15.

7. Perrie, 'The social composition', pp. 236–7.
8. 'Okhranka i chernye kabinety', *Revoliutsionnaia Mysl'*, no. 1 (April 1908) pp. 10–11.
9. Mikhail Gots to Miss Loid, Kiev, 26 November 1902, Okhrana Archives, XVII h, fol. 1.
10. Johnson, 'The Okhrana Abroad', p. 32.
11. 'Pamiati L. I. Zil'berberga i V. M. Suliatitskago', *Znamia Truda*, no. 30 (August 1910) p. 19.
12. Ibid.
13. 'K kharakteristike Letuchego Otriada Sev. obl.', Iz arkhiva Sledstvennoi komissii, Nicolaevsky Collection, no. 224, box 3.
14. Gerassimoff, *Der Kampf*, p. 126.
15. 'Protokoly parizhskoi konferentsii zagranichnoi organizatsii S-R', January 1907, pp. 22–3, Nicolaevsky Collection, no. 7, box 1.
16. Agafonov, *Zagranichnaia okhranka*, p. 136.
17. See above pp. 19–20.
18. Gerassimoff, *Der Kampf*, pp. 126–7.
19. Savinkov, *Memoirs*, pp. 150–6.
20. V. Ropshin [B. V. Savinkov], *Kon' blednyi* (Moscow, 1912).
21. 'K chitateliam "Bylogo" i "Revoliutsionnoi Mysl"', attached to Foreign Agency's report to Police Department, 13/26 December 1908, Okhrana Archives, XXIV b, fol. 5.
22. 'Otchet o deiatel'nosti Tverskoi gubernskoi organizatsii', 25 April 1907, PS-R Archives, no. 428.
23. N. M. Chernov, *Pered burei* (New York, 1953) p. 284.
24. Ibid., p. 280.
25. 'Evgenii Azef', *Znamia Truda*, no. 15 (February 1907), pp. 3–11.
26. Chernov, *Pered burei*, p. 280.
27. 'Iz istorii Partii S-R: Pokazaniia V. M. Chernova po delu Azefa v Sledstvennoi Komissii Partii SR', *Novyi zhurnal*, C (New York, 1970) p. 291.
28. 'Evgenii Azef', *Znamia Truda*, p. 3.
29. Chernov, *Pered burei*, pp. 287–8.
30. Gerassimoff, *Der Kampf*, p. 240.
31. 'Evgenii Azef', *Znamia Truda*, p. 3.
32. Savinkov, *Memoirs*, pp. 341–2.
33. V. Zenzinov, 'Razoblachenie provokatsii Azeva', Rukopis' (pechatalas' v amerikanskom evreiskom gazeta "Forward" v 1924 g.)', Nicolaevsky Collection, no. 132, box 3, fol. 18; *Zakliuchenie Sudebno-sledstvennoi Komissii po delu Azefa* (Paris, 1911) p. 34.
34. Chernov, *Pered burei*, p. 287.
35. 'Evgenii Azef', *Znamia Truda*, p. 4.
36. Zenzinov, 'Razoblachenie provokatsii Azeva', p. 3.
37. Intercepted letter from Egor Lazarev, Baugy (France), to Mark Natanson, Paris (January 1909), attached to Foreign Agency report to Police Department, 29 December 1908/11 January 1909, no. 519, Okhrana Archives, XII c, fol. 1/A.
38. V. Zenzinov, 'Iz nedalekago proshlago', *Delo Naroda*, no. 126 (13 August 1917).
39. Editorial, *Znamia Truda*, no. 15 (February 1909).

40. 'Otchet o sostoiavshemsia 1/14 ianvaria 1909 g. v Parizhe sekretnom zasedanii iskliuchitel'no chlenov "pravoi" gruppy partii Sotsialistov-Revoliutsionerov po delu Azeva', 6/19 January 1909, no. 8, Okhrana Archives, XVI c, fol. 9.
41. Foreign Agency to Police Department, 8/21 January 1909, no. 17, Okhrana Archives, XII c(1), fol. 1/B.
42. 'Rezoliutsii po delu Azefa', *Znamia Truda*, no. 17 (April 1909) p. 16.
43. 'Rezoliutsii po delu Azefa: Rezoliutsiia Severnago oblastnago biuro', *Znamia Truda*, no. 17 (April 1909) pp. 15–16.
44. 'Rezoliutsiia Kholomgorskoi gruppy', PS-R Archives, no. 116.
45. 'Rezoliutsii soveta Bakinskoi organizatsii PS-R priniataia v fevrale 1909 g.', ibid.
46. 'Protokol sobraniia Parizhskoi gruppy sodeistviia PS-R ot 2 fevralia 1909 g.', PS-R Archives, no. 31.
47. See pp. 153–5.
48. 'O detsentralizatsii', *Revoliutsionnaia Mysl'*, no. 4 (February 1909) pp. 1–5.
49. 'Urok', ibid., p. 14.
50. 'O detsentralizatsii', ibid., p. 2.
51. Spiridovich, *Partiia Sotsialistov-Revoliutsionerov*, pp. 512–14.
52. 'Ot Tsentral'nago Komiteta PS-R', *Znamia Truda*, no. 14 (December 1908) p. 36.
53. See below, pp. 138–9.
54. 'O provokatsii Azeva', *Izveshcheniia Parizhskoi gruppy Sotsialistov-Revoliutsionerov*, listok no. 1, PS-R Archives, no. 210.
55. A group of *émigrés*, Cavi di Lavagna, to the Central Committee, February 1909, PS-R Archives, no. 506.
56. E. Lazarev, Baugy, to M. Natanson, Paris, 4/17 January 1909, Okhrana Archives, XII c(1), fol. 1/B [a copy].
57. 'Izveshcheniia Tsentral'nago Komiteta o provokatsii E. F. Azeva', 7/20 January 1909, PS-R Archives, no. 168.
58. 'Izveshcheniia Tsentral'nago Komiteta PS-R', February 1909, ibid.
59. 'Tysiacha i odna gipoteza', *Znamia Truda*, no. 15 (February 1909) pp. 7–10.
60. B. Savinkov, 'Terror i delo Azefa', *Znamia Truda*, no. 15, p. 10.
61. 'Tysiacha i odna gipoteza', p. 8.
62. The Socialist Revolutionary slogan that appeared at the head of all official party publications.
63. Egor Sazonov: a member of the Battle Organization, took part in Plehve's assassination; committed suicide in prison in Siberia in 1910. Ivan Kaliaev: a member of the Battle Organization, took part in the assassination of the Grand Duke Sergei, sentenced to death and executed in May 1905.
64. Savinkov, 'Terror i delo Azefa', p. 12.
65. Spiridovich, *Partiia Sotsialistov-Revoliutsionerov*, p. 470.
66. 'TsK PS-R o sozyve soveta partii', January 1909, PS-R Archives, no. 168.
67. 'Protokol sobraniia Parizhskoi gruppy sodeistviia PSR ot 2 fevralia 1909 g.', PS-R Archives, no. 31.
68. 'Protokol sobraniia Parizhskoi gruppy sodeistviia PS-R ot 8 fevralia 1909 g.', ibid.

69. 'Piaty sovet partii', *Znamia Truda*, no. 19 (July 1909) p. 1.
70. Spiridovich, *Partiia Sotsialistov-Revoliutsionerov*, p. 470.
71. Ibid., p. 432.
72. The above description of the Fifth Council proceedings is based on 'Piaty sovet partii', *Znamia Truda*, no. 19.
73. Spiridovich, *Partiia Sotsialistov-Revoliutsionerov*, p. 487.
74. Foreign Agency to Police Department, 4/17 June 1909, no. 328, Okhrana Archives, XVI b(3), fol. 7.
75. Spiridovich, *Partiia Sotsialistov-Revoliutsionerov*, p. 496; 'Kratkaia zapiska o polozhenii Partii Sotsialistov-Revoliutsionerov, sostavlennaia po svedeniiam "Nikolia" v oktiabre 1913 goda', attached to Foreign Agency's report to Police Department, 8/21 October 1913, no. 1569, Okhrana Archives, XVI b(3), fol. 7.
76. Spiridovich, *Partiia Sotsialistov-Revoliutsionerov*, p. 487; Hildermeier on the other hand counts Bleklov among the traditional top leadership (*Die sotzialrevolutionäre Partei*, p. 282).
77. 'Vopros o terrore na V Soveta partii, mai 1909 g.', *Sotsialist-Revoliutsioner*, II (Paris, 1910) pp. 3–8.
78. Ibid., pp. 17–19.
79. Ibid., pp. 21–6.
80. Ibid., pp. 28–38.
81. Ibid., p. 31.
82. 'Iz istorii Partii S-R: Pokazaniia V. M. Chernova', p. 301.
83. Foreign Agency to Police Department, 23 November/6 December 1910, no. 1079, Okhrana Archives, XVI b(3), fol. 1/B.
84. 'Rezoliutsii V-go soveta', Okhrana Archives, XVI c, fol. 6.
85. Savinkov, *Memoirs*, p. 350.
86. 'Rezoliutsii V-go soveta'.
87. Hildermeir stresses the negative impact the Council had on the party's future. The majority of its participants had ignored the intra-party criticism and thereby missed the opportunity to save the unity of the party (*Die sozialrevolutionäre Partei*, p. 335).
88. *Zakliuchenie Sudebno-sledstvennoi komissii po delu Azefa*, p. 5.
89. Ibid., pp. 6–7.
90. Ibid., p. 12.
91. Ibid.
92. Ibid., p. 41.
93. Ibid., p. 35.
94. Ibid., pp. 42–6.
95. Ibid., p. 92.
96. Ibid., p. 94.
97. Ibid., p. 96.
98. The Judicial Investigation Commission to the former Central Committee, (n.d.), PS-R Archives, no. 408.
99. Intercepted letter of Rakitnikova to Petr Sidorov (n.d.), attached to Foreign Agency's report to Police Department, 8/21 June 1911, no. 760, Okhrana Archives, XVI b(3), fol. 10.
100. Foreign Agency to Police Department, 14/27 April 1911, no. 512, Okhrana Archives, XVII g, fol. 2.

101. 'V redaktsiiu "Znameni Truda"', *Znamia Truda*, no. 38 (October 1911) p. 31; PS-R Archives, no. 31.
102. Intercepted letter of Rakitnikova to Sidorov.
103. Ibid.
104. 'Rezoliutsiia Parizhskoi gruppy SR-ov', 28 April 1911, PS-R Archives, no. 210.
105. A. Lipin [Iudelevskii], *Sud nad Azefshchinoiu* (Paris, 1911).
106. Ibid., pp. 82–111.
107. L. Deutsch, *Der Lockspitzel Azew und die terrorishische Taktik* (Frankfurt/Main, 1909) p. 29. A similar line of argument regarding the police labour unions is to be found in Lenin's *What Is To Be Done* (*Polnoe sobranie sochinenii*) (Moscow, 1959) vol. 6, pp. 115–6.
108. Deutsch, *Der Lockspitzel*, pp. 29–30.
109. P. Kropotkin, 'Organizatsiia ili vol'noe soglashenie', *Khleb i Volia*, no. 13 (June 1905).
110. N. R. 'Bankrotstvo terrora i delo Azeva', *Burevestnik*, no. 15 (March 1909) pp. 12–14.

NOTES TO CHAPTER 3: CHAIN REACTIONS

1. For all details pertaining to Petrov's version see: 'K ubiistvu polkovnika Karpova', *Znamia Truda*, no. 25 (January 1910).
2. For all details pertaining to Martynov's version see Martynov, *Moia sluzhba*, pp. 183–7; for all details pertaining to Gerasimov's version see Gerassimoff, *Der Kampf*, pp. 240–53.
3. 'Delo Petrova', *Znamia Truda*, no. 25 (January 1910) p. 4.
4. Ibid.
5. Pribyleva-Korba, 'Sergei Petrovich Degaev', p. 5.
6. 'Delo Petrova', *Znamia Truda*, p. 4.
7. Ibid.
8. 'Iz zapisok N. V. Kletochnikova', *Byloe*, no. 7 (1908).
9. Circular no. 19 from the Organization Bureau of the Central Committee, 3 October 1908, PS-R Archives, no. 917.
10. 'Delo Petrova', *Znamia Truda*, p. 3.
11. Ibid.
12. 'K ubiistvu polkovnika Karpova', *Znamia Truda*, p. 9.
13. Foreign Agency's cables to Police Department, 15/28 November 1909, 20 November/3 December 1909, Okhrana Archives, XXVII (d), fol. 6.
14. Vassilyev, *The Ochrana*, pp. 78–82.
15. Gerassimoff, *Der Kampf*, pp. 252–3.
16. Ibid., p. 250.
17. See pp. 35–9.
18. 'Korrespondentsii', *Znamia Truda*, no. 26 (February 1909) p. 22.
19. 'V redaktsiiu "Znameni Truda"', *Znamia Truda*, no. 25 (January 1910) p. 23.
20. N. Bleklov, secretary of the Lausanne group for the SR Party to the Regional Foreign Committee, (n.d.) PS-R Archives, no. 730.

21. 'Rezoliutsiia Londonskoi gruppy SR-ov po delu ob ubiistve Karpova', *Oblastnoi zagranichnyi komitet zagranichnykh organizatsii SR-ov*, *4-oe tsirkuliarnoe pis'mo*, PS-R Archives, no. 210.
22. 'Delo Petrova', *Znamia Truda*, p. 6.
23. 'Po povodu tolkov o L. Men'shchikove (beseda s V. L. Burtsevym), *Parizhskii Listok*, no. 28 (18 September 1910).
24. 'Ivanov', *Novoe Vremia*, 1 September 1910; Police Department to Foreign Agency, 20 August/2 September 1910, no. 114725, Okhrana Archives, XXIV (b), fol. 6; 2/15 September 1910, no. 125978, ibid.
25. 'Spiski sekretnykh sotrudnikov Okhrany, vydannykh Men'shchikovym v 1909–1910 gg', Nicolaevsky Collection, no. 111, fol. 3.
26. '"K delu Zhuchenko", pis'mo v redaktsiiu V. L. Burtseva', *Znamia Truda*, no. 21–2 (September 1909) pp. 31–2.
27. Pribylev, *Zinaida Zhuchenko*, pp. 44–5.
28. '"K delu Zhuchenko", pis'mo Burtseva', *Znamia Truda*.
29. 'Kopii pisem Z. Zhuchenko k V. Burtsevu 1909–1910', Nicolaevsky Collection, no. 95, box 6.
30. '"K delu Zhuchenko", pis'mo Burtseva', *Znamia Truda*.
31. Pribylev, *Zinaida Zhuchenko*, pp. 39–40.
32. Foreign Agency to Police Department, 20 February/5 March 1910, no. 160, Okhrana Archives, XVII p, fol. 1/A.
33. Foreign Agency to Police Department, 25 August/7 September 1910, no. 850, ibid.
34. 'Pokazanie Natansona, protokol 6-go zasedaniia tovarishcheskago suda ot 28 dekabria 1913 g.', PS-R Archives, no. 218.
35. Foreign Delegation to V. M. Chernov (n.d.), PS-R Archives, no. 714.
36. 'Pokazanie Bilita, protokol 5-go zasedaniia tovarishcheskago suda ot 25 Dekabria 1913 g.', PS-R Archives, no. 218.
37. The correspondence between Burtzev and Gerasimov is reminiscent of the *Funkspiel* described in detail in Gilles Perrault's book *The Red Orchestra*. The intelligence heads of both rival parties each knew about the seizure of his own espionage net and yet they continued to use the previous communication system, feeding each other with false information, and attempting to draw conclusions from messages they received from the other side.
38. 'V. L. Burtsev o gen. Gerasimove', Nicolaevsky Collection, no. 95, box 4, fol. 4; a copy of the false document, ibid., no. 224, box 2.
39. According to Burtsev his conclusions were confirmed by Tatiana Tseitlin, who was personally associated with Dobroskok. Her role as a secret agent was exposed in 1909. 'Delo Leonovicha', PS-R Archives, no. 81.
40. V. Leonovich to the Central Committee, Paris, 31 January 1909, Nicolaevsky Collection, no. 224, box 2.
41. 'Pokazanie Natansona, protokol tovarishcheskago suda', PS-R Archives, no. 218.
42. 'Delo Leonovicha', PS-R Archives, no. 81.
43. For example, the secret investigation in the case of Bal'kanskii, Nicolaevsky Collection, no. 224, box 2.
44. See below, pp. 169–73.
45. E. Kolosov to T. Kolosova, Paris (n.d.), PS-R Archives, no. 307.

46. Foreign Agency to Police Department, 20 January/2 February 1909, no. 56, Okhrana Archives, XXIV c, fol. 1.
47. 'Pamiati tov. Tatiany Lapinoi', *Znamia Truda*, no. 19 (July 1909) pp. 15–16.
48. E. Kolosov to T. Kolosova, ibid.
49. 'Zaiavlenie II TsK PS-R', *Znamia Truda*, no. 20 (August 1909) p. 20.
50. Pribylev, *Zinaida Zhuchenko*, p. 40.
51. 'Pomiati tov. Tatiany Lapinoi', *Znamia Truda*.
52. Foreign Agency to Police Department, 28 October/10 November 1913, no. 1677, Okhrana Archives, XXIV c, fol. 2; 1/14 November 1913, no. 1712, ibid; 20 November/3 December 1913, no. 1837, ibid; V. L. Burtsev, *Moia bor'ba s provokatorami (1912–1914 g.g.)*, an unpublished manuscript, Nicolaevsky Collection, no. 95, box 3, fol. 8.
53. Police Department to Foreign Agency, 5/18 February 1914, no. 190162, Okhrana Archives, III f, fol. 12.
54. See chapter 4.
55. Foreign Agency to Police Department, 28 October/10 November 1913, no. 167, Okhrana Archives, XXIV c, fol. 2.
56. 'Protokol zasedaniia Zagranichnoi Delegatsii 1 marta 1914 g.', PS-R Archives, no. 20.
57. 'Pokazanie Vebera, protokol 2-go zasedaniia tovarishcheskago suda ot 25 dekabria 1913 g.', PS-R Archives, no. 218; 'Pokazanie Natansona, protokol 6-go zasedaniia 25-go dekabria 1913 g.', ibid.
58. Burtsev, *Moia bor'ba*, pp. 19–22; Foreign Agency to Police Department, 24 January/6 February 1913, no. 117, Okhrana Archives, III f, fol. 24.
59. Burtsev, *Moia bor'ba*, pp. 19–22; Foreign Agency to Police Department, 24 January/6 February 1913, no. 117, Okhrana Archives, III f, fol. 24.
60. Foreign Agency to Police Department, 20 April/3 May 1913, no. 620, Okhrana Archives, XVI d, fol. 1/B; 'Ot Zagran. Delegatsii TsK PS-R', *Znamia Truda*, no. 50 (April 1913) p. 15.
61. Pribylev, *Zinaida Zhuchenko*, p. 40.
62. 'Pokazanie Natansona, Protokol tovarishcheskago suda'.
63. M. Siniavskii to the Central Committee, Paris, 14 March 1910, PS-R Archives, no. 145; Agafonov, *Zagranichnaia okhranka*, p. 136.
64. Secretary of the Munich group for the SR party to the Foreign Delegation, Munich, 9 March 1910, PS-R Archives, no. 275.
65. Ibid.
66. Foreign Agency to Police Department, 26 November/9 December 1907, no. 519, Okhrana Archives, XVI b(3), fol. 1; 'Obzor Partii Sotsialistov-Revoliutsionerov sostoiania Tsentral'nago Komiteta Partii S-R-ov k kontsu 1908 g.', ibid., fol 1/B.
67. *Revoliutsionnaia Mysl'*, nos 1–6, Izdanie Gruppy Sotsialistov-Revoliutsionerov (1 April 1908–6 December 1909).
68. 'Politicheskii perevorot i initsiativnoe men'shinstvo', *Revoliutsionnaia Mysl'*, no. 2 (June 1908) pp. 4–7.
69. 'Postanovleniia Parizhskoi gruppy Sotsialistov-Revoliutsionerov na zasedanii 6 ianvaria 1908 goda', PS-R Archives, no. 216.
70. 'Zaiavlenie TsK PS-R', *Znamia Truda*, no. 20 (August 1909) p. 19.

71. 'Postanovleniia Parizhskoi gruppy Sotsialistov-Revoliutsionerov 6 ianvaria 1908 goda'.
72. The Paris Group of the Socialist-Revolutionaries to the Paris Group for the SR Party, 17 February 1908, PS-R Archives, no. 31.
73. Cited in 'Rezoliutsiia Parizhskoi gruppy Sotsialistov-Revoliutsionerov po povodu soobshcheniia oblastnago komiteta zagranichnykh organizatsii SR-ov za no. 1 ot 23 aprelia 1908 g.', PS-R Archives, no. 210.
74. Ibid.
75. 'Rezoliutsiia priniataia Parizhskoi gruppoi Sotsialistov-Revoliutsionerov 16-go marta 1908 po povodu provala Sev. Boev. Otriada', PS-R Archives, no. 210.
76. 'Tsirkuliarnoe soobshchenie ot OZK', 23 April 1908, Nicolaevsky Collection, no. 125, fol. 8.
77. 'Rezoliutsiia Parizhskoi gruppy SR-ov', 23 April 1908.
78. Chernov, *Pered burei*, pp. 280–1.
79. Foreign Agency to Police Department, 20 February/5 March 1910, no. 159, Okhrana Archives, XVI b(3), fol. 4.
80. Spiridovich, *Partiia Sotsialistov-Revoliutsionerov*, p. 433.
81. Foreign Agency to Police Department, 7/20 October 1908, no. 372, Okhrana Archives, XVI d, fol. 1.
82. Foreign Agency to Police Department, 25 September/8 October 1908, no. 362, Okhrana Archives, XVI c, fol. 2.
83. 'O provokatore Azeve', *Izveshchenie Parizhskoi gruppy Sotsialistov-Revoliutsionerov*, listok no. 1, PS-R Archives, no. 210.
84. 'Ko vsem Sotsialistam-Revoliutsioneram', 6 May 1909, PS-R Archives, no. 210.
85. Ibid.
86. Ibid.
87. 'Rezoliutsiia Briussel'skoi gruppy sod. PS-R', (n.d.) PS-R Archives, no. 269.
88. 'Oblastnoi zagranichnyi komitet Sotsialistov-Revoliutsionerov, tsirkuliarnoe pis'mo no. 7', Paris 10/23 June 1909, PS-R Archives, no. 210.
89. See above, pp. 96–8.
90. A certain similarity between the development of the Moscow opposition at the end of 1904 and that of the Paris opposition is noteworthy. Both groups protested against the monopoly of the traditional party leadership, and on the basis of their demand for greater organizational autonomy *vis à vis* the Central Committee brought about a final rift culminating in their respective attempts to form a new and independent party organization. Those of the Moscow opposition who had not joined the maximalists after the dissolution of their group, returned later to the SR party. For further details see Hildermeier, *Die sozialrevolutionäre Partei*, pp. 131–3.
91. Foreign Agency to Police Department, 20 February/5 March 1910, no. 159, Okhrana Archives, XVI b(3), fol. 4.
92. The description of this opposition group's secret deliberations are based on police reports. Yet bearing in mind that one of the group's chief protagonists, entrusted with the role of taking down the minutes of all the opposition's discussions, was the secret agent Andrei Demetrash-

vili, these reports can be taken as a reliable source. Moreover his reports about later developments of the affair are confirmed by SR party sources, thus lending them additional credibility.

93. Foreign Agency to Police Department, 13/26 November 1913, no. 1786, Okhrana Archives, XVI b(3), fol. 8; 25 November/8 December 1913, no. 1876, ibid.
94. Foreign Agency to Police Department, 30 November/13 December 1913, no. 1893, ibid.
95. Foreign Agency to Police Department, 20 November/3 December 1913, no. 1842, ibid.; Shabel'skii's report on the Veber-Argunov trial, 6 February 1914, PS-R Archives, no. 218.
96. Foreign Agency to Police Department, no. 1842.
97. Shabel'skii's report on the Veber-Argunov trial; N. Sletov and N. Madridov [Nikolaev] to Veber (n.d.) PS-R Archives, no. 218.
98. Pavlov and Fedorov to Madridov [Nikolaev] and Sletov, Paris, 23 November 1913, ibid.
99. See pp. 148–9.
100. 'Mikhnevich' – Gersh Iakobson – commenced his activity in the Okhrana at Saratov in 1908. Transferred to Paris in the summer of 1911, joined the Paris Group for the SR Party, and reported directly to Saratov, whence his reports were rerouted to Paris via St Petersburg. Because of the high regard in which he was held, the Foreign Agency in Paris was requested to employ him at 100 roubles per month. He was known as 'Minkhevich' among the SRs in Paris. Particularly active, he was several times appointed to the Group's committee. Initial suspicions against him surfaced in September 1913 when he suddenly purchased a car. There was also other evidence hingeing on unclear financial sources. An inquiry revealed his treachery, and Boris Bartold, of the Group's committee, took it upon himself to kill him. However, Burtsev, whether out of professional curiosity – a desire to talk to him first – or because he was not absolutely certain about Iakobson's guilt, prevented the execution. This delay allowed 'Mikhnevich' to flee from Paris. He was exposed publicly only in April 1914.
101. Shabel'skii's report.
102. Ibid.
103. 'Protokol tovarishcheskago suda, sobraniia 17 dekabria 1913 g. 3-go zasedanie', ibid.
104. See chapter 4.
105. Foreign Agency to Police Department, 31 May/13 June 1914, no. 1019, Okhrana Archives, XVI b(3), fol. 8.
106. Foreign Agency to Police Department, 5/18 June 1914, no. 1038, ibid.
107. Foreign Agency to Police Department, 31 May/13 June 1914, no. 1019, ibid.
108. Ibid.
109. See pp. 110–11.
110. Referred to throughout as Postnikova, although part of the events described here occurred before she acquired her married name.
111. 'Zakliuchenie Sledstvennoi komissii po delu Postnikovoi', 17/30 April 1914, PS-R Archives, no. 714.

112. Bilit to the Foreign Delegation, Paris, 13 April 1914, ibid.
113. Ibid.; Foreign Delegation to Chernov (n.d.) ibid.
114. Bilit to Foreign Delegation, 13 April 1914.
115. Foreign Delegation to Chernov.
116. Chernov to Moiseenko, 1 May 1914, ibid.
117. Intercepted undated letter from Chernov to Liubov Azef, attached to Foreign Agency's report to Police Department, 23 August/5 September 1912, no. 1079, Okhrana Archives, XVI d, fol. 1/A.
118. Ibid.
119. Chernov, *Pered burei*, p. 286.
120. Chernov to Moiseenko Paris (n.d.) PS-R Archives, no. 714.
121. Foreign Delegation to Chernov, Paris (n.d.) in reply to Chernov's letter to Moiseenko, ibid.
122. See pp. 124, 145–6.
123. Chernov, *Pered burei*, pp. 292–4.
124. B. Ropshin [B. Savinkov], *To chego ne bylo* (Moscow, 1914) p. 311.
125. Ibid., pp. 324–5.
126. Ibid., pp. 388–9.

NOTES TO CHAPTER 4: EXPOSURES AS A POLITICAL TACTIC

1. Foreign Agency to Police Department, 16/29 March 1910, no. 230, Okhrana Archives, XVI b(3), fol. 8; 7/20 December 1911, no. 1632, ibid.; 5/18 May 1914, no. 889, ibid.
2. Foreign Agency to Police Department, 22 June/5 July 1913, no. 1026, Okhrana Archives, XVI b(3), fol. 8.
3. Foreign Agency to Police Department, 28 March /10 April 1912, no. 124, Okhrana Archives, XVI b(3), fol. 4.
4. As dubbed by B. D. Wolfe, *Three who Made a Revolution*, p. 536.
5. Foreign Agency to Police Department, 11/24 April 1909, no. 211, Okhrana Archives, II a, fol. 1.
6. Foreign Agency to Police Department, 28 November/11 December 1913, no. 1892, Okhrana Archives, XXIV c, fol. 2.
7. Burtsev, *Moia bor'ba*, pp. 8–11.
8. V. L. Burtsev, *Bor'ba za svobodnuiu Rossiiu. Moi Vospominaniia 1882–1924 g.* (Berlin, 1924) p. 32.
9. *Narodovolets. Sotsial'no-politicheskoe obozrenie*, red. V. L. Burtseva, nos 1–4 (London, April 1897–August 1903).
10. Burtsev, *Bor'ba za svobodnuiu Rossiiu*, pp. 31–2.
11. Ibid.
12. Ibid., p. 32.
13. *Svobodnaia Rossiia*, pod redaktsiei V. L. Burtseva i Vl. Debagoria-Mokrievich, nos 1–3 (Zheneva, February–May 1889).
14. Burtsev, *Bor'ba za svobodnuiu Rossiiu*, p. 216.
15. *Obshchee delo*, izdaetsia pod red. V. L. Burtseva, nos 1–4 (Paris, 15 October 1909–15 August 1910).

16. *Budushchee, ezhenedel'naia gazeta*, red. V.L. Burtsev, nos 1–48 (Paris, 22 October 1911–4 January 1914).
17. Ibid., no. 1 (22 October 1911), editorial.
18. Ibid., no. 2 (29 October 1911).
19. Ibid., no. 4 (12 November 1911).
20. Ibid., no. 2 (29 October 1911).
21. Ibid., no. 1 (22 October 1911).
22. Ibid., no. 2 (29 October 1911).
23. Ibid.
24. Ibid.
25. Ibid.
26. Burtsev, *Bor'ba za svobodnuiu Rossiiu*, p. 6.
27. *Budushchee*, no. 2 (29 October 1911).
28. Ibid., no. 6 (26 November 1911).
29. Ibid., no. 7 (3 December 1911). My emphases.
30. Burtsev, *Bor'ba za svobodnuiu Rossiiu*, p. 286.
31. Shchegolev (ed.), *Padenie*, vol. I, p. 305.
32. Ibid., p. 296.
33. A copy of Lenin's note, 18 April 1912, Nicolaevsky Collection, no. 95, box 4, fol. 34.
34. B. Nikolaevskii, *Istoriia odnago predatelia* (New York, 1980) p. 361.
35. Intercepted letter from Chernov to Savinkov (n.d., n.p.) attached to Foreign Agency's report to Police Department, 11/24 August 1912, no. 1023, Okhrana Archives, XII c(1), fol. 1/C.
36. F. Volkhovskii to SR leaders in Paris, London, 12 October 1912, PS-R Archives, no. 506.
37. Intercepted letter from E. Kolosov to V. Kolosova, Paris (n.d.) attached to Foreign Agency's report to Police Department, 29 September/12 October 1912, Okhrana Archives, XII c(1), fol. 1/C.
38. Chernov to Savinkov.
39. *Budushchee*, no. 3 (5 November 1911).
40. Evgenii Kolosov, a former member of the SR party and at that time a member of the editorial staff of *Byloe*, maintained that no deception was involved, but only a misunderstanding. Kolosov to Kolosova, intercepted letter.
41. Ibid.
42. *Budushchee*, no. 4 (12 November 1911).
43. V. Figner to V. L. Burtsev, 12 May 1913, Nicolaevsky Collection, no. 95, box 4, fol. 34A.

Index

In some cases it has not been possible to ascertain the full names of people mentioned (*see* Preface, pp. xiii–xiv). In the case of code-names, if the real name is known, the index entry is under that name followed by the code-name in brackets, and with a cross-reference from the code-name.